NEW TERR NISM

CREW series of Critical and Scholarly Studies
General Editors: Kirsti Bohata and Daniel G. Williams (*CREW*, Swansea University)

This *CREW* series is dedicated to Emyr Humphreys, a major figure in the literary culture of modern Wales, a founding patron of the *Centre for Research into the English Literature and Language of Wales*. Grateful thanks are due to the late Richard Dynevor for making this series possible.

Other titles in the series

Stephen Knight, *A Hundred Years of Fiction* (978-0-7083-1846-1)
Barbara Prys-Williams, *Twentieth-Century Autobiography* (978-0-7083-1891-1)
Kirsti Bohata, *Postcolonialism Revisited* (978-0-7083-1892-8)
Chris Wigginton, *Modernism from the Margins* (978-0-7083-1927-7)
Linden Peach, *Contemporary Irish and Welsh Women's Fiction* (978-0-7083-1998-7)
Sarah Prescott, *Eighteenth-Century Writing from Wales: Bards and Britons* (978-0-7083-2053-2)
Hywel Dix, *After Raymond Williams: Cultural Materialism and the Break-Up of Britain* (978-0-7083-2153-9)
Matthew Jarvis, *Welsh Environments in Contemporary Welsh Poetry* (978-0-7083-2152-2)
Harri Garrod Roberts, *Embodying Identity: Representations of the Body in Welsh Literature* (978-0-7083-2169-0)
Diane Green, *Emyr Humphreys: A Postcolonial Novelist* (978-0-7083-2217-8)
M. Wynn Thomas, *In the Shadow of the Pulpit: Literature and Nonconformist Wales* (978-0-7083-2225-3)
Linden Peach, *The Fiction of Emyr Humphreys: Contemporary Critical Perspectives* (978-0-7083-2216-1)
Daniel Westover, *R. S. Thomas: A Stylistic Biography* (978-0-7083-2413-4)
Jasmine Donahaye, *Whose People? Wales, Israel, Palestine* (978-0-7083-2483-7)
Judy Kendall, *Edward Thomas: The Origins of His Poetry* (978-0-7083-2403-5)
Damian Walford Davies, *Cartographies of Culture: New Geographies of Welsh Writing in English* (978-0-7083-2476-9)
Daniel G. Williams, *Black Skin, Blue Books: African Americans and Wales 1845–1945* (978-0-7083-1987-1)
Andrew Webb, *Edward Thomas and World Literary Studies: Wales, Anglocentrism and English Literature* (978-0-7083-2622-0)
Alyce von Rothkirch, *J. O. Francis, realist drama and ethics: Culture, place and nation* (978-1-7831-6070-9)
Rhian Barfoot, *Liberating Dylan Thomas: Rescuing a Poet from Psycho-Sexual Servitude* (978-1-7831-6184-3)
Daniel G. Williams, *Wales Unchained: Literature, Politics and Identity in the American Century* (978-1-7831-6212-3)
M. Wynn Thomas, *The Nations of Wales 1890–1914* (978-1-78316-837-8)
Richard McLauchlan, *Saturday's Silence: R. S. Thomas and Paschal Reading* (978-1-7831-6920-7)
Bethan M. Jenkins, *Between Wales and England: Anglophone Welsh Writing of the Eighteenth Century* (978-1-7868-3029-6)
M. Wynn Thomas, *All that is Wales: The Collected Essays of M. Wynn Thomas* (978-1-7868-3088-3)

NEW TERRITORIES IN MODERNISM

ANGLOPHONE WELSH WRITING, 1930–1949

WRITING WALES IN ENGLISH

LAURA WAINWRIGHT

UNIVERSITY OF WALES PRESS
2018

www.uwp.co.uk

British Library CIP Data
A catalogue record for this book is available from the British Library.

ISBN: 978-1-78683-217-7
e-ISBN: 978-1-78683-218-4

The University of Wales Press acknowledges the financial support of the Welsh Books Council.

Typeset by Marie Doherty
Printed by CPI Antony Rowe, Melksham

For Arthur Celyn and Louie Heulyn

Contents

Series Editors' Preface

The aim of this series, since its founding in 2004 by Professor M. Wynn Thomas, is to publish scholarly and critical work by established specialists and younger scholars that reflects the richness and variety of the English-language literature of modern Wales. The studies published so far have amply demonstrated that concepts, models and discourses current in the best contemporary studies can illuminate aspects of Welsh culture, and have also foregrounded the potential of the Welsh example to draw attention to themes that are often neglected or marginalised in anglophone cultural studies. The series defines and explores that which distinguishes Wales's anglophone literature, challenges critics to develop methods and approaches adequate to the task of interpreting Welsh culture, and invites its readers to locate the process of writing Wales in English within comparative and transnational contexts.

Professor Kirsti Bohata and Professor Daniel G. Williams

Founding Editor: Professor M. Wynn Thomas (2004–15)

CREW (*Centre for Research into the English Literature and Language of Wales*)
Swansea University

ACKNOWLEDGEMENTS

For kind permission to include extracts from works I should like to thank the following: Gomer Press for Idris Davies's *Gwalia Deserta*; the Rhys Davies Trust for Rhys Davies's 'Arfon'; Literature Wales for 'Man' and 'Sande' by Glyn Jones; Maria Delgado for her translations of Valle-Inclán's *Bohemian Lights*; Angharard Rhys and Prydein Rhys for Lynette Roberts's 'Poem from Llanybri', 'Royal Mail', 'Crossed and Uncrossed', 'Seagulls', 'Plasnewydd' and 'Curlew'; David Higham Associates and New Directions Publishing Corporation for Dylan Thomas's 'I see the boys of Summer', 'The force that through the green fuse', 'A process in the weather of the heart', 'The Peaches', 'The Enemies', 'The Map of Love', 'A Prospect of the Sea'; David McDuff for his translation of Georg Trakl's 'Night'; and Gwendoline Mary Watkins for Vernon Watkins's 'Discoveries', 'The Collier' and 'Ophelia'. Despite my best efforts, I have been unable to trace the copyright holder for Patrick Bridgewater's translation of 'Guard Duty' by August Stramm. I apologise for this omission and encourage the copyright holder to contact me.

Thank you to my Mum and Dad for introducing me to the pleasures of literature, art and creativity. I also owe a debt of gratitude to Professor Katie Gramich, who supervised the Ph.D. thesis on which this book is based, and to Professor Daniel G. Williams for drawing my attention to Chana Kronfeld's *On the Margins of Modernism: Decentering Literary Dynamics*. I gratefully acknowledge the financial contribution of the Welsh Books Council in the publication of my work.

Finally, my love and thanks go to Darrell Thomas. This would all have been impossible without you.

INTRODUCTION

On 17 March 1987, Raymond Williams presented a lecture as part of a series convened by the University of Bristol. The lecture was called 'When Was Modernism?' – a title that Williams 'borrowed from a book by [his] friend Professor Gwyn Williams: *When Was Wales?*'[1] – and posited the following argument:

> After Modernism is canonized . . . by the post-war settlement and its accompanying, complicit academic endorsements, there is then the presumption that since Modernism is *here* in this specific phase or period, there is nothing beyond it . . . 'Modernism' is confined to this highly selective field and denied to everything else in an act of pure ideology, whose first, unconscious irony is that, absurdly, it stops history dead. Modernism being the terminus, everything afterwards is counted out of development. It is *after*; stuck in the post.[2]

Nowhere is the exclusionary force of conventional histories of Modernism more palpable than in the country of Raymond Williams's birth and the subject of Professor Gwyn Williams's book: Wales. With the exception of Saunders Lewis in the Welsh language, and Dylan Thomas, Caradoc Evans,[3] and David Jones (whose work is most often studied in the context of English or 'British' Modernism) in English, Wales's writers have, historically, been debarred from scholarly discussions of literary Modernism. In the case of Welsh writing in English, a minority of scholars have addressed the prospect of a Welsh Modernism as part of more discursive studies of the literature of Wales – notably M. Wynn Thomas in *Internal Difference:*

Twentieth-Century Writing in Wales (1992), *Corresponding Cultures: The Two Literatures of Wales* (1999) and *In the Shadow of the Pulpit: Literature and Nonconformist Wales* (2010); and Tony Conran in *Frontiers in Anglo-Welsh Poetry* (1997). In *Modernism from the Margins: The 1930s Poetry of Louis MacNeice and Dylan Thomas* (2007), Christopher Wigginton stresses that 'Welsh Modernism continues to be neglected, even within Wales';[4] and yet he limits the scope of his critical inquiry to Dylan Thomas, only mentioning other potentially Modernist Welsh writers in passing. The same can be said of John Goodby's *Under the Spelling Wall: The Poetry of Dylan Thomas* (2013). And although, more recently, Goodby and Wigginton have widened the scope of their inquiry, in their collaborative essay, 'Welsh Modernist Poetry: Dylan Thomas, David Jones and Lynette Roberts', this still cannot fully justify their substantial and complex claims, for example, that

> Welsh Modernism . . . is a heterogeneous, dispersed, irregularly recurring phenomenon, defined by a lack of the attributes which usually constitute a 'tradition', but distinctive because Welsh location, provenance, or identification led to a highly fruitful belated encounter between modernist techniques and 'the matter of Wales'.[5]

Daniel G. Williams has arrived at a more comprehensive and nuanced understanding of the forms that Modernism took in Wales, identifying its 'bourgeois, proletarian and folk strains',[6] and comparing these 'aesthetic and intellectual trajectories'[7] with those of African American Modernisms. Yet, still, no sustained or extensive study of Anglophone Modernism in Wales has been undertaken. My aims in this study are to build on Williams's scholarship and to afford the topic of Welsh Modernism the critical scrutiny that it deserves by considering a range of Anglophone Welsh writing from the 1930s and 1940s in the context of European Modernist literature and art.

Part of the reason why the notion of a Welsh Modernism has gone mostly unexplored, it seems, is the (often superficial) dissimilarity between canonical Modernist literature and art, and Anglophone Welsh writing of the first half of the twentieth century. Without a long and entrenched 'Anglo-Welsh' literary tradition to deviate from (an issue which I examine more closely in chapter one); flourishing, for the most part, after the high Modernist period, between 1930 and 1949; and tending to be concerned with rural and industrialised locations and milieux in a way that contravenes the popular conception of Modernism as 'an art of cities',[8] Anglophone Welsh writing, has, to use Williams's terms, 'been counted out of development' – 'stuck in the post' and on the periphery. Yet to exclude Welsh writing from discussions of Modernism on the basis of these narrow criteria is, now, in the current climate of Modernist studies, completely unjustifiable; for critics now recognise the divergent, multifaceted character of Modernism, and appreciate the complex relationship between Modernism, canonicity and geographical, social and cultural specificity. It is now common to hear critics talk of 'regional Modernisms'. In a book devoted to this subject, for example, Neal Alexander and James Moran have collected essays on Modernism from various different geographical spaces, including regions of Scotland, Ireland, England and Wales.[9] Laura Doyle and Laura Winkiel have coined the term 'geomodernisms', to denote such a 'locational' approach to Modernism's 'engagement with cultural and political discourses of global modernity'.[10] They argue that this 'unveils both unsuspected "modernist" experiments in "marginal" texts and suspected correlations between those texts and others that appear either more conventional or more postmodern'.[11] 'Across their differences', Doyle and Winkiel suggest, 'these works share something that allows them to be grouped together: a self-consciousness about positionality.'[12] Channa Kronfeld is similarly concerned with ideas about 'positionality' in *On the Margins of Modernism: Decentering Literary Dynamics* (1996). Using Gilles Deleuze and Félix Guattari's concept of 'minor literature'[13] as a starting point, she sets out to 'prepare the ground for . . . a less exclusionary theoretical and historical model of marginal modernisms, elaborated and applied to the production and reception of Hebrew and Yiddish poetic modernisms'.[14] I am centrally concerned in this book with bringing the progressive, expansive, 'less exclusionary' scholarship of Kronfeld, Doyle and Winkiel into dialogue with writing from Wales.

Fundamental to my argument is what I regard as certain key Anglophone Welsh writers' distinctively Welsh Modernist use of language. In chapter one, I read the diverse linguistic experimentation of Gwyn Thomas, Glyn Jones, Idris Davies and David Jones as manifestations of a particular modern 'crisis of language' in Wales,[15] generated by unprecedented social and cultural change in the country during this period. Adopting the kind of 'locational approach' espoused by Doyle, Winkiel and Kronfeld, I argue that these socio-cultural conditions made Wales an especially fertile territory for a burgeoning Welsh Modernism. I expand on this argument in chapter two, where I demonstrate how Lynette Roberts consciously embraced and utilised these circumstances in order to push linguistic boundaries and fully articulate her own experience as a female incomer in rural Wales during the Second World War. In chapter three, I also place Vernon Watkins's itinerant, intertextual poetic idiom within this developing picture of Welsh Modernism. Particulars of place and time continue to frame my comparison, in chapter four, of Dylan Thomas's use of Carmarthenshire and Salvador Dalí's use of Cadaqués, in rural Spain, as sites of transgressive, Modernist possibility. My use of the visual arts in this chapter – and indeed throughout this book – pertains to my overall aim to represent and appreciate Modernism in all its multiplicity and diversity. In chapter four, I challenge another common critical assumption: that late Modernism, such as that found in Welsh writing in English, is necessarily derivative in nature. I argue, moreover, that Modernism in Wales is, in Tony Conran's words, 'home-grown' – a product of unique geographical, social, cultural and temporal conditions – as well as being 'part of an international climate'.[16] This open, inclusive perspective continues to inform my analysis in chapter five, in which I explore, with reference to German Expressionism and Spanish *esperpento* theatre, the presence and significance of Modernist techniques of the grotesque in the short fiction of Gwyn Thomas and Rhys Davies. Here, I also expose the often socially engaged and politically ambitious impetus of Welsh Modernism, problematising, once again, narrow literary histories, of the kind that Raymond Williams critiqued in 1987, that view Modernism as essentially detached and rarefied in nature. My aim in this study is not to provide an exhaustive account of the entire trajectory of Modernism in Wales. Rather, I hope that the chapters in this book will speak to each other in thought-provoking ways and also shed light on the work of Welsh writers whose work I have not had space to discuss in more depth here. These might include slightly earlier writers such as Caradoc Evans, or later writers such as Tony Conran. In essence, the very purpose of this study is not to 'stop history dead', in Raymond Williams's words, but to generate and inspire future research and critical debate in Welsh Modernism and indeed Modernism studies more broadly, both within and outside Wales.

1

'THE DISSOLVING AND SPLITTING OF SOLID THINGS': WELSH MODERNISM'S 'CRISIS OF LANGUAGE'

Language and its deficiency in the context of the modern age preoccupy Modernist writers. This 'crisis of language'[1] can be traced back to the French Symbolist poets of the nineteenth century, who, as Elizabeth McCombie notes, shared 'a drive for artistic revolution . . . born of . . . a sense that everything had been done, written, and felt'.[2] Attempting to break away from what they perceived to be an exhausted poetic idiom, the French Symbolists pioneered a new kind of poetry in which language is approached in radically innovative ways.[3] Arthur Rimbaud, for example, reflects on this process in his collection of autobiographical prose-poetry, *Une saison en enfer*, or *A Season in Hell* (1873):

> I invented the colour of vowels! – *A* black, *E* white, *I* red, *O* blue, *U* green – I organized the shape and movement of every consonant, and by means of instinctive rhythms, flattered myself that I was the inventor of a new language, accessible sooner or later to all the senses.[4]

Paradoxically, however, the mood of this revelation is one of both artistic accomplishment and defeat. Indeed, *A Season in Hell* is pervaded with instances of linguistic failure. In 'Bad Blood' the narrator asks, 'Do I understand nature yet? Do I know myself? – *No more words*' (p. 219). And in 'Morning' he confesses, 'For my part, I can no more explain myself than a beggar with his endless *Pater Nosters* and *Ave Marias*. *I no longer know how to speak!*' (p. 251) Moreover, *A Season in Hell* seems to demonstrate how the French Symbolists' attempts at poetic rejuvenation ultimately served to compound their impression of linguistic crisis – not least because in Symbolist poetry, particularly, as McCombie explains, in the work of Stéphane Mallarmé,

> language [is] freed from conventional modes of denotation [and] assumes material existence independent of what it might signify; yet at the same time the word experienced as word creates an immediate consciousness of the absence of identity between word and sign. The word [therefore] points . . . to a thrilling Nothingness, a referential failure, at the heart of language itself.[5]

Writers and thinkers of the early twentieth century destabilised language in a similar way. Between the years 1907 and 1911, the Swiss linguist, Ferdinand de Saussure, posited a theory of language centred on the principle of arbitrariness. More specifically, Saussure argued that 'the bond between the signifier and the signified is arbitrary. Since I mean by sign the whole that results from the associating of the signifier with the signified,' he elaborated, 'I can simply say: *the linguistic sign is arbitrary*.'[6] Saussure disrupted traditional ideas about language further by proposing that 'in language there are only differences',[7] and no absolute values. 'Whether we take the signified or the signifier,' he concluded, 'language has neither ideas nor sounds that existed before the linguistic system, but only conceptual and phonic differences that have issued from that system.'[8] For Saussure, then, language has a fundamentally elusive quality, which is also underlined in the poetry of the early twentieth century – most famously, perhaps, in the work of T. S. Eliot. In 'The Love Song of J. Alfred Prufrock' (1917), for example, the speaker decides that 'It is impossible to say just what I mean!',[9] while the poetic voices of *The Waste Land* (1922) enact and reinforce the theme of faltering and failing language. This can be seen in 'The Burial of the Dead', where the speaker recollects:

> . . . when we came back, late, from the hyacinth garden,
> Your arms full, and your hair wet, I could not
> Speak, and my eyes failed, I was neither
> Living nor dead, and I knew nothing,
> Looking into the heart of light, the silence.[10]

Eliot's fragmentary closing lines provide another memorable example:

> I sat upon the shore
> Fishing, with the arid plain behind me
> Shall I at least set my lands in order?
> London Bridge is falling down falling down falling down
> *Poi s'ascose nel foco che gli affina*
> *Quando fiam uti chelidon* – O swallow swallow
> *Le Prince d'Aquitaine à la tour abolie*
> These fragments I have shored against my ruins[11]

Indeed, the same preoccupations re-emerge in 'East Coker' (1940) – the second of Eliot's *Four Quartets*:

> So here I am, in the middle way, having had twenty years –
> Twenty years largely wasted, the years of *l'entre deux guerres* –
> Trying to learn to use words, and every attempt
> Is a wholly new start, and a different kind of failure
> Because one has only learnt to get the better of words
> For the thing one no longer has to say, or the way in which
> One is no longer disposed to say it. And so each venture
> Is a new beginning, a raid on the inarticulate
> With shabby equipment always deteriorating
> In the general mess of imprecision of feeling,[12]

Echoing Rimbaud and Mallarmé, in all of these poems Eliot questions the effectiveness of language as a means of knowing and of expressing the world.

A feeling of disjunction between language and the world is often also expressed in Modernist fiction. In his short story, '*Die Verwandlung*' or 'The Metamorphosis' (1915), in which the protagonist, Gregor Samsa, awakens to find that he has been miraculously 'transformed in his bed into a giant insect',[13] Franz Kafka employs a strikingly laconic, matter-of-fact style in order to narrate extraordinary and terrifying external events. Kafka's work is most frequently aligned with Expressionism – an aesthetic first associated with visual art which I discuss more fully in chapter five – and several other Modernist movements that formed in continental Europe during the early decades of the twentieth century seem similarly to have been born out of a consciousness that language had become estranged from reality. In 'The Founding and Manifesto of Futurism' (1909), for instance, Filippo Tommaso Marinetti asserts: 'Up to now literature has exalted a pensive immobility, ecstasy, and sleep. We intend to exalt aggressive action, a feverish insomnia, the racer's stride, the mortal leap.'[14] 'No work without an aggressive character', he continues, 'can be a masterpiece. Poetry must be conceived as a violent attack on unknown forces, to reduce and prostrate them before man.'[15] Marinetti's proclamations register Futurism's attempt to liberate the written word from the structures of the past and reinvent literature for a new epoch of militarism, patriotism and technological advance; as he avowed in his 'Technical Manifesto of Futurist Literature' (1912), 'we make use of . . . every ugly sound, every expressive cry from the violent life that surrounds us . . . After free verse, here finally are *words-in-freedom*.'[16] This theme of creative freedom resurfaces in 'The First Manifesto of Surrealism' (1924), where André Breton proclaims:

> Under the pretence of civilisation and progress, we have managed to banish from the mind everything that may rightly or wrongly be termed superstition, or fancy; forbidden is any kind of search for truth which is not in conformance with accepted practices. It was, apparently, by pure chance that a part of our mental world which we pretended not to be concerned with any longer . . . has been brought back to light. For this we must give thanks to Sigmund Freud. On the basis of these discoveries a current of opinion is finally forming by means of which the human explorer will be able to carry his investigations much further, authorised as he will henceforth be not to confine himself solely to the most summary realities.[17]

Here, Breton calls for 'the mind' to extricate itself from the oppressive, 'accepted' discourses of 'civilisation' and 'progress', and access a more vital modern world, illuminated and invigorated by the Freudian unconscious. 'Language has been given to man', Breton argues, 'so that he can make Surrealist use of it,'[18] opening up literature to new areas of non-rational, subjective experience.

In a sense, both the Futurist and Surrealist manifestos are products of what Sheppard calls the 'disjunction between social discourse and literary discourse',[19] which he sees as fundamental to the modern 'crisis of language'. More specifically, Sheppard proposes that

> Where the 'surface' of classical [that is to say, traditional or long-established] writing takes strength from and corresponds with the social and linguistic structures which it presupposes and celebrates, the modern writer cannot assume this correspondence. He has to dismantle the structures of the conventional world and 'explode' language before he can create an adequate 'verbal ikon'.[20]

This idea of Modernist writers dismantling the conventional world and 'exploding' language is particularly relevant to the Italian Futurist movement, echoing its dictum of '*parole in libertà* and *tavole parolibre*, or liberated words and syntax',[21] and its aggressive rejection of tradition. Wyndham Lewis and Ezra Pound's Vorticist aesthetic, expounded in the appositely titled *BLAST* magazine in 1914 and 1915 is similarly called to mind; for as Andzej Gasiorek notes,

> the search [in *BLAST*] for a kind of 'radical purism' in words, to match the 'stark radicalism of the *visuals* found in Vorticist art, resulted in a [linguistic] 'play' that minimised the use of connectives, articles, pronouns, and prepositions, making it edgy and charging it with a visceral power.[22]

A linguistic 'explosion' is, we might argue, also an appropriate metaphor for the Surrealist movement's creation of its own incongruous, illogical and often shocking 'language' from dreams, hallucinatory states and other manifestations of the unconscious mind. Indeed, according to Walter Benjamin,

> it is [precisely] as magical experiments with words, not as artistic dabbling, that we must understand the passionate phonetic and graphic transformational games that have run through the whole literature of the avant-garde . . ., whether it is called Futurism, Dadaism, or Surrealism.[23]

The phrase 'crisis of language' takes on a wholly new resonance, however, when it is applied to Welsh authors writing in English in the first half of the twentieth century. This is because 'the disjunction between social discourse and literary discourse' underlying this modern anxiety is exacerbated in the Welsh context by an accompanying linguistic divide: a new social discourse derived from English-speaking Wales, and an established literary discourse rooted in native Welsh-language culture. As Tony Conran explains, Welsh writing in English

> shares its territory with another linguistic community which regards its tongue as the right and natural language of the country – a claim which Anglo-Welsh writers often accept, and which if they dispute, they cannot ignore.[24]

This situation was particularly difficult for Anglophone Welsh writers to ignore at a time when Welsh nationalists, such as the

Welsh-speaking writer, critic and political activist Saunders Lewis, were questioning the legitimacy of 'Anglo-Welsh' writing. As Lewis argued in 1938, in his provocative lecture and pamphlet, 'Is there an Anglo-Welsh literature?':

> Is there an Anglo-Welsh nation which has its own literature in its own language? It is unlikely that anyone would answer that question with a 'Yes', except possibly some native of South Pembrokeshire.
>
> A writer of literature belongs to a community. Normally he writes for that community. His instrument of expression – the speech he uses, – has been shaped for and given to him by that society. Moreover, there belong to that society traditions and experiences and a secular mode of life as well as a literary heritage which have impressed themselves not only on the language but on all those who so use it that their use of it is seen to be literature. Every separate literature implies the existence of . . . an organic community. Such a community, possessing its own common traditions and its own literature, we generally call a nation.
>
> Who, then, are the Anglo-Welsh? Actually we never think of an Anglo-Welsh people. The term is an abstraction, a literary abstraction, even as 'Britisher' is an abstraction, but a political one. Neither term has reference to an organic community. Neither term has any social or cultural connotation.[25]

Indeed, to adapt a phrase from Deleuze and Guattari's 1975 study, *Kafka: Toward a Minor Literature*, Anglophone Welsh writers of the early twentieth century might, in a sense, be said to have experienced a '*deterritorialization* of language [my emphasis]'[26] because, as representatives of the so-called 'first flowering'[27] of Anglophone writing in Wales – of an, as yet, as Saunders Lewis avers, indistinct 'Anglo-Welsh' literary tradition – they occupied a nomadic position within two established cultural spaces. In the words of M. Wynn Thomas, they shared a

> common experience – [arguably] simultaneously constructive and destructive, liberating and inhibiting – of belonging to a place apart; a historical region which was certainly not assimilable to England, but which could not be integrated into traditional Wales either. It was doubly separate – set apart on two counts and on two fronts – and its writers were perhaps accordingly doubly blessed and doubly cursed.[28]

The notion of Anglophone Welsh writers as, linguistically, both 'cursed' and 'blessed', 'inhibited' and 'liberated', also relates to what Tony Conran describes as the 'newness' of English for many

Anglophone Welsh writers in the early twentieth century.[29] As I discuss in this chapter, a number of these writers came from backgrounds where the English language 'was no more than a generation or two old',[30] and consequently their work manifests a creatively empowered delight in this linguistic novelty but also, relatedly, a kind of alienation, a strong feeling of the uncanny strangeness of language and of their own linguistic situation. Moreover, the specific tensions associated with the 'crisis of language' in Wales overlap with Deleuze and Guattari's ideas about 'minor literature' and, more specifically, with what they describe as the unfortunate[31] but, at the same time, 'revolutionary conditions for every literature within the heart of what is called great (or established) literature':[32] like 'a Czech Jew [who] writes in German, or an Ouzbekian [who] writes in Russian'[33] (to use Deleuze and Guattari's examples), a Welsh writer who writes in English is, we might argue, inevitably engaged in 'setting up a minor [and, in this respect, potentially transformational or "revolutionary"] practice of a major language from within'.[34] Indeed, because of this, Deleuze and Guattari contend, 'minor literature' has the capacity to act as 'the revolutionary force for all literature'[35] – an idea that connects Welsh writing in English, however marginal, with the international Modernist imperative to 'make it new'. Such an approach does not, as this chapter will demonstrate, entail an 'implicit dehistoricization of both the minor and the modernist',[36] which Kronfeld warns might result from this 'logical slippage'[37] between the two categories. Neither does it deny (as she claims Deleuze and Guattari's study does) 'minor [and, therefore, potentially, Modernist] status to . . . literatures in "indigenous" minority languages',[38] such as Welsh. On the contrary, this chapter will show how three Anglophone Welsh writers, Gwyn Thomas, Glyn Jones and Idris Davies, together with the English-born poet and visual artist, David Jones, engage in their work from the 1930s and 1940s with the modern linguistic crisis in early twentieth-century Wales – a crisis that affected both English- and Welsh-speaking communities – in a way that both expands and challenges our knowledge and understanding of Modernism.

I

Gwyn Thomas (1913–81), a writer known and widely admired for his verbal exuberance and inventiveness, might seem an unlikely figure to associate with a 'crisis of language'. Born in Porth in the industrialised

Rhondda Valley in South Wales, he was a short-story writer, novelist, playwright and essayist, whose better-known works include the novella, *The Dark Philosophers* (1946), the novel, *All Things Betray Thee* (1949) and the play, *The Keep* (1962). Thomas's contemporary, Glyn Jones, refers to Thomas's 'amazing gifts as a spontaneous speaker',[39] to 'the extraordinary vigour of [his narrative] style, the brilliance, the gusto, the torrential language, the inexhaustible imagery',[40] and describes him as possessing 'a mind . . . that uses metaphor as naturally, as abundantly and as persistently as do most of us the cliché'.[41] Similarly, for Stephen Knight, Thomas is 'the most verbally brilliant writer of Welsh fiction in English';[42] 'only Dylan Thomas', Knight insists, 'can challenge him'.[43] It is precisely this striking verbal individuality and ingenuity, however, which should encourage – and has recently, in the case of Dylan Thomas, led to – consideration of these writers in the context of the Modernist fixation with language. Walford Davies has argued in his essay, 'The Poetry of Dylan Thomas: Welsh Contexts, Narrative and the Language of Modernism', for example, that Dylan Thomas's position as a first-generation English-speaker in a Welsh-speaking family meant that his poetry 'represented a kind of [experimental] no-man's-land between two languages – one dead, the other powerless to be born. Or at least powerless to be born into any kind of natural ease'.[44] This, Davies suggests, explains 'not only why he [Thomas] appears so radically different from any other poet of the 1930s, but also why he found poetry more and more difficult to write'.[45] Gwyn Thomas may not, as Glyn Jones suggests, have found the process of writing particularly difficult, but his similarly complex socio-linguistic background, I would argue, demands that his literary output during the 1930s and 1940s be considered within the kind of conceptual framework that Walford Davies invokes, and this premise will form the basis of the discussion that follows.

Gwyn Thomas's parents were Welsh-speakers, from Welsh-speaking backgrounds, and their first six children were brought up with Welsh as their first language.[46] Immigration and the promotion of English in schools, however – from the late nineteenth century, Westminster government policy dictated that education should be conducted solely through the medium of English[47] – meant that, like the suburban Swansea in which Dylan Thomas grew up, industrial south Wales, including the Rhondda Valley where the Thomas family lived, was becoming increasingly Anglicised.[48] Sensing a need to adapt to this rapidly changing social environment, Thomas's mother and father brought up their subsequent children, Thomas included, as exclusively English-speaking, creating a linguistic rift in the family.[49] Thomas reflected on this situation in a television programme broadcast in 1969 called *It's a Sad but Beautiful Joke*:

> Our kitchen, about the size of an average hutch, was a busy, bi-lingual bomb of a place. The first six children spoke Welsh, the bottom six English, and all at the same time; politics in English, gossip in Welsh, and downright lies in both.[50]

Thomas, then, despite being unable to speak Welsh, was nevertheless immersed in the language and its culture while he was growing up, both at home and, as Glyn Jones points out, at the Welsh chapel that his family attended.[51] And this confluence of English and Welsh is manifested in his writing during the 1930s and 1940s. In *Sorrow for thy Sons*, for example, a novel which Thomas completed in 1936 and centred on the lives of three brothers, Alf, Hugh and Herbert, in the industrialised south Wales Valleys during the Depression years, English phrases and syntax are frequently juxtaposed with Welsh sentence structure: 'Alf noticed that the kitchen fire was still lit. It had sunk low. There was a kettle pressed down on it. Two towels, dirty, were hung from a brass bar, thick and running just below the mantel shelf.'[52] Here, the phrases 'two towels, dirty' and 'a brass bar, thick' seem to echo the way in which adjectives are positioned after the nouns that they describe in Welsh. And this is a common occurrence in the novel: Thomas also writes that 'on the table in the centre of the room there were twelve boy's suits, second hand, and half a dozen pairs of shoes, new' (p. 163), and he describes how 'the headmaster . . . pulled out a walking stick, thick, brown' (p. 112). The appearance of the sentence, 'around the barricade played children' (p. 20), instead of the more usual 'around the barricade children played' or 'children played around the barricade', provides another example of this linguistic interchange, calling to mind the way in which the verb is generally positioned before the subject in Welsh-language clauses. Verbs are usually located at the beginning of sentences in Welsh, and this also finds expression in Thomas's prose. It is perceptible during the account of Hugh's punishment at school:

> He heard the headmaster talking to him, gaspily. The small exertion of three strokes had winded him.

> 'This may seem . . . very stupid . . . to you, Evans. But . . . you've got . . . got to be taught.
>
> Came three more strokes. Hugh heard himself being told to get down. (p. 112)

Thomas disrupts the otherwise conventional English syntax by writing 'Came three more strokes' rather than 'Three more strokes came'. These grammatical patterns also occur, for instance, in Thomas's short story, 'Myself My Desert' (1946), in which the impoverished narrator imagines himself with 'nicer hair, a cleaner shirt, a body straighter',[53] and in the novella, *Oscar* (1946), when the narrator, Lewis, stands beside 'a lighted window, small'[54] and observes that his destitute friend, Hannah, 'looked no happier. Rather did she look as if the rain was beating a little harder on the wet mountain that she looked like' (p. 32). In this second example, Thomas positions a verb before the subject, initially placing 'did she look' rather than 'she looked'.

The effect of this 'seepage'[55] from Welsh into English in Thomas's prose is, as M. Wynn Thomas suggests, a 'kind of linguistic defamiliarization . . . which is a product of Welsh biculturism'[56] – a sense that 'language [has become] other to its ordinary self'.[57] Thomas undoubtedly transcribes some instances of contemporary language usage in the south Wales Valleys. Indeed, Parnell traces 'the individuality' of Thomas's 'particular brand of English' back to the 'family idiolect which the Thomas children learned from their father . . . whose peculiar delivery, not quite Welsh and not quite English, made memorable and comical his interpretation and presentation of . . . ideas'.[58] Stephen Knight, on the other hand, has considered the broader social history of the bicultural Rhondda Valley in his analysis of Thomas's oeuvre, demonstrating how his hybridised narrative style lends itself to a postcolonial reading.[59]

But Thomas's mode of writing can also be viewed in another way. More specifically, it might be said to represent that point of modern linguistic crisis, born out of a heightened feeling of 'disjuncture between social and literary discourse', at which language – both English and Welsh – is 'exploded' in an attempt to create a new, more adequate mode of expression. Thomas's fictional world becomes, in a different sense, like his childhood home: 'a busy bi-lingual bomb of a place'. Moreover, Thomas's new, bicultural 'verbal ikon' seems to reflect how, as Deleuze and Guattari suggest, 'minor literature' is particularly concerned to develop or experiment with '*intensives* or *tensors*'[60] – defined as the various 'linguistic elements . . . that express the "internal tensions of a language"'[61] – and the following passage from *Sorrow for thy Sons* also creates this impression:

> Gwyneth had funny lips, twisted a bit, made her talk like a woman who's hiring a maid. That wasn't her fault. Gwyneth was too fond of hard work to think of hiring a maid. It was a touch of paralysis she had had as a kid that made her talk funny like that. Screwed her lips up into a curious shape, gave Alf the itch to be always touching them with his. But more than that, nothing. (p. 13)

With the phrase 'Screwed her lips up', Thomas begins a sentence with a verb, once again effecting the permutations of Welsh grammar. And the phrases, 'twisted a bit' and 'But more than that, nothing', where conventional word order is similarly inverted, also have this defamiliarising effect; these phrases would usually be expected to read 'a bit twisted' and 'But nothing more than that'. Moreover, tremors from these small but symptomatic linguistic detonations radiate through Thomas's narratives, and the unfamiliar and unpredictable idiom that results allows Thomas to circumvent and, in doing so, continue to dismantle linguistic paradigms.[62] In *Sorrow for thy Sons*, Alf does not feel a desire 'to kiss' Gwyneth, but experiences 'the itch to be always touching [her lips] with his'. As Glyn Jones notes, Thomas's narrative style 'enlarges and enlivens',[63] and here the verb 'kiss' is turned inside out and presented in the form of its constituent units of meaning. In *Oscar*, the verb 'teach' is broken apart in a similar way, as Lewis recalls how 'the teachers . . . had vanished after a few months of trying to put some knowledge into Clarisse' (p. 14). Thomas's deconstruction of 'kiss' and 'teach', in fact, pushes towards an almost Brechtian 'alienation effect'[64] within language; his technique seems to announce, as the German Expressionist playwright, Bertolt Brecht, did in his writings on the theatre, that

> the familiar must be stripped of its inconspicuousness; we must give up assuming that the object [or action] in question needs no explanation. However frequently recurrent, modest, vulgar it may be it will now be labelled as something unusual.[65]

Forms somewhat other than standard usage are similarly employed in *Sorrow for thy Sons* when Lloyd falls over a classmate in school, and the narrator perceives him 'resting on one hand, looking at his other to see if there were any splinters and letting out a violent murmured rat-tat-tat of curses' (p. 102); Thomas incongruously employs a hard sound, 'rat-tat-tat', to describe a 'murmur' – a technique that he replicates in the novella, *Simeon* (1946) in his description of 'the plain, distant rattle of [Simeon's daughter, Bess's] sobs' (p. 275). Similarly, in *Sorrow for thy Sons* he writes that 'the street . . . was full, full of men . . . parading back and fro' (p. 80), rather than 'to and fro' or 'back and forth', and tells how 'Jones the ostler'

> passed by with his stick that had a piece of loose clicketing metal on the end of it. That would make the time about half past four. Alf felt like shouting to Jones to see why in the name of holy Joe he didn't get a nail from somewhere in the colliery and put that bit of metal right. It had been clicketing and getting on people's nerves for five years or more. But Jones was a bit deaf, and as obstinate as some of the horses it was his job to feed underground. The metal would keep on clicketing until Jones passed over or the stick crumbled. (p. 21)

'Clicketing' is an unfamiliar word reconstructed from a dismantled English equivalent, 'clicking'; and Thomas's recursive use of this neologism underscores its deconstructive effect.

This process of linguistic fission and 'creative reassembly'[66] is also palpable in *Sorrow for thy Sons* when Thomas describes how the headmaster talked 'gaspily' (p. 112), creating a new adverb from the English verb 'to gasp', and identifies the music at a local dance as a 'bellocking, tuneless combination of piano, trombone and cymbals' (p. 11). In this second example, 'bellocking' appears to be an amalgam of 'bollocking', or perhaps 'bullock', and 'bellowing' and suggests the robustness and physical energy of the music. This further energises Thomas's language itself and he makes similar attempts, as T. S. Eliot puts it in his analysis of the praxis of the modern poet, 'to force, to dislocate . . . language into his meaning'[67] in his short fiction. In *Oscar*, Lewis perceives 'the bawl of singing that splurched out of [Oscar's] mouth' (p. 85), and observes Danny standing on the coal tip 'his sack dangling in his hand, the other hand keeping the mouth of the sack open to admit the ribblings of coal he picked up' (p. 57). Here, 'Splurch' – another neologism possessing a distinct physical energy – seems to originate from 'lurch' and 'splurge', and 'ribblings' from 'dribbling' and 'ribs', from orthodox English words that, in the hands of Thomas, are, to use a phrase from *Myself My Desert*, 'pulled miles out of shape and plumb' (p. 184).[68] In this respect, Thomas's approach to language can be compared to that of James Joyce in his high Modernist novel *Ulysses* (1922) – a text which, as the following passage evinces, flouts the rules of standard English in a comparable way:

> Men, men, men.
>
> Perched on high stools by the bar, hats shoved back, at the tables calling for more bread no charge, swilling, wolfing gobfuls of sloppy food, their eyes bulging, wiping wetted moustaches. A palled suetfaced young man polished his tumbler knife fork and spoon with his napkin. New set of microbes. A man with an infant's saucestained napkin tucked round him shovelled gurgling soup down his gullet. A man spitting back on his plate: halfmasticated gristle: no teeth to chewchewchew it.[69]

Like Thomas (whose non-standard usages are, arguably, the more imaginative), Joyce conflates words – for example in 'suetfaced', 'saucestained' and 'halfmasticated' – creating a kind of grotesque prose that exaggerates the grotesqueness of his subject.[70] Moreover, according to Deleuze and Guattari, Joyce, as an Irish writer who writes in English, exploits 'the genial [or liberating] conditions of minor literature'[71] in his work – conditions which, as previously discussed, facilitate a '[transformational] utilization of English',[72] or 'a minor practice of a major language from within'. Clearly, this argument can also be applied to the narratives of Gwyn Thomas. Moreover, we might construe the similarly unfettered or 'revolutionary' practice of English seen in the work of Joyce and Thomas as manifesting a 'deterritorialization of language' (to invoke Deleuze and Guattari's critical vocabulary again) – an uprooting of a major language, or its radical transposition beyond the territorial boundaries of 'the major culture'.[73]

Not only does Thomas display a Joycean disregard for the boundaries of the English language in *Sorrow for thy Sons*, but the novel is also shot through with what appear to be self-conscious references to the simmering potential of words. Herbert suggests to Alf, for example, that 'the language [he uses] on the road is enough to blow the roof off a chapel' (p. 51), to which Alf replies, 'That's why I use it. I haven't seen any roofs blowing off yet. It must be a matter of patience or I'm not using the right words' (p. 51). Alf is clearly expressing his opposition to what he perceives as the puritanical nature of chapel culture here. But his remarks are also applicable to Thomas's own Welsh Modernist praxis: the chapel is entrenched in native, Welsh-language culture and, as previously shown, Thomas's narrative unbalances traditional linguistic models. There is evidence here of what M. Wynn Thomas calls the 'assumption [amongst many Anglophone Welsh writers of Thomas's generation] of complete complicity between chapel and [the Welsh] language'[74] – a credence that, he argues, incited those writers to concoct a 'subversive counter-discourse'. Indeed, according to Wynn Thomas, 'Welsh writing in English emerged, in its modern form, by constituting itself as a counter-hegemonic practice', calling to mind the often iconoclastic designs of Modernist writers and artists.

Gwyn Thomas's narrator in the novel avers that 'Metaphors were powder barrels of disaffection. They exploded under one's nose' (p. 40) – a strikingly accurate analysis of Thomas's own metaphorical language in *Sorrow for thy Sons*. The excess of discursive, loosely associated and even incongruous metaphor and simile in his work is itself best elucidated in metaphorical terms: the impression formed is of a 'shell-burst'[75] of imagery, which is an expression of 'disaffection', of estrangement from conventional language. Glyn Jones also seems to be referring to this effect when he describes Thomas as possessing 'a mind . . . which shoots up all its material as it were into massive and spectacular fountains, and plays upon them always the dazzling illumination of his wit'.[76] And we witness this in *Oscar*, when, referring to Oscar's treatment of his housekeeper, Meg, Lewis predicts that

> the sight of her flesh, which was very white and soft, would coax all his snoring desires from their rat-holes and he would come lunging to his feet like some element who has just been brought back from the dead, a solid sheet of flame with all his appetites barking like dogs from him, hungry for food and Meg and Christ knows what. (p. 26)

Here, and indeed throughout his work, Thomas uses the word 'element' to refer to a person: another original and idiosyncratic usage that suggests the dehumanisation of a people and the subsumption of the individual within a wider socio-political machine (ideas which I return to in chapter five). Thomas's language is not always this extravagant, but its very unpredictability gives it continuously seismic potential. In *Sorrow for thy Sons*, Alf recalls how, when a child injured himself while attempting to climb over the wall of a policeman's house to retrieve a ball, 'the policeman came out and stood there like a lighthouse taking the poor little devil's name and address' (p. 38), and in 'And a Spoonful of Grief to Taste', the narrator suggests that the sound of his voice in the choir caused 'the hair of the choir leader to drop out like hail'.[77] Similarly, in *Oscar*, Lewis compares the face of a regular customer at the local pub to 'chalk writing something on the air' (p. 16) and accuses a fruit and vegetable seller of being 'drunk as a wheel' (p. 8). Thomas's use of metaphor and simile in these examples elicits an almost Saussurean awareness of the arbitrariness of language, and might be compared to what Glyn Jones recognised as the Surrealists' 'dramatic placing of objects, words, ideas never before associated, to achieve a sense of shock, strangeness, wonder'.[78]

This connection between Thomas's idiom and European Surrealism is strengthened as his figurative language assumes increasingly surprising and outlandish forms. Thomas writes, in *Sorrow for thy Sons* that 'Alf had long ago come to the conclusion that Mrs Taylor had a stomach full of crab apples that twisted her life into all shapes except the right one' (p. 178), and he identifies Alf's neighbour as

> a robust woman, with a throat as deep and resonant as a pit shaft. Alf thought that if you fell down that woman's throat you'd come to no harm, because her inside was full of the sunlight she got down her every time she swallowed, and you'd come up as the first line of a sentimental song. (pp. 18–19)

Linguistically, these passages again seem to actualise what M. Wynn Thomas has described as Gwyn Thomas's desire 'to dramatize the sense of a decisive break with the past, of a radical new departure':[79] Thomas's English is no longer subject to that language's mechanisms of sense. This effect is not dissimilar, in fact, to that created through the Surrealist practice of 'express[ing] – verbally, by means of the written word . . . – the actual functioning of thought . . . in the absence of any control exercised by reason'.[80] The following, dream-like monologue from 'Myself My Desert' certainly has a Surrealistic tenor:

> I know now that to live is only gradually to become, in ways and looks, part of the earth that only let you go for a little canter and is waiting like

> a lusting thing to be on top of you again, stopping up your laugh, your groan and all your foolery of seeking food and sureness in a slipping, fruitless wilderness; of clutching fear's hand in the dark you share and bawling lullabies to make it sleep that sound so loud they keep the world awake and finding, when you take the trouble to glance, that your hand is gone and the hand you clutched is now your own. It looks alien and feels dead for it is yours and yet not yours. (p. 183)

In particular, the sinister hand in this extract evokes Dylan Thomas's Surrealistic short story, 'The Lemon' (1936), in which a young boy explores the dark corridors of a remote house:

> Nant, the boy, was not alone; he heard a frock rustle, a hand beneath his own scrape on the distemper. 'Whose hand?' he said softly. Then, flying in a panic down the dark carpets, he cried more loudly: 'Never answer me.' 'Your hand' said the dark, and Nant stopped still.[81]

Both passages, in fact, call to mind Salvador Dalí and Luis Buñuel's Surrealist film, *Un Chien Andalou* (1929), discussed in more detail in chapter four, which features a number of shots of disembodied and macabre hands. Whereas Dylan Thomas's knowledge of Surrealism is well documented, Gwyn Thomas's familiarity with the movement is less certain. Nevertheless, it seems highly likely that, as a lifelong cinema enthusiast and a teacher of Spanish and French, he would have been aware of Dalí and Buñuel's groundbreaking film.

Gwyn Thomas, then, can be seen as a writer who is engaging with a heightened sense of modern linguistic crisis in early twentieth-century Wales, circumventing conventional linguistic structures and constructing a 'new verbal ikon' reminiscent of the alternative 'languages' of European Modernism. The religious trace discernible in Sheppard's phrase, 'verbal ikon', may be especially pertinent to Thomas's case and, in varying ways, to the cases of other modern Anglophone Welsh writers, many of whom I discuss in this book. For Gwyn Thomas can, in M. Wynn Thomas's words, be regarded as a 'first-generation, *post-Nonconformist* [my emphasis], Anglo-Welsh writer, wanting to create a new discourse that will name his world into different, singular existence'.[82] M. Wynn Thomas is actually referring to Gwyn Thomas's famously Modernist contemporary, Dylan Thomas, here – for whom, he argues, language acted as a kind of 'saving religion'.[83] But the same might be said for Gwyn Thomas and other Modernist writers besides. Moreover, what is clear is that Thomas utilises what Deleuze and Guattari view as the 'revolutionary conditions' of 'a literature within the heart of what is called great (or established) literature': he makes 'a minor or intensive use of [language]'[84] – a practice that pushes it beyond the 'territory' of the dominant culture(s). As this impulse constitutes the inception of a new Anglo-Welsh discourse or 'verbal ikon' – a new mode of expression that establishes or marks out a distinct *territory* for Anglophone Wales and Anglophone Welsh literature – however, we might argue that Thomas's narratives are, in fact, animated and propelled by what Deleuze and Guattari describe as 'a double movement of [linguistic] deterritorialization and reterritorialization'.[85] And this also finds expression in the work of Glyn Jones and Idris Davies.

II

Glyn Jones (1905–95) was born in the south Wales mining town of Merthyr Tydfil. His more famous works include the novels, *The Valley, The City, The Village* (1956) and *The Island of Apples* (1965), as well as his seminal introductory study of English-language literature in Wales, *The Dragon has Two Tongues* (1968). He was, however, also a prolific poet and short story writer. Unlike Gwyn Thomas, Jones came from a Welsh-speaking family.[86] By the time that he had reached his teenage years, however, the same process of Anglicisation that prevented Thomas from speaking Welsh had also caused Jones to lose his native language; 'English, the language of school and street, and of chapel activities,' as Tony Brown has pointed out, 'finally and inevitably, became the language of his home.'[87] When he moved to Cardiff in the 1930s to become a schoolteacher, Jones started to attend a Welsh-speaking chapel and made friends there who introduced him to Welsh-language poetry. He gradually became fascinated by Welsh-language literature, recalling later how he was 'swept off [his] feet by the unfamiliar music of the *cywyddau*',[88] and how he read the *cywyddwyr* and *The Mabinogion* 'in a sort of blaze of glory'.[89] He later attended evening classes on Welsh culture taught by Saunders Lewis.[90] At the same time, however, Jones was acutely aware of, and deeply troubled by, the effects of economic depression on the working-class people of English-speaking south Wales. 'How', he later asked in the unpublished manuscript, 'Remembering Aloud',

> do you persuade people who have lived on the dole, and suffered the Means Test, for perhaps ten years – how do you make them realise that the language and Welsh culture are important? What they want is a job and a good standard of living for themselves and their children . . .[91]

As this note suggests, Jones was a writer for whom the modern 'crisis of language' in Wales was an immediate concern. Indeed, in *The Dragon has Two Tongues*, he proffered suggestions of ways in which this predicament might be allayed:

> What I myself would welcome in Anglo-Welsh writers is . . . a wider knowledge of the past and present of our country, particularly of our native literature, and a deeper sense of her destiny. This would surely result ultimately in closer unity between Welsh and Anglo-Welsh, so that the two groups could recognise each other as Welshmen and not merely antagonists.[92]

When Jones brings together English- and Welsh-language culture in this way in his own short stories from the 1930s and 1940s, the overall effect is often contiguous with the linguistic rupture seen in Gwyn Thomas's early writing. In his 1935 short story, 'Porth-y-Rhyd', for instance, it becomes clear from the outset that Jones is purposively attempting to connect with Welsh-language culture. He constructs the narrative in two parts: '*Machludiad*',[93] meaning 'a going down, a setting (of the sun)',[94] and *Codiad* (p. 88), meaning 'a getting up, an arising'[95] in Welsh. The story's title, which is also in Welsh and translates into English as 'gateway to the ford',[96] is the name of the place that its protagonist, Tudur, comes from, and is used, according to Welsh custom, as a substitute for his actual surname. On a more subtle level, the name 'Tudur' calls to mind the medieval Welsh bard, Tudur Aled; and Tudur's apprehension of the view from his cottage as 'lovely, a thing for praise' (pp. 88–9) later in the story echoes the central theme of praise in the Welsh poetic tradition.[97] Additionally, Tudur's surroundings appear to ground the narrative in rural, Welsh-speaking Wales and, more specifically perhaps, in Llansteffan, Carmarthenshire – a region that Jones was drawn to throughout his life – as opposed to the industrialised, English-speaking south:[98]

> Tudur was going in the sunshine down the steep little road from his cottage to the bay. It was so hot there was nothing out, no creatures and hardly any birds, only a dusty snake rowing his way across the path, and

> the baggy cormorants. The coast there was lovely in parts, and then lonely again, and a bit terrifying; and the bay itself was a curve of tigered sand between the headland and the line of pitch cliffs that the water shawled, bubbled with woods behind, whose brambles mixed with the sea-pinks and the blue thistles. (p. 85)

This knowable external world, however – already vaguely awry (Tudur's environment is unusually and oppressively hot and empty, and envisaged through resonant but faintly discordant imagery such as 'baggy cormorants', a 'rowing' snake, 'tigered sand' and 'bubbled with woods') – is soon made utterly strange. The narrator recounts how a raven perched in the 'stony branches' of a tree, 'pulled his skin lids down his flat eyes for the sun', and 'made himself finished and entire' (p. 86) – a series of events which, in turn, causes Tudur to hear 'his blood shouting the tide has gone out for the last time' (p. 86) and exposes the reader to what might be described as the linguistic uncanny or 'an experience of being disorientated, of not feeling entirely at home'[99] with the type of language being used. And we experience a similar sense of 'shock, strangeness, wonder' when Tudur, alone in his cottage, gazes out of the window at the bay:

> Slowly the light smoked up between the clouds, and Tudur saw with excitement the bay full of water between the headland plastered with irregular fields and the sliced cliffs on the left . . . It was lovely, a thing for praise, although the air was dull and filled with small rain cold as dust, and there were no waves, only the sea with light floating on it like a wafer, heaving gently and the skin of the water never broken. He rose to run down to the beach, but as he lifted the latch he saw a quiet woman in the room, holding out her long hair to dry it like a net before his fire . . . To see her first was wonderful, yet he was disappointed somehow, displeased that she was standing there like that before his face as though he were nothing, ignoring him. But she was wet with rain, her hair and her dress.
>
> 'So there is a woman on the earth,' he said, trying to please her. 'I am glad. Where have you come from? Who are you?'
>
> He thought she said, 'Yourself,' but he wasn't sure. (pp. 88–9)

Here, phrases such as 'the light smoked up' (in which Jones reinvents the verb 'smoke'), 'the air was dull', 'small rain cold as dust' and 'the skin of the water' have a deeply estranging effect which is compounded by the almost Surrealistic absence of conventional, logical narrative causality. As Nicholas Royle notes, the uncanny is 'inextricably bound up with thoughts of home and dispossession, the homely and the unhomely, property and alienation'.[100] And here, Jones's uncanny idiom seems to manifest a fascination with, and yet also a feeling of remoteness, separation and dispossession – of 'alienation' – from Welsh-speaking Wales and its culture. In capturing this psychological state, Jones effectively both 'deterritorialises' the language – alienates or casts it adrift from the 'major culture' – and 'reterritorialises' or grounds it in the form of a new 'verbal ikon' that is truer to his experience as a modern Anglophone Welsh writer.

This process is also observable in 'The Apple-Tree' (1940), a short story centred on a family of three children, Sibli, Trystan and Robyn. Echoing 'Porth-y-Rhyd', all three of these names demonstrably reflect Jones's aspiration to reconcile Welsh writing in English with Welsh-language culture, though 'Sibli' and 'Trystan' are especially revealing. Sibli is a character in the medieval Welsh tale 'Proffwydolyaeth Sibli Doeth' or 'The Prophecy of Sibli the Wise',[101] recorded in *The White Book of Rhydderch* and *The Red Book of Hergest*,[102] and she also appears in *Trioedd Ynys Prydein*, or *The Triads of the Island of Britain*.[103] 'Trystan', on the other hand, is derived from *Trystan ac Essyllt*, the Welsh version of the Arthurian legend of *Tristan and Isolde*. The quiet, coastal environment introduced in the opening paragraph of 'The Apple-Tree' – a setting which echoes that of 'Porth-y-Rhyd' – once again seems to focus Jones's narrative in rural, Welsh-speaking Wales:

> Two brilliant hills stood on the coast, with the river swollen between them carefully swallowing the sea. Over the fields of one were spread the shadows of the clouds with the slow wind peeling at them, skinning slowly back off the grasses their dark membrane of shadow, but the sea-thorns were plastered flat and brown in a bush-crust against the round rock of the other, caking its bareness, although a red tree grew on the curve of its only field. A burning sun poured out of the sky on the thick liquid of the sea, and on the ripples of the eating river, and on the shore-pool with its darn of groundwind, and on the sea-sand, and the timber, and the flesh.
>
> Down at the foot of the field-bearing hill stood a grey cottage. Three children lived there, and the eldest was called Sibli.[104]

Following the same pattern as 'Porth-y-Rhyd', however, this knowable world is disarranged by the 'uncanny strangeness'[105] of Jones's style, which captures Jones's complex feelings of enthralment and alienation in relation to Welsh-speaking Wales and Welsh-language culture. The narrator observes an 'eating river', 'the thick liquid of the sea', fields with 'a slow wind peeling at them', and 'sea-thorns . . . plastered flat and brown in a bush-crust against the round rock'. New, hybrid words such as 'bush-crust', 'shore-pool' and 'sea-sand' are wrought, with 'shore-pool' and 'sea-sand' seeming to reinvent established English nouns such as 'seashore', 'beach' and 'bay'. Tony Brown provides another example of this transformational linguistic play in 'The Apple-Tree', pointing out that, in his reference to 'the last tawn of the pointed sandbar' (p. 94), Jones extracts 'tawn' from the standard English words, 'tawny' and 'tawniness';[106] and this is also a feature of 'Porth-y-Rhyd', in which Jones envisages 'a thin white sky-skin' (p. 87) and 'a laddered sea-sun' (p. 87). Recalling the work of Gwyn Thomas, Jones also uses Welsh in 'The Apple-Tree' as 'a prism through which to fracture'[107] standard language: his reference, later in the narrative to how 'a bird dived into the back of the sea' (p. 94), for example, is 'an echo of a literal translation of the Welsh *cefnfor*', meaning '(the deep of) the ocean'.[108] In fact, Jones creates estranging effects through literally translating Welsh colloquial uses in this way throughout many of his short stories.

The imaginative scope of Jones's 'new verbal ikon' becomes apparent when Trystan returns from a trip to 'the city' (p. 92) to find that his sister's lover has drowned:

> Trystan listened in agony . . . He heard Sibli go on with her speaking, the steady anguish of her voice as she held her face close to the yellow lamplight.
>
> 'My spirit ached, I heard the creak of the well-rope. I could not speak, my mouth was dust like the blackened flower-tongue, my eyes dry as the barren finger-nail. And I saw my hands were orchards fruited with grief. I wished for thick darkness, for this day to drain like sand back into the sun, or for the bright hand of the rain around me. I saw the torn mouth of the poppy mouth my knee and the stumps of the fractured bridge sticking out of the sides of the hills. The waterbirds cried, the arum's frosted gold was snapped, the lily-bell showed the blood-veins red in her aching throat. I was naked in a bleak island of spotted thistles and my heart was broken like a heart in a picture. I saw on the coasts a drowned body wrapped in red rock under the hawk-hang of my heart . . . (pp. 94–5)

While the mystical, nostalgic tone of Jones's narrative here, as in the previous passages considered, is quite different from the black, often outrageous comedy of Gwyn Thomas's prose, the kind of language used is of a piece with Thomas's most ambitious and outlandish verbal experiments. Disorientating sentences are again interspersed with new, uncanny and estranging lexical admixtures such as 'hawk-hang', 'flower-tongue' and 'blood-veins'; though the appearance and cadence of these words call to mind Gerard Manley Hopkins's 'dapple-dáwn-drawn Falcon'[109] in his innovative poem of 1918, 'The Windhover'. Interestingly, in this text Hopkins also 'experiment[s] . . . with rhythm, and rhyme influenced by . . . Welsh patterns'.[110] The causal and chronological relationships that traditionally lend narratives cogency and verisimilitude are subverted in 'The Apple-Tree', so that Sibli's narrative seems closer to Modernist poetry than to prose; indeed, her declaration, 'I could not speak' (as previously noted) and also her reference to 'red rock' echo the first part of Eliot's *The Waste Land.*

Trystan is also the name of the protagonist in Jones's novel, *The Valley, the City, the Village*, which he was working on throughout the 1940s (though it was not published until 1956). In this narrative Jones again covets the uncanny in language, his narrator observing 'the back of the black river oiling down the cwm'[111] (*cwm* being Welsh for 'valley'); noting how 'a beam of sun like a foot-thick slice of talc, stretches in glass-like rigidity' (p. 265); and how some colliers, their 'liquid lustrous eyeballs glistening in the sunshine, ground out a cud-chewed sound as their hobnailed boots grunted past me on the road' (p. 26). Another strategy that Jones uses to defamiliarise language in this text is to texture his prose with obscure and esoteric words. When recalling his boyhood in the Ystrad Valley, the narrator describes how he and his friends 'covered the mountain's sunlit back with the patterns of our exultation and delirium, with the bedlam choreography of our dizzy eleutheromania' (p. 29); and Jones employs a similarly elaborate vocabulary to convey the experience of a train-ride to Pencwm School:

> We dive in darkness on dithyrambic wheels through the gathering crescendo of jangling gongs, bells, and deafening siren shrieks, we clamour two hours for Pencwm and hear the drum of detonations and the uproar of some interminable calliope . . . (p. 58)

These examples demonstrate how, as Stevie Davies suggests,

> Jones's inventiveness with the English language [in *The Valley, the City, the Village*] yields a spree of language, riotous, saturnalian . . . explosive,

> expressive, in which English is forced to mix its registers promiscuously, in defiance of taste and common usage.[112]

In several of Jones's poems from the 1930s, too, we witness the effacement of orthodox language in favour of an alternative, abstruse idiom. 'Man' (1934), a poem, tellingly, originally published under the title 'Half an Ancestor',[113] provides a particularly memorable example:

> The crucifix's shortest armstump points up.
> He noticed. Knew much ghost-talk flim-flam. Blew
> Buckshot; picked fish for his bucket near
> Chucked lime off the lizard pools. Sucked small
> Sea-honey; swallowed the workers' pabulum,
> The fishy porridge of a snake. Hated
> The mounted squires' duck, the hatted knee.
> Gulped at some baggy tits for suck and love.
> Felt his half-children screaming in his loins
> For entry, entry into grassy bone,
> And fed them cold pudding by his catmint
> And the sleepy apples. Sliding sea-stars were good,
> So Saturdays, entires, bitters, and
> Though some vicar's mason cut the chancel
> Cross-arms equal, church, working the bell-wheels.[114]

The linguistic character of this poem is captured in Jones's own phrase, 'ghost-talk flim-flam': Jones's language is an unfamiliar, unquiet 'ghost-talk' that is perhaps closest, in its effect, to Surrealist 'psychic automatism', or verbal expression 'dictated by thought, in the absence of any control exercised by reason'.[115] In his 1934 poem, 'Sande', Jones again, as in 'Porth-y-Rhyd' and 'The Apple-Tree', explicitly draws on native Welsh literary culture and, more specifically, on the tales of *The Mabinogion*: 'Sande' is derived from the character of Sandde Bryd Angel, or Sandde Angel-Face, in *Culwch ac Olwen*,[116] whom no man will fight because he is so beautiful.[117] The poem goes on to frustrate these cultural signifiers, however. Sande is recast as the emaciated skeleton of a saint and linguistic norms prove to be equally friable:

> Sande's crucifix, that crisscross star.
> The risking saint, naked and upright, scans
> His crop of hills and prays against the dark.

> The winds pluck off his ripened flesh like leaves,
> And then his upright bone-shrub chants, the rigid
> Thicket of his skeleton repeats
> Its praises from a lip of bone, and through
> The lantern holes of both his eyes, his ghost
> Erect and vivid, sees his morning star.
> The melted lightnings yellow round his head;
> The vigour of his dropped bones burns the rocks;
> Scattered he prays and sees his pulsing star.[118]

Jones's particular aptitude to amass strange, hybrid neologisms from the rubble of familiar language is again evinced in both 'Sande' and 'Man' – in 'bone-shrub', 'sea-stars', 'sea-honey', 'lightnings' and 'armstump'. And as with Gwyn Thomas, the religious timbre of Sheppard's term, 'new verbal ikon', seems especially relevant to Jones's work. The Christian imagery in 'Sande', in particular, seems to dramatise what M. Wynn Thomas has described as Glyn Jones's psychic 'struggle towards [Nonconformist] belief'[119] in the 1930s, which became, for him, also a struggle to reidentify with a sundered ancestral or indigenous Welsh cultural past. Wynn Thomas notes 'the persistent identification, in his [Jones's] mind, of Welshness with Nonconformity and with the Welsh language'.[120]

Clearly, then, both Gwyn Thomas and Glyn Jones can be viewed as writers who are responding to a distinct and complex sense of modern socio-linguistic crisis in early twentieth-century Wales. They are writers who are negotiating and utilising the fraught yet 'revolutionary conditions' of a 'minor literature' that is both positioned within a 'major language' and adjunct to an established, native literary culture, and – in the absence of an established Anglo-Welsh literary discourse or 'a recognisably indigenous English-language literature'[121]– searching for a mode of expression that is appropriate to the modern, Anglicised Wales of their experience. Their work is, in a effect, a riposte to Saunders Lewis's assertion in 'Is there an Anglo-Welsh Literature?':

> there is not a separate literature that is Anglo-Welsh, and . . . it is improbable that there ever can be that . . . For if the Anglo-Welsh by writing in English have wider fame, more worldly honours, more social success, and more money, the writers in Welsh have the prestige of a national literature, and still some sense of assurance that comes from belonging to a great tradition.[122]

Lewis seems to have based his opinion, at least in part, on his own experience of writing about Wales in English in his 1921 play, *The Eve of St John*. In this text – 'a . . . one-act comedy set amongst the peasantry of nineteenth-century Wales' – as Bruce Griffiths points out, 'the influence of [the Irish playwright] J. M. Synge is plain',[123] suggesting that Lewis was casting about for, and failing to produce, what he felt to be an appropriate voice or mode of non-standard English in which to express Welsh experience. 'I couldn't be satisfied with its diction,' Lewis later said of the play, 'and I settled the issue by turning and learning to write in Welsh. It was the logical thing to do.'[124] We might argue, moreover, that the Anglo-Welsh 'verbal ikon' that Lewis felt simply could not exist was even more disposed to linguistic creativity by virtue of the fact that Glyn Jones and Gwyn Thomas *were* among those 'men' of industrialised, Anglicised Wales who, according to Lewis, had 'lost one tongue without acquiring another'.[125] They were first-generation English speakers, who, as Tony Conran emphasises, were 'essentially dealing with a new language'.[126] Jones seems to be registering this propensity in *The Valley, the City, the Village* when Welsh-speaking Zachy is said to have 'kept a little black book in which he collected big English words' (p. 114), and in his characterisation of Gwydion – a figure who he identifies as 'above all, Welsh' and 'deeply conscious of it' (p. 304):

> In Gwydion there is the childish love of words . . . He seemed sometimes as though mankind's ancient and universal faculty of speech were to him a new and enchanting discovery. He was a dictionary reader, a neologist, an inventor of nicknames . . . Any such oddity as an adjective embedded in the middle of a noun delighted him. (p. 298)

'Gwydion' is of course the name of a sorcerer in the *Mabinogion*, and so there is a sense that Jones's character, like his creator, is a kind of verbal magician, conjuring spectacles and transformations in language.

III

Idris Davies (1905–53) was born in the town of Rhymney, in the Rhymney Valley, and published three books of poetry, *Gwalia Deserta* (1938), *The Angry Summer* (1943) and *Tonypandy and Other Poems* (1945). Like Gwyn Thomas and Glyn Jones, he came from a

Welsh-speaking family.[127] In contrast to Jones and Thomas, however, the Anglicisation of the south Wales Valleys did not cause Davies to lose his native language completely; his parents continued to speak Welsh to him at home, and, as Dafydd Johnston notes, he ultimately only lacked 'the ability to express himself confidently and satisfactorily in [the language] in written' form.[128] Like Glyn Jones, Davies later attended evening classes in an attempt to improve his knowledge of literary Welsh, and he wrote several Welsh-language poems during the 1930s.[129] But he continued to use poetry as a medium through which to voice the experiences of the many people in south Wales who spoke only English. The following verse from 'I was Born in Rhymney' (1943) is a well-known example:

> I lost my native language
> For the one the Saxon spake
> By going to school by order
> For education's sake.[130]

Davies's poetic sequence, *Gwalia Deserta* (1938), has been described by Conran as a 'collage'[131] of discourses, manifesting a 'dislocation and contrast of registers',[132] which, he suggests, reflect the disintegration of 'the *buchedd*'[133] or 'the Welsh way of life'[134] in the south Wales Valleys during the early decades of the twentieth century. Conran draws attention, for example, to Davies's juxtaposition, in the opening four lines of the first poem in the sequence, of documentary,[135] Surrealistic, Welsh hymnological, and modern cinematic styles respectively:[136]

> The Commissioners depart with all their papers
> And the pit-heads grin in the evening rain;
> The white deacons dream of Gilead in the Methodist vestry
> And the unemployed stare at the winter trees.[137]

In transcribing the dissolution of '*buchedd*-culture'[138] in this way, Conran opines, Davies created a 'modernism' which, while it 'never quite got into top gear', 'sit[s] quite happily with the craggier works of Dylan Thomas and Glyn Jones'.[139] While Daniel G. Williams, comparing Davies's poetic technique with that of the African American poet, Langston Hughes, argues that 'both poets juxtapose voices and points of view, 'high' and 'low' cultures, and in the fragmentary, heteroglossic, form of their poetic sequences both can be seen to manifest a number of characteristics that are today recognised as distinctively "modernist"'.[140] Conran's exegesis certainly connects Davies's poetic technique with wider trends in European and Anglo-American Modernism. Collage performed an important role in the development of the new 'languages' of Futurism, Dadaism and Surrealism – as the work of the visual artists, Carlo Carrà, Raoul Hausmann, Joan Miró and Kurt Schwitters attests – and T. S. Eliot also invokes a collage-like technique in the closing lines of *The Waste Land*, 'shoring' 'fragments' of languages against the ruinous, 'arid plain' of modern consciousness. Indeed, with its central trope of contemporary south Wales as a desolate land, *Gwalia Deserta* might even be construed as a kind of reply or Welsh counterpart to Eliot's famous poem.[141] The parallel that Conran draws between Davies's early work and that of Glyn Jones, however, should also be considered within the context of what Conran describes as the 'social and linguistic convulsions churning around the individual consciousness'[142] in contemporary Wales. For the collage, by its very nature, entails a process of rupture and reinvention comparable with that witnessed previously in both Glyn Jones's short stories and poetry and in the fiction of Gwyn Thomas. As Jones himself wrote in 'Nodiadau ar Surrealistiaeth' or 'Notes on Surrealism' (1937), an essay published in the Welsh-language avant-garde magazine *Tir Newydd* or *New Ground*, collage represents 'a new way of creating pictures of objects and people by cutting out bits of pictures of objects and people from newspapers and magazines and then gluing them together on paper to form a new picture.'[143] Moreover, if *Gwalia Deserta* amounts to a kind of linguistic collage, then it too can be interpreted as an expressive conduit for and response to the modern 'crisis of language' in Wales, and, more specifically, as a text where language, like the 'bits of pictures of objects and people' that comprise a pictorial collage, is simultaneously 'deterritorialised' or dislocated, and 'reterritorialised' or 'glued together' to form an experimental 'new picture' – a manifestly fissiparous and discursive new literary discourse or 'verbal ikon' appropriate to contemporary south Wales.

This process is decipherable in the opening four lines of the sequence, cited at the beginning of this section, and it is similarly apparent in the first stanza of poem XXVII:

So we're all Welsh boys gathered together,
Boys bach, boys bach
We have roamed from the rain and the ruins,
Boys bach, boys bach (p. 15)

Here, conversational, working-class camaraderie ('So we're all Welsh boys gathered together') is juxtaposed with the poetic and notably Romantic 'We have roamed from the rain and the ruins'.[144] Indeed, the tone and style of this line can be compared with that of section XIV – a poem which Dafydd Johnston has suggested echoes the work of the English Romantic poet, William Wordsworth[145] – demonstrating how the collage-like 'textual instability and epistemological uncertainty'[146] of *Gwalia Deserta* manifests itself both within the fabric of each individual poem and at a holistic level:

Roaming the derelict valley at dusk
Breathing the air of desolation
Watching the thin moon rise behind the mountain church,
I seek in the faces of men glimpses of early joy,
I seek in the sounds of human speech
The echoes of some far forgotten rapture ... (p. 9)

The linguistically uneven and protean character of poem XXVII is also evidenced in the repeated bilingual phrase, 'boys bach', and similarly in poem XXV:

Who seeks another kingdom
Beyond the common sky?
Who seeks the crystal towers
That made the martyrs sigh?

On earth alone your towers,
By human strength, shall stand,
And the waters of your mountains
Alone shall save the land.

Your cities shall be founded
On human pride and pain,
And the fire of your vision
Shall clean the earth again. (p. 14)

Both the content and the form of these stanzas seem to have their origins in Welsh Nonconformist hymnology: the pattern of 'the four-line stanza, with short second and fourth lines rhyming', as Johnston notes, 'is very common in the work of [the eighteenth-century Nonconformist hymn-writer] Williams Pantycelyn'.[147] Embedded in this Welsh religious idiom, however, is secular, Socialist discourse,[148] and this also occurs in poem IV:

> O timbers from Norway and muscles from Wales,
> Be ready for another shift and believe in co-operation,
> Though pit-wheels are frowning at old misfortunes
>
> And girders remember disasters of old;
> O what is man that coal should be so careless of him,
> And what is coal that so much blood should be upon it? (p. 4)

In the last two lines cited, Davies offsets rhetorical language, familiar from newspaper headlines and political speeches or manifestos, with biblical discourse and, more specifically, with psalm 8, verse 3: 'What is man, that thou art mindful of him? And the son of man, that thou visitest him?'[149] In poem XV, on the other hand, ecclesiastical cadences give way to the English nursery rhyme, 'Oranges and Lemons':

> Oh what can you give me?
> Say the sad bells of Rhymney.
>
> Is there hope for the future?
> Cry the brown bells of Merthyr.
>
> Who made the mineowner?
> Say the black bells of Rhondda
>
> And who robbed the miner?
> Cry the grim bells of Blaina.
>
> They will plunder willy-nilly,
> Say the bells of Caerphilly.
>
> They have fangs, they have teeth!
> Shout the loud bells of Neath.
>
> To the south, things are sullen,
> Say the pink bells of Brecon.

Even God is uneasy
Say the moist bells of Swansea.

Put the vandals in court!
Cry the bells of Newport.
(pp. 9–10)

The at once naive and polemical tone of this poem – 'They will plunder willy-nilly, / Say the bells of Caerphilly' – endows it with a discordant and occasionally jarring quality, reminiscent, once again, of collage. Indeed, Davies's choice of individual words – his references, for instance, to the 'pink' bells of Brecon and to the 'moist' bells of Swansea – educes an uncanny strangeness similar to that generated by this Modernist technique, a comparable sense that things are not quite 'at-home'. Tony Conran seems to observe a similar effect in his introduction to Davies's later poetic sequence, *The Angry Summer* (1943), noting how sometimes, in this work too, 'ideas . . . don't altogether fit' and 'metaphors . . . splay out from the signifier in too many directions at once'.[150] Again, this effect seems to be facilitated and augmented by what Conran describes as the 'newness' of the English language for Welsh writers such as Davies, in whose work, he suggests, 'words are [perhaps] . . . without the *patina*' – the 'trace elements of pathos, irony or snob-value' – 'that English writers would instinctively give them'.[151] Moreover, to return to poem IV, Davies's piecemeal method is again palpable in the shift from archaic folk-song ('O timbers from Norway and muscles from Wales' – a line that also structurally presages the reference to psalm 8, discussed earlier) to the decontextualised, prosaic instructions of a modern industrialist ('Be ready for another shift and believe in co-operation'); and from this quotidian mode back to the 'Surrealistic' or more accurately perhaps, Expressionistic style that Conran apprehends in the opening of the sequence. 'Though pit-wheels are frowning' subjectively distorts a 'social image'[152] in a manner characteristic of European Expressionist literature and art.[153]

The 'double movement[s] of [linguistic] deterritorialisation and reterritorialisation' which drive the early writings of Idris Davies, Glyn Jones and Gwyn Thomas can then be seen as a Modernist dynamic, which indexes these writers' creative engagement with, and utilisation of, the modern 'crisis of language' in early twentieth-century Wales. This connection with the international cultural context of Modernism problematises narrow critical approaches to these writers, which tend to recycle, in various forms, the idea of the *bardd gwlad* –

> that is, of the poet [or writer] as serving his/her [Welsh] community, deliberately cultivating versatility, regularly producing what in English culture tends to be dismissed as 'occasional' verse [or writing] (much of it knowingly disposable), even while capable of functioning at an altogether more 'sophisticated' literary level.[154]

But it also, in a sense, entails a recasting of the concept of Modernism itself. As Laura Doyle and Laura Winkiel suggest, under these circumstances 'the *term* modernism' – historically, and often still, employed to signify a principally transnational, metropolitan, high-cultural phenomenon that began at the turn of the century and ended in the early 1930s – 'breaks open', like a conventional word or phrase in the hands of Gwyn Thomas and Glyn Jones,

> into something we [might] call geomodernisms, which signals a locational approach to modernisms' engagement with cultural and political discourses of global modernity. The revelation of such an approach is double. It unveils both unsuspected 'modernist' experiments in 'marginal' texts and suspected correlations between those texts and others that appear either more conventional or more postmodern.[155]

'Across their differences', Doyle and Winkiel continue,

> these works share something that allows them to be grouped together: a self-consciousness about positionality. Here, positionality is onto-social as well as geographical, entailing a sense of situated and disrupted social presence. Thus in some sense, however local their settings, their horizon is global and their voicing is refracted through the local-global dialectic of inside and outside, belonging and exile . . .[156]

As I have demonstrated, the largely 'unsuspected' Modernist experiments of Davies, Jones and Thomas are inspired by these writers' awareness of their own 'disrupted social presence' – 'refracted through the local-global dialectic' of native Welsh-language and English-language culture, and fuelled by a conflicting sense of both 'belonging' and 'exile'. In essence, their Modernism is the product of an acute 'self-consciousness about positionality', or (to use Deleuze and Guattari's word) 'territoriality',[157] that is at once geographical, social and cultural. The 'conditions' in which Davies, Jones and Thomas operate as writers are indeed, as Deleuze and Guattari suggest, 'revolutionary'. They point towards a 'logical slippage' between the 'minor' and 'the Modernist' – a nexus that should encourage consideration of more Welsh writing in English from this period in relation to Modernism – which is firmly grounded in 'temporal' and 'cultural specificity'.[158] This 'self-consciousness about positionality', moreover, can also be said to inform the work of the widely acknowledged Modernist writer and visual artist, David Jones, as I will suggest in the final section of this chapter, with reference to Jones's book-length war poem, *In Parenthesis* (1937).

IV

David Jones differs from Gwyn Thomas, Glyn Jones and Idris Davies in the sense that he was neither born nor brought up in Wales. Although his father came from a Welsh-speaking family based in Flintshire, north Wales,[159] Jones was born in Kent[160] and lived in London for much of his life.[161] Additionally, Jones was not exposed to the Welsh language in the same way that Gwyn Thomas, Glyn Jones and Idris Davies were; his father had been discouraged from speaking Welsh as a child, and so he was unable to pass the language on to his son.[162] Despite his English upbringing, however, David Jones felt an intense personal and artistic connection with Wales, and he developed a close affinity with Welsh-language tradition. This relationship finds constant expression in his work, which includes visual art as well the book-length poems, *In Parenthesis* (1937), *The Anathémata* (1952) and *The Sleeping Lord* (1974). As Jeremy Hooker points out, he also 'spent one of the most emotionally intense and intellectually fertile periods of his life living . . . at Capel-y-ffin in the Black Mountains in 1925–6'.[163] 'Here,' Hooker adds, 'through his paintings, he acquired a strong sense of the rhythms of Welsh landscapes, while . . . his literary and historical studies enhanced his feeling for Wales as a many-storied land.'[164] To some extent, then, Jones self-consciously 'positioned' himself as – or elected to inhabit the 'territory' of – a modern Anglophone Welsh writer. Like his contemporary, Lynette Roberts, his Welshness was, in Patrick McGuinness's words, essentially 'a combination of choice and imaginative will'.[165]

Jones's 'imaginative will' to integrate Wales and Welsh culture into his oeuvre is nowhere more apparent than in *In Parenthesis*, a poem based on his own experiences as a soldier in the First World War. Conveying and experimentally interweaving the external and psychological reality of conflict on the Western Front, Jones focuses on the Third Battalion of what was his own regiment, the Royal Welch Fusiliers,[166] whom he identifies in his preface as 'mostly Londoners with an admixture of Welshmen'.[167] Through frequent references and allusions, Jones compares the plight of this regiment to that of the 300 warriors from the *Gododdin* tribe in Aneirin's sixth-century Welsh-language heroic poem, *Y Gododdin*.[168] Indeed, Aneirin's poem, which chronicles the heroic defeat of the *Gododdin* by English armies at the battle of Catraeth around the year 600,[169] is a key piece – to reapply Conran's metaphor for Idris Davies's *Gwalia Deserta* – in the 'collage' of discourses or 'languages' that comprises Jones's text, functioning, in part, as a commemoration of the bravery of the soldiers who fought in the Great War. The epigraph to part six of the poem, for example, is taken from *Y Gododdin* and includes the lines, 'Men went to Catraeth . . . death's sure meeting place, the goal of their marching.'[170] Jones also hints at the eulogistic function of this intertext in his essay, 'Welsh Poetry' (1957), stating:

> the poetry of the 'first-bards' was concerned with a recalling and appraisement of the heroes in lyric form'[171] – '*Gwyr y aeth Gatraeth*, Men went to Catraeth'; how natural it is for us of this generation to substitute for Catraeth, *y ffosydd*, 'the trenches'.[172]

As previously noted, however, *In Parenthesis*, like *Gwalia Deserta*, actually presents the reader with a melange of discourses, both literary and non-literary. In the following extract from part three, for example, a conversation between a Welsh corporal and a soldier on sentry duty visibly splinters, scattering shards of language which collectively recall the verbal experiments not only of Idris Davies, but also of Glyn Jones and Gwyn Thomas:

> Can you see anything, sentry.
> Nothing corporal.
> '01 Ball is it, no.
> Yes corporal.
> Keep a sharp outlook sentry – it is the most elementary
> disciplines – sights at 350.
> Yes corporal.
> 300 p'r'aps.
> Yes corporal.
> Starving as brass monkeys – as the Arctic bear's arse –

> Diawl! – starved as Pen Nant Govid, on the confines of
> hell. (p. 52)

In this passage, the phrase 'Starving as brass monkeys', as Jones informs the reader in his notes on the text, is derived 'from the popular expression among soldiers, 'Enough to freeze the testicles off a brass monkey'.[173] But echoing the deconstructive techniques of Glyn Jones and Gwyn Thomas, this English colloquialism is – to use David Jones's own words in the poem – 'unmade' (p. 60) and 'made newly real' (p. 28): 'brass monkeys' is used to convey hunger instead of cold. This new metaphor then accrues a bizarre, almost Surrealistic and, in this sense, again, strikingly Gwyn Thomas-like dint through the phrase, 'Starving . . . as the Arctic bear's arse', with 'Arctic bear' connoting both a polar bear and Arcturus, the Great Bear of the solar system.

Subsequently, the corporal – we assume that we are hearing the voice of the corporal, although, as Paul Fussell notes, 'as readers, we don't always know who's speaking, and to whom'[174] in this text – adds to this defamiliarised English slang a Welsh-language expletive, '*diawl*', meaning 'Devil, one deprived of light',[175] and then, in an abrupt change of register that again recalls Idris Davies's collage-like praxis in *Gwalia Deserta*, shifts into the language of Welsh mythology: 'Pen Nant Govid, on the confines of / hell' is derived from the dialogue between Culhwch and the giant Ysbaddaden Bencawr in the medieval Welsh tale *Culhwch ac Olwen*. In this story, Ysbaddaden Bencawr sets a number of tasks for Culhwch to complete before he will allow him to marry his daughter, one of which is to retrieve 'the blood of the Very Black Witch, daughter of the Very White Witch, from Pennant Gofid in the uplands of hell'[176] so that he may 'straighten out'[177] his beard in preparation for it to be shaved for the wedding. There is an element of absurdity to Ysbaddaden Bencawr's request, which is consistent with what Dafydd Johnston calls the often 'extravagantly hyperbolical'[178] style of *Culhwch ac Olwen*;[179] and, on one level, its appearance in Jones's text alongside the similarly dislocated and outlandish English-language simile, 'Starving . . . as the Arctic bear's arse', seems to represent Jones's attempt to recreate the idiolect of the Welsh soldiers in his battalion. As he later suggested, the Londoners and the Welsh 'both speak in parables, [and] the wit of both is quick'.[180] Equally, however, from another vantage point, these lines embody – in a kind of 'consummation of all burstings-out'

(*In Parenthesis*, p. 24) – the manifold linguistic innovations previously observed in the work of Idris Davies, Gwyn Thomas and Glyn Jones. As Jones reveals in his preface to the poem, 'this writing is called "In Parenthesis" because I have written it in a kind of space between'.[181] To some extent, this interstitial zone is temporal: it is the 'space between' the Battle of Catraeth and the Battle of Mametz Wood, and also, perhaps, between 1914–18 and 1937. But it is also linguistic: like his Anglophone Welsh contemporaries, David Jones tendentiously conceives an alternative, Modernist idiom in this poem through refracting his voice through 'the local-global dialectic of inside and outside, belonging and exile', through purposively locating his writing within, and utilizing the 'revolutionary conditions' expedited by the 'space between' English-language and Welsh-language literary culture.

The ensuing 'conversation' between corporal and soldier lends support to such a reading:

> Unwise it is to disturb the sentinel.
> Do dogs of Annwn glast this starving air – do they ride the trajectory zone, between the tangled brake above the leaning walls.
> This seventh gate is parked tonight.
> His lamps hang in this black cold and hang so still; with this still rain slow-moving vapours wreathe to refract their clear ray – like through glassy walls that slowly turn they rise and fracture – for this fog-smoke wraith they cast a dismal sheen.
> What does he brew in his cauldron,
> over there.
> What is it like. (p. 52)

Here, Jones strays further away from the realistic, conversational mode in which this exchange began into an allusive, oneiric idiom that is self-consciously positioned, like Glyn Jones's equally estranging narrative in 'The Apple-Tree', between Welsh-language and English-language culture. 'Unwise it is to disturb the sentinel' is derived from the line, 'Difficult was a conversation with its sentinel'[182] in the medieval Welsh bard Taliesin's poem, *Preiddeu Annwn*,[183] and the word order of both lines again reflects Welsh-language sentence structure. This text documents Arthur's descent into *Annwn* or *Annwfn* – the 'hell' to which Ysbaddaden Bencawr refers in *Culhwch ac Olwen*, and which Jones identifies in his notes as 'the frozen regions of the Celtic underworld',[184] and it is also echoed in Jones's line, 'His lamps hang in this black cold and hang so still': Taliesin writes in *Preiddeu Annwn* that 'before the door of the gate of Uffern the lamp was / burning' (p. 265).[185] The interrogative 'Do dogs of Annwn glast this starving air' sustains this interplay with *Preiddeu Annwn*, although it originates, Jones reveals in his notes, from Lady Charlotte Guest's claim that 'dogs of Annwn' are 'still heard by the peasants of Wales, riding the night sky'[186] – a superstition which finds parodic expression in Caradoc Evans's short story, 'Be this Her Memorial' (1915):

> Mice and rats, as it is said, frequent neither churches nor poor men's homes. The story I have to tell you about Nanni – the Nanni who was hustled on her way by the Bad Man . . . who saw the Spirit Hounds and heard their moanings two days before Isaac Penparc took wing – the story I have to tell contradicts that theory.[187]

Evans's reference to the 'Spirit Hounds' of Annwn, like Jones's, pertains to a general, idiomatic contravention of normative language – though Jones does not construct 'a made-up language which mocks Welshness',[188] in the way that Tony Conran has concluded Evans does. On the contrary, he invokes an 'obsolete'[189] Welsh word, 'glast', meaning 'to bark a lot',[190] which disrupts both the syntax and the logic of the question, and produces a Glyn Jones-like Delphic effect that is enhanced by the presence of a full stop instead of a question mark. The analogously closed questions, 'What does he brew in his cauldron / over there. / What is it like.', also function in this way, reinscribing and obfuscating two more lines from *Preiddeu Annwn*: 'Is it not the cauldron of the chief of Annwyn? What is / its intention?' (p. 265). Although 'This seventh gate is parked tonight' entrammels Taliesin's poem in a similar way (Arthur and his men pass through a series of gates as he journeys into the underworld), this intertext is juxtaposed with another Gwyn Thomas-esque reinvented English expression: 'parked', as Jones indicates, is created from 'parky',[191] meaning 'cold'.[192] And finally, again evoking Idris Davies's *Gwalia Deserta*, Jones stirs English Romantic discourse into his linguistic 'cauldron'; 'for this fog-smoke wraith they cast a dismal sheen' is plainly concocted from part one of Samuel Taylor Coleridge's ballad, 'The Rime of the Ancient Mariner' (1817):

And now there came both mist and snow,
And it grew wondrous cold:
And ice, mast-high, came floating by,
As green as emerald.

And through the drifts the snowy clifts
Did send a dismal sheen:
Nor shapes of men nor beasts we ken –
The ice was all in between.

At length did cross an Albatross,
Thorough the fog it came;
As if it had been a Christian soul,
We hailed it in God's name.

. . . In mist or cloud, on mast or shroud,
It perched for vespers nine;
Whiles all the night, through fog-smoke white,
Glimmered the white Moon-shine.[193]

Coleridge's poem also resounds in Jones's subsequent portrayal of a soldier named 'Old Adams, Usk':

> Old Adams, Usk, sits stark, he already regrets his sixty-two years. His rifle-butt is a third foot for him, all three supports are wood for him, so chill this floor strikes up, so this chill creeps to mock his bogus 'listing age.
>
> Forty-five – Christ – forty five in Her Jubilee Year, before the mothers of these pups had dugs to nourish them.
>
> He grips more tightly the cold band of his sling-swivel; he'd known more sodden, darker ways, below the Old Working. He shifts his failing flanks along the clammy slats . . . (p. 53)

Ostensibly, the reference here to Old Adams's 'listing age' recreates the speech patterns of soldiers in the trenches: 'listing' seems, at first glance, to be an abbreviated form of 'enlisting'. But 'listing', connoting both a stricken ship and the posture of 'Old Adams' himself, leaning heavily on his 'rifle-butt', also seems to invoke and invert the following simile from 'The Rime of the Ancient Mariner':

With sloping masts and dipping prow,
As who pursued with yell and blow

> Still treads the shadow of his foe,
> And forward bends his head,
> The ship drove . . . (i. 45–9)

These enmeshed colloquial and English Romantic discourses are, in turn, also amalgamated with native Welsh literary tradition; 'His rifle-butt is a third foot for him' is sourced from the following 'ninth-century Welsh stanza'[194] from *The Red Book of Hergest*:

> Mountain snow – the hart on the slope;
> The wind whistles over the ash-tops.
> A third foot for the aged is his stick.[195]

Here again we witness, in Jones's words, a 'dissolving and splitting of solid things' (*In Parenthesis*, p. 24), as assorted discourses collide and conflate to engender a poetic bricolage in which language is always unstable and diffuse, and therefore perpetually just beyond easy apprehension. In essence, language in *In Parenthesis* appears distanced – at times, remote – and the 'uncanny' prose of Glyn Jones is again called to mind in lines such as 'all three sup / ports are wood for him, so chill this floor strikes up' and 'He shifts his failing flanks along the clammy slats'.

David Jones's free-floating mode of expression is perhaps most memorably displayed, however, at the scene of Corporal Aneirin Lewis's death in part seven:

> And the place of their waiting a long burrow,
> in the chalk, and steep clift –
> but all too shallow against his violence.
> Like in long-ship, where you flattened face to kelson for
> the shock-breaking on brittle pavissed free-board, and the gunnel stove, and no care to jettison the dead.
>
> No one to care there for Aneirin Lewis spilled there
> who worshipped his ancestors like a Chink
> who sleeps in Arthur's lap
> who saw Olwen-trefoils some moonlighted night
> on precarious slats at Festurbert,
> on narrow foothold on le Plantin marsh –
> more shaved he is to the bare bone than
> Yspaddadan Penkawr.

> Properly organised chemists can let make more riving
> power than ever Twrch Trwyth;
> more blistered he is than painted Troy Towers
> and unwholer, limb from limb, than any of them fallen at
> Catraeth
>
> (p. 155)

'The Rime of the Ancient Mariner' continues to figure prominently in this section of the poem; the 'long burrow' in which the soldiers lie, 'flattened face' to the ground, is compared to a 'long-ship' and the enemy fire is likened to waves crashing or 'shock-breaking' on the deck. Furthermore, just as the storm in 'The Ancient Mariner' is personified – 'And now the STORM-BLAST came, and he / Was tyrannous strong' (ll. 41–2) – the narrator of Jones's text regards the burrow as 'too shallow against *his* violence, [my emphasis] and the 'steep ["chalk"] clift' of this fragile hideaway comports with the 'snowy clifts' encountered by the Mariner and his crew. The phrase, 'no care to jettison the dead', on the other hand, itself echoes the following vignette from part four of Coleridge's ballad:

> I looked upon the rotting sea,
> and drew my eyes away;
> I looked upon the rotting deck;
> And there the dead men lay. (iv. 240–3)

These echoes from the phantasmagorical 'ghastly tale' (l. 585) of the mariner and his crew emphasise the disorientating, alienating and terrifying world of the trenches. Whereas 'No one to care there for Aneirin Lewis spilled there' maintains the Romantic tenor, the ensuing description of the corporal as a man 'who worshipped his ancestors like a Chink' first marks an abrupt diversion into contemporary army slang, and then again, more subtly, integrates historic Welsh-language literature. The lines, 'who worshipped his ancestors like a Chink / who sleeps in Arthur's lap / who saw Olwen-trefoils some moonlighted night' seem to emulate the often repetitive syntax of *Y Gododdin*:

> It was usual on a spirited horse to defend Gododdin
> In the forefront of the battle of the ardent ones,
> It was usual that on the track of a deer he was swift,
> It was usual that before the war-band of the Deirans
> He would attack,[196]

. . .

He charged before three hundred of the finest,
He cut down both centre and wing,
He excelled in the forefront of the noblest host,
(ll. 947–9)

'Olwen-trefoils', on the other hand, is a reference to the 'Four white clovers [that] would spring up behind . . . [Olwen] wherever/ she went' (p. 192) in *Culhwch ac Olwen* (Jones cites this line in his notes as 'Four white trefoils sprang up wherever she trod').[197] And 'Who sleeps in Arthur's lap' brings another intertext into the fray, invoking the following passage from Shakespeare's *Henry V*, where, on the eve of war with France, Ensign Pistol, Lieutenant Bardolph, Corporal Nim and the Hostess lament the death of the knight, Falstaff:[198]

PISTOL . . . my manly heart doth erne. Bardolph,
Be blithe; Nim, rouse thy vaunting veins; boy, bristle
Thy courage up. For Falstaff he is dead,
And we must earn therefore.
BARDOLPH Would I were with him, wheresome'er he is, either in heaven or In hell!
HOSTESS Nay, sure, he's not in hell: he's in Arthur's bosom, if ever a man went to Arthur's bosom.[199]

This euphemistic Shakespearean language is shadowed, however, by Welsh mythological references freighted with the brutal physicality of death; 'more shaved he is to the bare bone than / Yspaddadan Penkawr', for example, foregrounds the giant's demise in *Culhwch ac Olwen*:

And then Culhwch set out with . . . those who wished harm to Ysbaddaden Bencawr, and took the wonders with them to his court. And Caw son of Prydyn came to shave off Ysbaddaden's beard, flesh and skin to the bone, and both ears completely.

And Culhwch said, 'Have you been shaved, man?'

'I have,' he replied.

'And is your daughter now mine?'

'Yours,' he replied . . . And then Gorau son of Custennin grabbed him by the hair and dragged him to the mound and cut off his head and stuck it on the bailey post. And he took possession of his fort and his territory. (p. 213)

Again, the explosive force of Jones's 'strenuously allusive'[200] and esoteric style dissipates through the account of Corporal Aneirin Lewis's death. The lines, 'Properly organised chemists can let make more riving / power than ever Twrch Trwyth', for instance – in which the speaker opines that not even Twrch Trwyth, 'the mysterious destroying beast'[201] from *Culwch ac Olwen*, could realise the carnage of modern warfare – are syntactically discomposed. And, recalling the work of Glyn Jones and Gwyn Thomas, an invented word, 'unwholer', replaces the standard English, 'more unwhole'.

Indeed, in occupying this linguistic 'space between' English-language and Welsh-language culture, *In Parenthesis* can be regarded, as Chris Wigginton contends, as 'writing which deals with the condition of Welshness'[202] in the 1930s and 1940s, and, more specifically, as writing which indexes the 'epochal rupture'[203] of language and culture in Wales during this period. Jones's linguistic preoccupations could, as Jeremy Hooker writes, be said to 'illuminate the complex situation of the modern Anglo-Welsh writer, a situation brought about by the social . . . pressures behind Anglicisation in his father's generation'.[204] Moreover, *In Parenthesis* can be viewed as a text that not only inhabits and dramatises the modern Welsh 'crisis of language', but also, effectively, turns it into a 'language of crisis', harnessing its explosive, estranging potential in order to create a 'new verbal ikon' capable of 'overcoming the futility felt by David Jones and all other combatants when trying to tell civilians what the war was really like'.[205] For Jones, the linguistic 'parenthesis' or 'space between' – the deterritorialised, no-man's land – in which he self-consciously positions himself as a Welsh author writing in English, in a sense, becomes paradigmatic – representative of a more general feeling of disintegration, disjuncture and disorientation roused by the events of the First World War. Essentially, moreover, in *In Parenthesis*, as Duncan Campbell has said of Jones's later book-length poem, *The Anathémata* (1952), war is 'linked to *cultural* chaos and instability [my emphasis]';[206] and Jones's association of the modern Welsh 'crisis of language' with the soldier's experience in the trenches is made explicit in part four of the text:

> Lance-Corporal [Aneirin] Lewis looked about him and on all this liquid action.
>
> It may be remembered Seithenin and the desolated cantrefs, the sixteen fortified places, the great cry of the sea,

> above the sigh of Gwyddno when his entrenchments stove in. Anyway he kept the joke to himself for there was none to share it in that company, for although Watcyn knew everything about the Neath fifteen, and could sing *Sospan Fach* to make the traverse ring, he might have been an Englishman when it came to matters near to Aneirin's heart. (p. 89)

The 'liquid action' that the narrator records here pertains to the 'continuing rain' (p. 88) and the failure of the 'trench-drain' (p. 88) to prevent flooding – a situation, which Lance-Corporal Lewis ironically likens to 'the inundation of [the city of] Cantref Gwaelod ruled over by Gwyddno, whose drunken dyke-warden, Seithenin, failed to attend his duties'[207] in a poem from *The Black Book of Carmarthen*. The following extract from the poem illustrates 'the sigh of Gwyddno' 'above':

> A cry from the roaring sea
> Impels me from my resting-place this night;
> Common after excess is far-extending destruction.
>
> The grave of Seithenin the weak-minded
> Between Caer Cenedir and the shore
> Of the great sea and Cinran.[208]

The corporal, however, is unable to share this 'joke' with Watcyn, who embodies the disjunction between traditional Welsh literary discourse and the new social discourses of south Wales. Watcyn's knowledge of native Welsh-language culture, it seems, is limited to *Sospan Fach*, a song adopted by rugby supporters, and sung at matches.[209] Indeed, as the narrator observes, Watcyn 'might have been an Englishman when it came to matters near to Aneirin's heart' – 'Aneirin' connoting both the corporal and the poet.

In this sense, just as the 'new verbal ikon[s]' of Gwyn Thomas, Glyn Jones and Idris Davies were compared to the new 'languages' of European Modernism, so Jones's alternative idiom might be likened to the experimental evocations of war by other Modernist artists and writers: to the violent, chaotic dynamism represented in Tullio Crali's Futurist painting, *Air Battle I* (1936–8),[210] for example, or the sinisterly Expressionist use of colour in Otto Dix's painting *Self-Portrait as a Soldier* (1914–15). We might also place Jones's alternative 'language' alongside that exhibited in the war poetry of the German

Expressionist writer, August Stramm, who fought, and was ultimately killed, in the First World War. 'Guard-Duty' (1915), a poem that strongly evokes part three of *In Parenthesis*, provides a particularly thought-provoking example:

> A star frightens the steeple cross
> a horse gasps smoke
> iron clanks drowsily
> mists spread
> fears
> staring shivering
> shivering
> cajoling
> whispering
> You![211]

Here, lines such as 'A star frightens the steeple cross' and 'a horse gasps smoke' have an estranging effect, which is amplified through the lack of punctuation and conventional syntax. The language of the poem is, therefore, fragmented, both in terms of its form and its meaning, with each word or phrase's relationship to the next seeming ambivalent. The reader is left unsure, for example, whether to read the final two lines as 'whispering, "You!"', or to view 'whispering' as another impression or perception, like 'shivering' and 'cajoling', and 'You!' as an intruding voice. Significantly, as Richard Sheppard notes, studying Stramm's poetry in the original German reveals how, like David Jones, he 'was [also] prepared to mutate and mutilate the conventional forms of words'[212] in order to reify the experience of war. Indeed, Jones's praxis also has much in common with that of the Austrian writer, Georg Trakl, in his poem, 'Night':

> The fires of the nations gold-blaze
> all over, and across
> black streaked cliffs, drunken with death,
> plunges the glowing vortex,
> the blue glacier's wave.
> In the valley drones the huge
> bell-sound: flames, curses,
> and the occult games
> of voluptuousness.
> The sky
> is stormed by a petrified head.[213]

Here, Trakl dreams up a nightmarish and- abstract language of 'symbols and colours'[214] in an attempt to verbalise the horror and delirium of world war.

This chapter has demonstrated how, in accreting his own particular language of crisis, David Jones inhabits and, like Gwyn Thomas, Glyn Jones and Idris Davies, utilises the Modernist 'conditions' established by the 'crisis of language' in early twentieth-century Wales. Moreover, as I have illustrated, David Jones's 'new verbal ikon' operates by means of the very explosive, transformational linguistic practices witnessed in the writing of his marginalised Welsh contemporaries, foregrounding what Kronfeld recognises as 'the decentering, deterritorializing, indeed the revolutionary and innovative force of minor writing',[215] particularly the 'minor writing' of early twentieth-century Wales. Gwyn Jones, editor of the English-language Welsh journal *The Welsh Review*, sensed this creative potency at the end of the 1930s:

> A year or so ago I was writing in these words of the Welsh contribution to modern literature, and I see no reason to change them: ". . . the last few years have seen the emergence of a group of young writers (young in age or work) who for the first time are interpreting Wales to the world. They are as diverse as the land that gave them their rich if ragged heritage, but I believe firmly that they will soon be recognised as the most valuable leaven in English literature since the Irishmen opened insular eyes at the beginning of the century. Thus South Wales, in the nineteenth century the matrix of Great Britain's industrial and imperial expansion, in this new age will shake with new impulse the weary body of English Literature."[216]

Moreover, this chapter has shown that, when considered in relation to the work of all these writers, Modernism, too, is no longer a 'solid thing', but a fluid concept, open to interrogation and diversification. In the words of Peter Nicholls, Modernism emerges 'not [as] one thing but [as] many and . . . its divergent forms are profoundly determined by specificities of time and place'.[217] This inclusive and searching approach to Modernism will continue to inform all of the discussions of Anglophone Welsh Modernism that follow.

2

'ALWAYS OBSERVANT AND SLIGHTLY OBSCURE': LYNETTE ROBERTS AS WELSH MODERNIST

David Jones was not, in fact, the only writer from outside Wales to avail himself of the potentially Modernist 'conditions' of Anglophone Welsh writing. Neither was he the only artist to assimilate these conditions in a bid to render the experience of war. His contemporary, Lynette Roberts (1909–95), was born in Buenos Aires and spent much of her early childhood in South America. Her family, however, was English-speaking (though her parents were of Welsh descent), and she received an English education in Bournemouth and then London, where she studied at the Central School of Arts and Crafts.[1] In 1939, Roberts married the Welsh poet Keidrych Rhys, who had established the seminal Anglo-Welsh literary magazine *Wales* in 1937, and the couple took up residence in the small village of Llanybri in Carmarthenshire. Although Rhys was frequently called away on military service, and both he and Roberts made intermittent excursions to London,[2] Llanybri remained their home throughout the Second World War. During this period, Roberts produced a body of poetry that was published by T. S. Eliot's Faber and Faber Press in two volumes: *Poems* (1944) and *Gods With Stainless Ears: A Heroic Poem* (1951). Faber and Faber had also published David Jones's *In Parenthesis* in 1937. Indeed, just as Capel-y-ffin and the Black Mountains became sites of artistic inspiration for David Jones, Llanybri and the wider landscape of West Wales were formative to Lynette Roberts's poetry.[3] 'Poem from Llanybri' (1944), where the poet-speaker gently encourages her friend, the poet Alun Lewis, to visit her in the village, attests to the centrality of this locale in her work:

If you come my way that is . . .
Between now and then, I will offer you
A fist full of rock cress fresh from the bank
The valley tips of garlic red with dew
Cooler than shallots, a breath you can swank

In the village when you come. At noon-day
I will offer you a choice bowl of cawl
Served with a 'lover's' spoon and a chopped spray
Of leeks or savori fach, not used now,

In the old way you'll understand. The din
Of children singing through the eyelet sheds
Ringing smith hoops, chasing the butt of hens;
Or I can offer you Cwmcelyn spread

With quartz stones from the wild scratchings of men:
You will have to go carefully with clogs
Or thick shoes for it's treacherous the fen,
The East and West Marshes also have bogs . . .[4]

It is not only the topography of this area – the 'valley' and its flora, the 'village', and the sweeping marshland of 'Cwmcelyn' – but also Welsh tradition that Roberts fondly and enthusiastically invokes here: the poet-speaker resurrects the 'old way[s]' of the region, offering 'cawl / Served with a "lover's" spoon and a chopped spray / Of leeks or savori fach'. And the form of the poem, too, owes much to Welsh literary history. Tony Conran notes that 'Welsh poetry is full of [the] social ritual' of 'asking', citing 'An Invitation to William Parry to visit Northolt' by the eighteenth-century poet Goronwy Owen as an example of this style.[5] Conran also suggests that 'Poem from Llanybri' is adapted from the fifteenth-century Welsh 'request poem (*cywydd gofyn*), in which the poet would ask a patron for a gift (such as a horse, a weapon, or a garment), sometimes for himself but more often on behalf of a nobleman'.[6] Roberts also seems to adapt stylistic techniques from ancient Welsh poetic tradition in this text; her use of assonance and rhyme in 'The din / Of children singing through the eyelet sheds', for example, is reminiscent of the *cynghanedd* or 'sound correspondences' of 'Welsh strict-metre poetry'.[7]

Indeed, Roberts draws freely on native Welsh literature in her work, embracing it with what Conran has described as 'an inspired curiosity',[8] and resisting its effacement and marginalisation both within and outside Wales. In 'The Circle of C' (1944), for instance, in which the poet-speaker seeks reassurance and consolation from the ancient, 'many-storied'[9] landscape of Wales during wartime, she writes:

> I walk and cinder bats riddle my cloak
> I walk to Cwmcelyn ask prophets the way.
>
> 'There is no way they cried crouched on the hoarstone rock
> And the Dogs of Annwn roared louder than of late.'[10]

Here, we witness the re-emergence of the 'Dogs of Annwn', who, Roberts informs the reader in her notes accompanying the poem, 'appear in early [Welsh] triads, and in the first story of *The Mabinogion*, (Pwyll Prince of Dyved)'.[11] Roberts also makes extensive use of numerous Welsh-language literary sources in her book-length poem *Gods With Stainless Ears*, including the medieval poetry of Dafydd ap Gwilym, Aneirin's *Y Gododdin*, *Canu Llywarch Hen* or 'The Song of Llywarch the Old' (a collection of ninth-century *englynion*),[12] and the Bible of William Morgan (1545–1604). Some of these texts she cites in the original Welsh, as epigraphs. Moreover, Roberts was clearly inspired by Welsh culture in all its forms, for she also analysed Welsh architecture in a commentary entitled 'Simplicity of the Welsh Village' (1945), and turned her attention to Welsh craft in her article, 'Coracles of the Towy', which was published in *The Field* magazine in 1945.[13] Furthermore, in her essay accompanying the seven prose pieces that comprise her 1944 collection, *An Introduction to Village Dialect* – a piece that is testament to Roberts's fascination with language – she sets out to prove, to those who would occlude the distinctive culture of Wales, that there is 'a tradition and root to the Welsh dialect',[14] and expresses her intention to 'discuss, at a later interval, the history, mythology, weather, craft, custom, literal syntax and idiom of the Cymric language, in relation to the contemporary dialect in [Llanybri]'.[15]

Several of Roberts's poems, however, reveal that her relationship with Wales and Welsh culture was not always entirely harmonious. In 'Lamentation' (1944), she recalls how

> To the village of lace and stone
> Came strangers. I was one of these

Always observant and slightly obscure.
I roamed the hills of bird and bone
Rescuing bees from under the storm:[16]

In these lines, Roberts conflates her move to Llanybri – 'the village of lace and stone' – with the dispersive tide of the Second World War, and her poetic voice, in contrast to the rooted, homely speaker of 'Poem from Llanybri', sounds like that of a wandering exile. Indeed, among the 'strangers' with whom Roberts identifies in 'Lamentation' are the women and children who were evacuated to west Wales to escape the bombing in London, and whose disparity she contemplated in her *Evacuee's Report*, a diary entry for 2 February 1941. Here she writes: 'A grown-up evacuee called on me this morning and this was roughly her opinion': "What could they [that is, the people of Llanybri] have talked about before we came? Have you heard I sit on my ass all day and smoke?" (In Llanybri no woman smokes).'[17] Another 'stranger' and, by extension, a figure with whom the poet-speaker feels a close affinity in 'Lamentation' is a young pilot named Petwick Lawrence, who, Roberts also reveals in her *Evacuee's Report*, was 'killed as his plane crashed into a meadow behind [her Llanybri] cottage'.[18] Roberts's empathy with the airman is subtly and movingly communicated in the poem as she associates his violent death with the miscarriage that she suffered in March 1940:

For I met death before birth:
Fought for life and in reply lost
My own with a cold despair.
I hugged the fire around the hearth
To warm the beat and wing
Yet knew the symbol when it came
Lawrence had found the same. (p. 8)

Roberts conflates this event with the destructiveness of warfare in a similar way in part four of *Gods With Stainless Ears* (1951), composed between 1941 and 1943, – though her poetic style is more obviously experimental and challenging in this text:

Rising ashly, challenge blood to curb – compose –
Martial mortal, face a red mourning alone.
To the star of the magnitude O my God,

Shriek, sear my swollen breasts, send succour
To sift and settle me. – This the labour of it . . .

But reality worse than the pain intrudes,
And no doctor for six days. This
Also is added truth. Razed for lack of
Incomputable finance. For womb was
Fresh as the day and solid as your hand.

BLOOD OF ALL MEN. DRENCHED ANCESTORS OF WAR
WHETHER GERMAN. BRITISH. RUSSIAN. OR HIDE
FROM SOME OTHER FOREIGN FIELD: REMEMBER AGAIN
BLOOD IS HUMAN. BORN AT COST. REMEMBER THIS[19]

Here, the trauma of miscarriage is paralleled with the bloodshed of war. And Roberts uses her personal tragedy, as she informs the reader in the prose 'argument' that accompanies this section,[20] to show '*that the birth of flesh and blood is everywhere a noble event and that lives of all nationalities must be considered sacred – not to be callously destroyed*' (p. 60).

The poet-speaker's isolation – 'And no doctor for six days' – adds a particular poignancy to these lines. Indeed, isolation is a recursive theme in Roberts's work. In the lines from 'The Circle of C' noted previously, for example, Roberts again casts herself as a 'stranger' and interloper in Wales. The poet-speaker 'ask[s] prophets the way' to Cwmcelyn, but they avow that 'There is no way', as if to render her a permanent outsider. This impression is compounded by the attendance at this scene of the 'Dogs of Annwn'. Roberts glosses this in her textual notes as 'an interpretation of raiders droning over estuary and hill; their stiff and ghostly flight barking terror into the hearts of the villagers';[21] but the way in which these spectral dogs 'roar louder than of late' also intimates that they have been roused and provoked by the poem's mysterious 'cloak[ed]' intruder. The 'cinder bats' that 'riddle' the poet-speaker's 'cloak' have a similar effect. On one level, Roberts seems to be comparing these dark, flitting shapes to cinders jumping in a riddle or sieve as it is shaken; but to 'riddle' can also mean 'to talk in riddles', suggesting that the Welsh environment is somehow conspiring to bemuse and exclude her. The mention of a 'cloak' is significant here. Roberts dressed in a bright red cloak when she went out walking in Llanybri and the surrounding area, suggesting, as John Pikoulis speculates, that she 'made a vivid [and, surely, to some people at this frightening time, vaguely unsettling] impression'.[22] Indeed, such was Roberts's perceived eccentricity that some villagers decided that she was really a German spy,[23] a slight that she responded to in her poem, 'Raw Salt on Eye' (1944):

> Stone village, who would know that I lived alone:
> Who would know that I suffered a two-edged pain,
> Was accused of spycraft to full innate minds with loam,
> Was felled innocent, suffered a stain as rare as Cain's.
>
> . . .
>
> Hard people, will wash up now, bake bread and hang
> Dishcloth over the weeping hedge. I can not raise
> My mind, for it has gone wandering away with hum
> I shall not forget; and your ill-mannered praise.[24]

This situation calls to mind Jean Rhys's pertinently titled 1966 short story, 'I Spy a Stranger', in which Laura, an unconventional, artistic, cosmopolitan woman from Prague, is suspected of being a spy by the residents of an English town during wartime. As Mrs Hudson, Laura's sympathetic though circumspect cousin and landlady in the town, apprises:

> Then the day came when I was going to give her [Laura] another hint, she said 'I've started packing'. And all her things were piled on the floor. Such a lot of junk to travel about the world with – books and photographs and old dresses, scarves and all that, and reels of coloured cotton.
>
> *A cork with a face drawn on it, a postcard of the Miraculous Virgin in the church of St Julien-le-Pauvre, a china inkstand patterned with violets, a quill pen never used, a ginger jar, a box full of old letters, a fox fur with the lining gone, silk scarves each with a history – the red, the blue, the brown, the purple . . . the bracelet bought in Florence because it looked like a stained glass window . . .*[25]

The coloured garments that the narrator catalogues here seem to function as markers of Laura's difference in a way that invests with further symbolic significance the vision of Roberts's red cloak against the 'stones' of Llanybri. Indeed, Jean Rhys's background is markedly similar to Roberts's. Rhys was born to a Welsh father and a Dominican Creole mother of British descent, on the Caribbean island of Dominica,[26] and was sent to school in London at the age of seventeen. She spent the ensuing years moving between London and Paris and, later, between various towns and villages in England;[27] and her fiction, beginning with her Modernist novels of the 1930s and 1940s, turns on themes of deracination, itinerancy and apartness. In her 1934 novel *Voyage in the Dark*, for example, Rhys's heroine, Anna, moves to England to begin a new life, yet experiences a nostalgic longing for the Caribbean home that she has left behind:

> Sometimes I would shut my eyes and pretend that the heat of the fire, or the bed-clothes drawn up round me, was sun-heat; or I would pretend I was standing outside the house at home, looking down Market Street to the Bay. When there was a breeze the sea was millions of spangles; and on still days it was purple as Tyre and Sidon. Market Street smelt of the wind, but the narrow street smelt of niggers and wood-smoke and salt fishcakes fried in lard. (When the black women sell fishcakes on the savannah they carry them in trays on their heads, 'Salt fishcakes, all sweet an charmin', all sweet an' charmin'.') It was funny, but that was what I thought about more than anything else – the smell of the streets and the smells of frangipani and lime juice and cinnamon and cloves, and sweets made of ginger and syrup, and incense after funerals or Corpus Christi processions, and the patients standing outside the surgery next door, and the smell of the sea-breeze and the different smell of the land breeze.[28]

This passage is strikingly similar, both in its subject matter and in its impressionistic, almost stream-of-consciousness style, to Lynette Roberts's 1944 poem, 'Royal Mail', in which the poet-speaker recalls the South America of her childhood:

> I would see again São Paulo;
> The coffee coloured house with its tarmac roof
> And spray of tangerine berries.
> I again climb the mountain cable
> And see Pernambuco with its dark polished table
> The brilliance of its sky piercing through the trees
> . . .
> The peacock struts and nets mimicrying butterflies,
> And the fazenda shop clinking like ice in an enamel jug
> As you open the door. The stench of wine-wood,
> Saw-dust, maize flour, pimentos, and basket of birds,
> With the ear-tipped 'Molto bien signorit' and the hot mood
> Blazing from the drooping noon. Outside sweating gourds
> Dripping rind and peel; yet inside cool as lemon,

Orange, avocado pear.
While in this damp and stony stare of a village
Such images are unknown:
So would I think upon these things
In the event that someday I shall return to my native surf
And feel again the urgency of sun and soil.[29]

Rhys and Roberts's comparable geographical and cultural displacement seems to account, at least in part, for their shared Modernist aesthetics: as Chana Kronfeld points out, 'Modernism is famous for its affinity for the marginal, the exile, the "other".'[30] Nonetheless, Roberts's, in some ways, apparently wilful 'outsider's [appearance] and perspective'[31] is balanced by a countervailing impetus to be accepted and assimilated into the Llanybri community, as suggested in the following lines from her diary entry for 20 March 1940: 'The wind was cold,' she reflects. 'I drew my scarlet cape around me and walked leisurely, as village people do.'[32]

While Roberts clearly gained some sense of belonging during her time in Llanybri through emulating the habits and customs of its residents, her awareness of her similarly peripheral position as a writer seems to have been difficult to assuage. As previously established, Roberts was a resolute explorer of Welsh literary culture, 'roaming' – as she writes in 'Lamentation' – its ancient terrain and salvaging or 'rescuing' it from homogenisation and elision by creatively invoking it in her own work. The image of the poet-speaker rescuing 'bees from under the storm' in 'Lamentation' also possesses a quasi-allegorical timbre, for the bee positively embodies this potential for dissemination, vitality and survival. Despite her dedication to Welsh literature, however, Roberts never learnt [to speak] Welsh';[33] rather, her husband, who was a native Welsh-speaker, seems to have been the main conduit for her knowledge of the language. Moreover, it would be fair to say that Roberts effectively remained, as she suggests in 'Lamentation', a kind of cultural '*stranger*' in Wales – a cosmopolitan outsider who produced avant-garde English-language poetry and prose. When we consider the 'Dogs of Annwn' from 'A Circle of C' with this in mind, they may be seen as prohibitive avatars and custodians of an ultimately inaccessible established Welsh literary tradition; and the isolated space occupied by the poet-speaker suggests Roberts's participation in a remote, hermetic form of Anglophone Welsh writing, which is only able to speak *for* and not *to* Welsh-speaking Wales. A similar sense of cultural alienation underlies Roberts's description of herself in 'Lamentation' as 'Always observant and slightly obscure'. These words are freighted with the opinions of Roberts's urbane, Anglo-American literary mentors, Robert Graves and T. S. Eliot, who remarked on her 'unusual gift for observation'[34] and her tendency towards opacity and abstruseness respectively. As Graves wrote in a letter to Roberts on 3 December 1944:

> You are saying [in your poetry that] 'To interpret the present god-awful complex confusion one must unconfusedly use the language of god-awful confusion'. . . [T]here are a great many small points I'd like to question you about: such as your views on how much interrelation of dissociated ideas is possible in a single sentence without bursting the sense.[35]

It is this notion, imaged in 'Lamentation' and 'The Circle of C', of Lynette Roberts, the poet, as cultural 'stranger' that I intend to pursue and expand in the remainder of this chapter in relation to the subject of Anglophone Welsh Modernism. For, in effect, the opening lines of both 'Lamentation' and 'A Circle of C' illustrate the culturally 'deterritorialized' position of the Anglophone Welsh writer, analysed in the previous chapter: that 'common experience', to reiterate M. Wynn Thomas's thesis – 'simultaneously . . . liberating and inhibiting – of belonging to a place apart; a historical [and cultural] region which was certainly not assimilable to England, but which could not be integrated into traditional Wales either'.[36] The two poems, in a sense, manifest twentieth-century Anglophone Welsh writers' proclivity to find themselves – or actively become – in Deleuze and Guattari's words, 'stranger[s] *within* [their] own [and also within the Welsh] language'.[37] Indeed, Roberts's multinational background may well have elicited even more profound feelings of cultural 'deterritorialisation' than those experienced by the writers discussed in the foregoing chapter. Whereas Gwyn Thomas, Glyn Jones and Idris Davies were purposefully 'deterritorialising' language and simultaneously 'reterritorialising' it in the form of a new, self-consciously Anglo-Welsh 'verbal ikon', Lynette Roberts also appears to have distanced her work from that of her English-speaking Welsh literary peers. In 'An Introduction to Welsh Dialect', for instance, she identifies the term 'Anglo-Welsh' as '*having no origin but a superficial one*',[38] and in her 1955 sketch of the contemporary English- and Welsh-language literary scene in Wales for the *Times Literary Supplement*, 'The Welsh Dragon' – an article in which she only very briefly mentions her own publications[39] – she concludes: 'Many Welsh writers have not been mentioned, but however wide the net is stretched it is unlikely to include a higher proportion of the forceful and the unexpected. For what the Welsh dragon lacks at present is fire . . .'[40] Thus, while Roberts's creative relationship with Wales was always founded on a genuine interest in and admiration for its culture and its people, she was also fully aware of the creative potential of Anglophone Welsh writing – even if, in her opinion, the 'Anglo-Welsh' scene at the time lacked the incendiarists to fully untap this potential – and like David Jones, she made extensive use of these 'liberating', transformational circumstances in her poetry. In essence, through adopting the position of 'Anglo-Welsh' writer – and it is important to remember that, as Patrick McGuinness stresses, Roberts was 'Welsh by a combination of choice and imaginative will'[41] – she harnessed the Anglophone Welsh writer's potentiality to become 'a stranger within . . . language' and cultivated the edgy or (again, in her own words) 'unexpected' and 'forceful' modes of writing that this entailed. Whereas Saunders Lewis, who also fought to preserve and promote the indigenous culture of Wales, accused 'Anglo-Welsh' writers of being 'too clearly deracinés',[42] it was precisely the artistic potential of the Anglophone Welsh writer's deterritorialised position that Roberts sought to utilise in her poetry.

This is apparent, for example, in the poem, 'Crossed and Uncrossed' (1944), in which Roberts recalls walking through the East End of London after a bombing raid. In these stanzas specifically, she imaginatively poeticises her diary account from 12 June 1942, where she observes 'library buildings . . . still smouldering' and a burnt-out church, 'wet and empty like a grotesque seashell':[43]

> Heard the steam rising from the chill blue bricks
> Heard the books sob and the buildings huge groan
> As the hard crackle of flames leapt on firemen
> and paled the red walls.
>
> Bled their hands in anguish to check the fury
> Knowing fire had raged for week and a day:
> under the storm.
>
> Fled the sky: fragments of the Law, kettles and glass:
> Lamb's ghost screamed: Pegasus melted and fell
> Meteor of shining light on to stone court
> and only wing grave.

Round Church built in a Round Age, cold with grief,
Coloured Saints of glass lie buried at your feet:
Crusaders uncross limbs by the green light of flares,
burn into Tang shapes.

Over firedrake floors the 'Smith' organ pealed
Roared into flames when you proud window
Ran undaunted: the lead roof dripping red tears
curving to crash.[44]

Roberts acknowledges her debt to Greek poetry – more specifically, to the Sapphic stanza form – in her notes to 'Crossed and Uncrossed';[45] and the style of this poem is also reminiscent at times of H.D.'s 'The Walls Do Not Fall' (1944), another poetic meditation on the devastation of parts of London during the Second World War:

ruin everywhere, yet as the fallen roof
leaves the sealed room
open to the air,

so, through our desolation,
thoughts stir, inspiration stalks us
through the gloom:

. . .

trembling at a known street-corner,
we know not nor are known;
the Pythian pronounces – we pass on

to another cellar, to another sliced wall
where poor utensils show
like rare objects in a museum;

Pompeii has nothing to teach us,
we know crack of volcanic fissure,
slow flow of lava[46]

The subject matter, elegiac mood and religious thematics of 'Crossed and Uncrossed' also call to mind Dylan Thomas's 'Ceremony After a Fire Raid', which was written in the same year. The greater 'frequency of initial verbs' in 'Crossed and Uncrossed', however, as Conran has also argued, seems to indicate that Roberts is invoking 'a Welsh-language sentence structure' of 'verb-subject-object'. This, in turn, produces an exploded, defamiliarised English syntax that is distinct from that of both H.D.'s 'The Walls Do Not Fall' and Thomas's 'Ceremony After a Fire Raid', and that mirrors the estranging, detrital cityscape of the poem. Indeed, we could say that, like David Jones, Roberts creatively utilises Welsh to engender her own new 'verbal ikon' of war; and this process is also discernible in the equally elliptical phrase, 'for week and a day'. Here, instead of adhering to the conventional English phrase, 'for a week and a day', Roberts seems to mirror the syntactical pattern of the Welsh, *am wythnos ac am ddiwrnod.* More specifically, Roberts is experimenting in this poem with '*intensives* or *tensors*' (as Deleuze and Guattari call them): using Welsh as a means to become 'a stranger within her own language' in a similar way to her contemporaries, Glyn Jones and Gwyn Thomas. She employs the same technique in another poem, 'Seagulls' (1944):

> Seagulls' easy glide
> Drifting fearlessly as voyagers' tears:
> Quay and ship move as imperceptibly,
> Without knowing we weep.
>
> Cry gulls who recall
> An ocean of uncertainty;
> Greed of rowing men
> Mere flies at the ship's sides.[47]

Although the form of these lines is broadly conventional, 'Cry gulls who recall / An ocean of uncertainty' replicates the Welsh 'verb-subject-object' paradigm seen in 'Crossed and Uncrossed' and underscores, on a syntactical level, both the temporal dislocation of the stanza, and the 'uncertainty' of the archaic seascape that it envisages. Indeed, again, as in 'Crossed and Uncrossed', Roberts seems to effect '*intensive*' syntactical disarray in order to formally enact the upheaval of war: the avaricious 'rowing men' evoke armies of invaders bound for enemy shores, and 'Quay and ship move as imperceptibly / Without knowing we weep' seems to connote the modern-day deployment of soldiers and the distress of wives, mothers and sisters left behind. As previously noted, Roberts herself spent long periods alone in Llanybri while Keidrych Rhys was away on military postings.

Keidrych Rhys's 'Poem for a Green Envelope' (1942) documents his own wartime experiences:

> . . . too soon I stumble over rough ground to the guns
> slip past the Command Post dragon flag to the tune of whistles
> respirator under arm, shell in fuse-setter for tray
> inside emplacement report
> 'Ready for action'
> under the extraordinary blue of the breech-light
> warm hands at the white of cartridge shell cases
> while others placed cooled charge-cases aside
> and box them methodically
> oh surely we won't go back to a pre-war world
> every night killing becomes more automatic
> as we rest huddled in beach huts like animals
> writhing in the equality of barrackroom language[48]

The concrete realism of Rhys's poem counterpoints Roberts's 'Seagulls', in which the poet-speaker can only conjure vague, mental apprehensions of war from the quotidian tableau – the wheeling 'gulls' – that surround her. Roberts's poem, in a sense, demonstrates how, as Gill Plain contends,

> just as the poets of 1914–18 [David Jones included] struggled to find a language adequate to express the unprecedented extent of their suffering, so, in the Second World War, the average person was confounded by the impossibility of articulating the scale of the conflict that confronted them.[49]

This sense of the remoteness of war re-emerges in 'Plasnewydd' – a poem in which Roberts transcribes or poetically inhabits the idiom of Rosie, her Welsh-speaking friend in Llanybri, enabling the poet, once again, to become a 'stranger within her own language' and, therefore, to give verbal expression to the oddity of wartime:

> WAR. There's no sense in it.
> Just look at her two lovely eyes
> Look at those green big big eyes
> And the way she hangs her tail.
> Like a weasel. Ferret. Snowball
> Running away on the breast of a hill.
> WAR. There's no sense in it
> For us simple people
> We all get on so well.
> Hal-e-bant.

The cows are on the move.
I must be off on the run:
Hal-e-bant. *Pussy drwg.*
Hal-e-bant Fan Fach
Hal-e-bant for the day is long
We must strengthen it:
Ourselves:
To the cows
Fetch them in.[50]

Like 'Crossed and Uncrossed', this poem has its origins in a diary entry which Roberts wrote on 17 July 1940. The precise passage is cited below:

> 'Well, you see, it's like this, Mrs Rhys' . . . and Rosie stands on one foot with her hand on her hip, she licks around her mouth, then begins talking again and it is always the same, 'Well, you see, it's like this, Mrs Rhys. I can't imagine the war or fighting at all, I've never travelled at all, only go to Cardiff, so I can't imagine this war at all. She's very wrong mind you (meaning the WAR), and what I feel is they're all flesh and blood like you or I, Mrs Rhys, aren't they? If you were to be stabbed you would feel it just as much as they, wouldn't you? WAR there's no sense in it. We're simple people we all get on. War there's no sense in it.'[51]

In both this passage and the poem, the War is referred to as 'she', a usage that Roberts also explicitly points out in 'An Introduction to Village Dialect', recognising 'she is not very well, the broccoli I mean' as one local's attempt 'to express herself directly out of the Cymric tongue' – an attempt, Roberts reveals, that 'left me as delighted and vague as Puttenham'.[52] Roberts also uses village colloquial expression in 'Poem from Llanybri' – in phrases such as '*If you come my way that is* . . .' and 'it's treacherous the fen'. Similarly, a more orthodox, familiar English-language rendering of 'Just look at those big big green eyes' in 'Plasnewydd' would be 'Just look at those big green eyes', or, more accurately in this context perhaps, 'Just look at those great big green eyes.' Just as Glyn Jones uses language in a way that elicits 'a sense of shock, strangeness, wonder',[53] then, in 'Plasnewydd' Roberts seems to revel in the linguistic oddness and expressive potency of this vernacular mode, registering what she describes in her literary memoir, 'Visit to T. S. Eliot', as 'the metallic *convergence* of words, heavy, colourful, rich and unexplored'.[54] As these diverse individual words – words such as 'WAR', 'Ferret', 'Snowball' and the Welsh phrase, 'Pussy drwg' (meaning 'naughty cat') – are singled out for emphasis, they collectively enact and underscore the intangibility and, as the voice of the poem insists, senselessness of the war to people in this small rural community. Roberts's use of the Welsh dialectal phrase, 'Hal-e-bant', meaning 'send it away' or 'shoo it away' in relation to both an errant cat and to world war amplifies this sense of the remoteness and insubstantiality of the conflict to those people – the majority of whom were women – not directly involved. This also finds typographical expression in the poem. Through capitalising 'WAR', Roberts draws our attention to each individual letter, endowing the word with a solid and ominous but, at the same time, starkly one-dimensional, almost abstract quality. In 'Seagulls' and 'Plasnewydd', then, Roberts's new 'verbal ikon' – her own 'language of crisis' – is not that of the embattled soldier, as is the case in David Jones's *In Parenthesis*. Rather, it is a language 'of those left behind [both] in rural Wales',[55] and in provincial locations the length and breadth of Britain; as she writes in her preface to the poem, 'the background [to *Gods With Stainless Ears*] is similar to any rural village: only the surface culture is superimposed or altogether distinct' (p. 43). So Roberts's Modernism is chiefly a rural Modernism which, like the work of Glyn Jones and also Caradoc Evans, along with that of Gwyn Thomas and Idris Davies, set in the industrialised Valley communities of south Wales, problematises the conventional critical view that Modernism was essentially metropolitan in character. In particular, through adopting the peripheral, estranged position of the 'Anglo-Welsh' poet, Roberts is able to engender a 'new verbal ikon', which articulates the 'problematic relationship',[56] identified above, between war 'and the women who stay[ed] behind'[57] – an uneasy relationship which, Gill Plain argues, was 'repressed and disguised [during the Second World War] by the veneer of national [or British] unity', of 'superficial togetherness' in the face of a common threat.[58]

Roberts's 1944 poem, 'Curlew', can also be read in this way:

> A curlew hovers and haunts the room.
> On bare boards creak its filleted feet:
> For freedom intones four notes of doom,
>
> *Crept, slept, wept, kept*, under aerial gloom:
> With Europe restless in his wing beat,
> A curlew hovers and haunts the room:

Fouls wire, pierces the upholstery bloom,
Strikes window pane with shagreen bleat,
Flicking tongue to a frenzied fume

Splints hís curved beak on square glass tomb:
Runs to and fro seeking mudsilt retreat;
Captured, explodes a chill sky croon

. . .

*Wail-íng…pal- íng…*a desolate phantom
At the bath rim *purring burbling trilling soft sweet*
Syllables of sinuous sound to a liquid moon[59]

Roberts wrote in a letter to Robert Graves, dated 18 December 1944, that her main objective in this poem – which at times, like Glyn Jones's prose, also faintly echoes the rhythms of Hopkins's verse – was 'to use the exact [qualities] of the curlew's call which so often breaks with . . . four shrill notes';[60] and this technique is clearly visible in the reference to 'four notes of doom, / *Crept, slept, wept, kept*' in stanzas one and two. Yet the manner in which the poem's speaker lingers over these, and other individual words – most notably '*purring burbling trilling*' and '*Wail-íng… pal- íng…*' – experiencing and exploring their sound, texture and composition, almost as if she were turning objects never before seen over in her hands, also recalls the linguistic praxis of the Anglophone Welsh writers discussed in the previous chapter. Tony Brown has observed how Glyn Jones, for example, employs a similar approach in his work, positing that he handles 'words in a way which is . . . almost tactile'.[61] Moreover, Roberts seems to be recreating in 'Curlew' the Anglophone Welsh writer's sense of a new, unexplored domain of English, which in turn verbally enacts the poet-speaker's and, more broadly, many women's experience of the Second World War. The strange remoteness of the war to the women left at home to continue with their day-to-day lives is also symbolically conveyed through the curlew itself. Within the secluded, domestic and obviously feminine space of the poem, the presence of war is figured as an elusive, phantasmal bird bearing ominous, encrypted news. Just as Branwen's starling carried news of her imprisonment in Ireland across the sea to her brother in Wales in *The Mabinogion*, there is a message of disturbance and urgency across the water on the continent of 'Europe' in the curlew's insistent 'wing beat', and the suggestion of aerial assault as it 'explodes a chill sky croon'. Indeed, it seems likely that Roberts is consciously drawing on this Welsh mythological tale in her poem; like Branwen, embroiled in and yet secluded from a simmering conflict between Ireland and Wales,[62] Roberts's female poet-speaker feels herself intensely involved and yet detached from, and disempowered in the face of world war. Roberts's strategy of becoming a stranger within language in order to express this, as well as a wider feminine, material and psychological estrangement from the war, in this poem is especially salient in her treatment of the pronoun 'his' in her references to the curlew: she places an accent instead of the usual dot above the 'i', which both abnormally stresses the sound of the vowel (in imitation, perhaps, of the curlew's cry) and defamiliarises the word in a typographical as well as an aural sense.

It is in *Gods With Stainless Ears*, however, that Roberts exploits the experimental conditions of 'Anglo-Welsh' writing to greatest effect:

> This is Saint Cadoc's Day. All this Saint Cadoc's
> Estuary: and that bell tolling, Abbey paddock.
> Sunk. – Sad as ancient monument of stone.
> Trees vail, exhale cyprine shade, widowing
> Homeric hills, green pinnacles of bone.
>
> Escaping from these, tomb and cave, quagmires
> Migrate; draw victim eyes with lustre sheen, suck
> Confervoid residue from gillette veins: who talk
> Now yield, calling others, those who walk
> From Llanstephan, Llangain, and Llanybri.
>
> No watereyes squinting or too near madness
> Could fail such a trek. In this same old soddenness
> In deep corridor graves culverts open; their
> Gates kedged in mud, preening feathered air
> Elucidating shapes flecked with woolglints
>
> And small affiliated tares. – So walk swiftly by,
> For today, *pridian*, tears ravens wings to grate
> The bay, and John Roberts covered with lingustrum,
> Always sanitary and discreet, rows to and fro from
> Bell house to fennel, floating quietly on the tide. (pp. 44–5)

In the prose 'argument' accompanying this section, Roberts elucidates the above stanzas as follows:

> The poem opens with a bay wild with birds and somewhat secluded from man. And it is in front, or within sight of this bay that the whole action takes place: merging from its natural state into a supernatural tension within the first six stanzas. War changes its contour. (p. 44)

The 'supernatural tension' that Roberts refers to here recalls the mood of 'Curlew', and, as in that poem, the uncanny atmosphere is generated by the absent presence of war. More specifically, again, we experience wartime from the perspective of the female poet-speaker – the rural west Wales coast, like the home in 'Curlew', becoming imbued with, or assuming the 'contours' of, her own, diffuse awareness of the conflict. Here, this awareness is configured as an adumbrative preoccupation with death and mourning. The tolling bell, to which Roberts's syntax lends particular emphasis, is like a death knell resounding across the estuary, and the funereal mood is enhanced by the 'Sad' Abbey paddock; the 'exhal[ing]' and 'vail[ing]' trees – to 'vail' is to 'bow or bend'[63] out of 'respect or submission',[64] and conjures images of mourners standing before a coffin or grave – the 'widowing [of] / Homeric hills'; and the portrayal of John Roberts as 'a benign Charon'[65] or 'Old Charon and his coracle' (p. 49). Charon was, of course, the 'ferryman of the dead, who transported the spirits over the marsh of Acheron'[66] in Greek mythology. Another reference to ancient Greece, to the epic poet, Homer, more explicitly associates this threnodic atmosphere with the theme of war, evoking the battles between the Greeks and the Trojans that are the focus of the *Iliad* and from which Odysseus returns in the *Odyssey*. Roberts even points towards an actual historical connection between these Bronze Age wars and the landscape of *Gods With Stainless Ears*, writing in her notes on the poem:

> there are historians who believe the Trojans came and settled on this coast. In years to come archaeologists may discover both the Temples and City as Sir Arthur Evans and Schliemann discovered Knossos and Troy – by studying the legends in the locality.[67]

Whereas David Jones draws on the battle of the *Gododdin* in *In Parenthesis* in order to proximate the soldier's experience of war, Roberts invokes these conflicts from antiquity in a way that elicits and maintains a sense of distance, of remoteness, from contemporary hostilities. And this remoteness also finds expression in the traces of violence that the speaker, her mind nevertheless troubled by this more immediate conflict, detects or invests in her environment. The 'gillette veins' are, presumably, channels in the saturated earth, along which water from 'migrat[ing]' 'quagmires', teeming with 'conferva' or 'freshwater algae',[68] runs. But this collocation also evokes injury, blood loss and suicide, Gillette being a manufacturer of razors. Roberts reinvokes this line of imagery later in the poem, when the speaker directs that 'the whaleback of the sea / Fall back into a wrist of ripples, slit' (p. 57). Roberts's descriptions of the hills as 'pinnacles of bone' and the trees' 'cyprine shade' have similarly brutal undertones. Cyprine is a 'blue vesuvianite',[69] a mineral pertaining to the infamous volcano, Mount Vesuvius, whose eruption in AD 79 obliterated the Roman city of Pompeii. We recall that H.D. contemplates this event in her own long war poem, 'The Walls Do Not Fall', cited previously:

> Pompeii has nothing to teach us,
> we know crack of volcanic fissure,
> slow flow of lava

Whereas the metropolitan poet-speaker of H.D.'s poem confidently 'know[s] crack of volcanic fissure / slow flow of lava' – or feels that she truly knows the experience of war – for Roberts's speaker this violence is ossified in mineral form: taciturn, dormant, remote. Roberts again speaks as a rural woman who feels herself a stranger to the actuality of war.

As in 'Seagulls', 'Plasnewydd' and 'Curlew', Roberts identifies and reifies this experience by assuming the Anglophone Welsh writer's position as a stranger within language. The manner in which Roberts treats Welsh words in these stanzas recalls her approach to individual words in 'Curlew'. The speaker seems to scrutinise the sound and texture of the Welsh place names, 'Llanstephan, Llangain, Llanybri', just as she meditatively intones the English verbs, '*Crept, slept, wept, kept*' in 'Curlew'. It is as if (to cite Roland Barthes) these 'words *glisten*, [as if they were] distracting, incongruous apparitions'.[70] The speaker seems to treat the archaic English noun, '*pridian*', with a similarly ennobling curiosity, italicising it and affording it particular emphasis in the line by isolating it between two commas. This syntactical sleight of hand further underlines Roberts's cultivation in this poem of the role of linguistic stranger. *Pridian* means 'on the previous day',[71] yet the syntax of the line leads us to assume, or at least momentarily anticipate, that this is an antiquarian or esoteric synonym of the preceding word, 'today'; the result is a moment of linguistic uncanniness, where the poetic voice does not seem quite 'at home' in the English language. Roberts also creates a sense of the linguistic uncanny that is cognate with that generated by Glyn Jones in his Modernist poetry and short stories; like Jones, Roberts conjoins orthodox English words to fashion hybrid neologisms such as 'watereyes' and 'woolglints'. Roberts's account in her notes on the poem of the etymology of 'woolglints' only accentuates its pecularity:

> I had the image of iridescent bits of dust which float about in the sunbeams like pieces of flock. As the estuary is covered with sheep, and the atmosphere I wanted to create, a supernatural one, I felt that there was bound to be some density – a stifling quality in the air. I therefore imagined these woolglints, which were bound to float about from the backs of the sheep, and the minute weeds – almost-green invisible cells – hovering over the quagmires.[72]

Moreover, 'even when the meaning is clear', as Conran observes, language in Roberts's poem acquires 'a curiously rootless quality . . . almost as if English were being used by a foreigner with a very large vocabulary learnt entirely from dictionaries';[73] we recall, from chapter one, Glyn Jones's description of the Anglophone Welsh character, Gwydion, in *The Valley, the City, the Village*, as 'a dictionary reader, a neologist' (p. 298). In the above stanzas this quality emanates from esoteric geological and biological words such 'cyprine' and 'confervoid', and also 'lingustrum', which, Roberts informs us in her notes, is 'the botanical name for privet'.[74] Roberts also points out here that privet is 'one of the sacred trees mentioned in Taliesin's *Battle of the Trees*',[75] or *Câd Goddeu*, referring the reader to Robert Graves's *The White Goddess: A Historical Grammar of Poetic Myth* (1948) for a translation of this medieval Welsh poem:

> When the trees were enchanted
> There was hope for the trees,
> That they should frustrate the intention
> Of the surrounding fires . . .
>
> . . .
>
> The alder trees in the first line,

> They made the commencement.
> Willow and quicken tree,
> They were slow in their array.
> The plum is a tree
> Not beloved of men;
> The medlar of a like nature,
> Overcoming severe toil.
> The bean bearing in its shade
> An army of phantoms.
> The raspberry makes not the best food.
> In shelter live,
> The privet and the woodbine,
> And the ivy in its season.
> Great is the gorse in battle.
> The cherry-tree had been reproached.
> The birch, though very magnanimous,
> Was late in arraying himself;
> It was not through cowardice,
> But on account of his great size.[76]

This gnostic intertextual allusion both subtly upholds the theme of war and augments the overall sense in Roberts's stanzas of the poet-speaker's removal from its real, contemporary form. This is made more explicit later in the section when the speaker asks, 'To what age can this be compared?' (p. 46). Indeed, the poet-speaker's sequestered, indeterminate position in relation to the war, which she shares with the ethereal ferryman, John Roberts, 'covered with lingustrum' and 'floating quietly on the tide', is echoed in Taliesin's poem. Whereas the alder, willow and birch trees 'array' themselves and the gorse is 'great . . . in battle', the privet 'in shelter live[s]', along with the ivy and the woodbine; as Graves puts it in his own arrangement of the poem:

> In shelter linger
> Privet and woodbine
> Inexperienced in warfare;
> And the courtly pine.[77]

Graves supports the scholarly position, moreover, that *The Battle of the Trees* is not, in fact, 'a battle physically fought, but a battle fought intellectually in the heads and with the tongues of the learned'.[78] This again contributes to the pervasive sense, in the opening stanzas of Roberts's poem, of the war as a psychological construct, gleaned from the rural female poet-speaker's imagination, knowledge and immediate surroundings, rather than a graspable reality.

Indeed, war is represented in Roberts's poem as a kind of dreamed or hallucinated surreality:[79]

> In fear of fate, flying into land Orcadian birds pair
> And peal away like praying hands; bare
> Aluminium beak to clinic air; frame
> Soldier lonely whistling in full corridor train,
> Ishmaelites waling through the windowpane,
>
> O the cut of it, woe sharp on the day
> Scaled in blood, the ten-toed woodpecker,
> A dragon of wings 1 6 2 0 B 6
> 4 punctuates machine-gun from the quarry pits:
> Soldiers, tanks, lorry make siege on the bay.
>
> Freedom to boot. CONCLAMATION. COMPUNCTION.
> Kom-pungk'-shun: discomforts of the mind deride
> Their mood. Birds on the stirrups of the waterbride
> Flush up, and out of time a tintinnabulation
> Of voice and feather fall in and out of the ocean sky. (p. 45)

In these lines the tranquil bay becomes more obviously coloured by war: Birds 'bare / Aluminium beak to clinic air', evoking the aluminium bodies of planes, and inducing thoughts of soldiers lying wounded in hospital wards, and these associative images, in turn, 'frame', or blur and refocus in the mind of the speaker, to form a cinematic vision of a 'Soldier lonely whistling in full corridor train'. Similarly, as Roberts indicates in the 'argument' that elucidates this section, a 'machine-gun is suggested by the tapping of a woodpecker' ('the ten-toed woodpecker /. . ./ punctuates machine-gun') and 'gives out the identity of the gunner' (p. 44): '1 6 2 0 B 6 / 4' was Keidrych Rhys's army number.[80] Moreover, the poet-speaker effects her movement into this projected 'martial zone'[81] – this imaginatively conceived (sur)reality of war – through immersing herself still further in her role as deterritorialized 'Anglo-Welsh' writer. The Welsh grammatical patterns of 'verb-subject-object' and 'noun-adjective' (outlined in the previous chapter) are again clearly decipherable in 'frame / Soldier lonely', and Roberts continues to overturn normative English grammar in the second half of this line – 'whistling in full corridor train'.

Indeed, Roberts re-employs and exaggerates all of the strategies of lexical defamiliarisation seen in 'Plasnewydd' and 'Curlew'. Conran's figuration of the speaker of *Gods With Stainless Ears* as 'a foreigner' who has internalised an English dictionary rings true again here: the words 'CONCLAMATION' and 'COMPUNCTION', though arresting and polemically expressive, are not regularly heard or seen, and their capitalisation lends them the same stark patina as the word 'WAR' in 'Plasnewydd'. Roberts produces even more linguistic 'alienation effect[s]' (to borrow Brecht's phrase)[82] in the following line. Here she spells 'compunction' phonetically, as 'Kom-pungk'-shun', regarding language, once again, with the concentrated, analytical attention of a non-native-speaker or student, and generating, in the process, what Nigel Wheale terms 'the challenging vocabulary of a new synthetic English',[83] with its own unorthodox orthography.

This 'new synthetic English' is also visible in the description of 'Birds on the stirrups of the waterbride' – a phrase that also estranges in the way that Robert Graves identified in his epistolary appraisal of Roberts's work. Recalling the work of her 'Anglo-Welsh' contemporaries Gwyn Thomas, Glyn Jones and also David Jones, Roberts interrelates many 'dissociated ideas . . . in a single sentence', amassing and inflating language almost to the point (in Graves's words) of 'bursting' its 'sense'. Graves could, plausibly, also have cited the following stanzas from *Gods With Stainless Ears* to illustrate his concerns:

Trees crisp with Maeterlinck blue, screen
Submarine suns and baskets of bees: but
Men nettled with pie-powdered feet, angry
As rooks on their pernickety beds 'training
For another Cattraeth' said Evans shop.

DISSIMILAR. DISSUNDERED. CRANCH-CRAKE CRANCH-CRAKE
ASHIVER. ANHUNGERED ANHELATION.
CERAUNIC CLOUDS CRACK IN THEIR BRAIN.
Who was to be ring carrier for Jerrymandering
Gerontocracy. The officer yellow with argyria? (p. 46)

These stanzas are not vessels for linguistic iconoclasm and anarchy, however – for 'the language of god-awful confusion', as Graves put it. While they demonstrate how, as Roland Barthes observes, 'the text can, if it wants, attack the canonical structures of the language . . .

lexicon (exuberant neologisms, portmanteau words, transliterations), syntax (no more logical cell, no more sentence)',[84] they also index a carefully wrought, progressive 'verbal ikon' of rural women's wartime experience, made possible through Roberts's self-conscious choice to utilize the peripheral 'Anglo-Welsh' writer's position as a stranger within language. 'Maeterlinck blue' seems to allude to the Belgian playwright and poet, Maurice Maeterlinck's play *L'Oiseau bleu* or *The Blue Bird: A Fairy Play in Six Acts* (1909), a theatrical fairy-tale centred on two children's quest to find a bluebird that promises happiness. The 'Maeterlink blue' of the trees, therefore, suggests the childlike innocence and naiveté of the rural locale juxtaposed with the realities of the contemporary, war-torn world. The way in which these trees 'screen' or obscure 'submarine suns' and 'basket of bees' – Maeterlinck also wrote *La Vie des abeilles* (1901), 'a protracted tragedy of the life of the bee', which earned the admiration of the French Surrealist playwright and 'theorist of the 'theatre of cruelty'', Antonin Artaud[85] – corroborates this reading. This sense of distance between the speaker's environment and the realities of war is enhanced through the description of the trees as 'crisp' and 'blue'. This imagery gestures towards coldness and ice, whereas the war – represented by the 'submarine *suns* [my emphasis]' – is associated with heat and fire. Moreover, once again, Roberts displays (to reuse Nigel Wheale's phrase) a 'high-risk word associative' poetic mode in these stanzas, where language is governed by an abstruse new logic. Characteristically, Roberts's 'verbal ikon' in these lines is made all the more alienating by her recondite lexical choices – most notably 'pie-powdered', 'ANHUNGERED', 'CERAUNIC' and 'argyria'. These last two examples are derived from scientific discourses, with 'ceraunic' pertaining to 'a branch of physics that deals with heat and electricity' and 'argyria' denoting 'silver poisoning'.[86] This defamiliarising technical vocabulary also enables Roberts to envisage a barely imaginable, dystopian image of the future in part five of the poem, where the Carmarthenshire landscape is blighted by 'progressing' 'industrial [and] chemical' war ('Argument', p. 64):

> Air white with cold. Cycloid wind prevails.
> On ichnolithic plain where no step stirs
> And winter harden into plate of ice:
> Shoots an anthracite glitter of death
> From their eyes, – these men shine darkly.

. . .

Over wails of boraic and tundra torn wounds,
Darkening 'peaked' Fuju-yama, clearing
Cambrian caves where xylophone reeds hide
Menhir glaciers and appointed feet.
Out of this hard. Out of this zinc.
We [the speaker and her lover] by centrifugal force . . . rose softly . . .
(pp. 64–5)

Here, along with the more well-known 'zinc' and 'centrifugal force', Roberts assimilates 'cycloid', which denotes 'the curve traced in space by a point in the circumference of a circle as it moves along a straight line'; 'ichnolithic' ('the science of studying fossil footprints'); 'anthracite', 'a kind of coal'; and 'boracic', a 'white salt crystal'.[87] In 'CRANCH-CRAKE CRANCH-CRAKE', from part two of the poem cited previously, moreover, Roberts invokes and conjoins two more 'definitively obscure'[88] words – 'cranch', meaning 'to crunch', and 'crake' meaning 'to utter a harsh grating cry: said of the crow, quail [and] corn-crake'.[89] Together, these words have a kind of linguistic *déjà-vu* effect, visually estranging and yet aurally prompting the reader by onomatopoeically evoking the familiar sound of tramping or marching footsteps.

In *Gods With Stainless Ears*, then, and in many more of her poems, Roberts exploits the revolutionary conditions of Welsh writing in English in order to reach new plains of Modernist experimentation. Through actively embracing the Anglophone Welsh writer's potentially liberating position as linguistic stranger or 'déraciné', she is able, like her 'Anglo-Welsh' contemporaries Gwyn Thomas, Glyn Jones, Idris Davies and David Jones, to engender a 'new verbal ikon' of modernity, of a rural women's day-to-day life during the Second World War – the 'very eccentricity and obscurity' of which, as Tony Conran contends, 'arise[s] from a truly modern unwillingness to be less than totally open to [this neglected] experience, even the [for her, remote] experience of total war'.[90] As Chana Kronfeld points out, although Modernism 'valoriz[es] . . . the marginal and the eccentric',[91] 'the representative examples of this marginality typically are those writers who have become the most canonical high modernists'.[92] The synchronic poetry of Lynette Roberts demands that we look beyond the canonical outsiders of high modernism and recognise Wales, and particularly marginal Anglophone Welsh writing, as a rich and important site of Modernist innovation.

3

Vernon Watkins's 'Modern Country of the Arts'

I have argued that Gwyn Thomas, Glyn Jones and Idris Davies utilise the 'revolutionary conditions' associated with the 'crisis language' in Wales in the early twentieth century to forge experimental new modes of expression, appropriate to the modern, Anglicised Wales of their experience. I then went on to suggest that the various linguistic innovations of these writers converge in David Jones's *In Parenthesis*, as Jones also exploits the revolutionary potential of the 'space between' English-language and Welsh-language culture, developing a disorientatingly intertextual, fragmentary poetic idiom that verbally enacts the soldier's experience of the First World War. In chapter two, I showed that David Jones was not the only writer to recognise the expressive and creative vibrancy of Anglophone Welsh writing: Lynette Roberts, too, through actively embracing the Anglophone Welsh writer's position as linguistic 'stranger' in her poetry, conceives her own 'new verbal ikon' of modernity – of rural women's experience of the Second World War. This Modernist pursuit of a new 'verbal ikon' essentially entails a process of linguistic deterritorialisation and *reterritorialisation*, where language is uprooted from the territory of the established culture in a move to delineate a separate and defined cultural territory for Wales and its Anglophone literature. In the present chapter I will propose that, in a related but distinct way, this pattern also underlies the Modernism of the poet, Vernon Watkins.

Like many of the writers discussed, 'Swansea's other poet',[1] Vernon Watkins (1906–67), was born into a family in which English was relatively new. Watkins's mother and father, who were living in the industrial town of Maesteg in south Wales at the time of his birth,[2] were Welsh-speakers, whose families originated in Carmarthenshire and Breconshire respectively.[3] Indeed, as Glyn Jones adduces in his commemorative essay on Vernon Watkins, 'Whose Flight is Toil' (1970), '[Watkins] was closely related [through his mother] to a family well known in Wales for their devotion to Welsh culture, particularly Welsh drama and poetry, the Phillips family of Gwaelodygarth, near Cardiff . . .'[4] Following a social trend that has already featured prominently in this book, however, Watkins's parents did not pass the Welsh language on to their son. In fact, Watkins was, arguably, particularly bereft of contact with Welsh culture during his youth. As Roland Mathias elaborates, Watkins's father (who was a successful bank manager) and his mother (who had attended school in London, where she had studied both English and German)[5] were, like other 'more educated'[6] Welsh parents, 'peculiarly susceptible to the feeling that to remain inside the Welsh cocoon was to be deliberately "parochial", uninterested in world issues, and devoid of ambition'.[7] This sentiment seems to have led Watkins's parents to decide largely to withhold the rich literary history of Wales from their child – though his father did read to him sporadically from English translations of Aneirin and Taliesin[8] – and to send him to preparatory school in Sussex, and then to Repton, a public school in Derbyshire.[9]

Watkins became more estranged from Welsh culture at school, where his Anglican religious education set him apart from his Nonconformist family, and his mind became 'stocked', in Mathias's words, 'with material [that his parents presumed to be] of greater importance'[10] than that which Wales had to offer – particularly English, German and French poetry.[11] Indeed, Watkins developed a keen interest in European languages, and went on to study for a degree in German and French at Cambridge. Finding the course to be more focused on language than on literature,[12] and the university unsupportive of his growing poetic ambitions, however, he withdrew after a year,[13] and returned to Wales, finally settling on the Gower peninsula near Swansea. Watkins remained in Wales for most of his life – though he died in Seattle in 1967, having moved to the American city that year to take up the position of Visiting Professor of Poetry at its University of Washington.[14] Despite his obvious attachment to Wales, however, Watkins did not learn Welsh as his contemporary Glyn Jones did.[15] Jones later wrote, in fact, that 'in spite of some rudimentary *cynghanedd* in "The Sure Aimer" [1968] it is vain to look in his [Watkins's] work for the influence of Welsh-language poetry, ancient or modern'.[16] Jones's observation is not strictly accurate: Watkins memorably invokes the Welsh bard, Taliesin, in poems such as 'Taliesin in Gower' (1954) and 'Taliesin and the Spring of Vision' (1959). 'So sang the grains of sand,' he writes in the second of these later poems,

> and while they whirled to a pattern
> Taliesin took refuge under the unfledged rock.
> He could not see the cave, but groped with his hand,
> And the rock he touched was the socket of all men's eyes,
> And he touched the spring of vision . . .[17]

In these lines, Watkins invokes the image of Taliesin, constructed in the mythological tale, *Hanes Taliesin*, and in *The Book of Taliesin* (a collection of Welsh poetry from the fourteenth century), as a 'wild inspired seer' and 'possessor of arcane knowledge'[18] yet, essentially, as M. Wynn Thomas argues, the minutiae of Watkins's early life form an impression of a 'socially and culturally displaced person',[19] in relation to whom the notion of linguistic and cultural 'deterritorialisation' rings especially, and poignantly, true: Wynn Thomas even links these circumstances to the psychological breakdown that Watkins suffered at the age of twenty-three, suggesting that 'it seems likely that the instabilities of his [Watkins's] early background had long been preparing the way for his collapse'.[20]

Unlike Gwyn Thomas, Glyn Jones and Idris Davies, Watkins did not even appear to feel at home within the newly forming 'territory' of Anglophone Welsh writing. Just as Lynette Roberts dismissed the term 'Anglo-Welsh' as '*having no origin but a superficial one*',[21] Watkins 'did not relish inclusion' in the roll of 'Anglo-Welsh poets of the twentieth century . . . preferring to call himself *a Welshman and an English poet*' [emphasis in the original]'.[22] According to M. Wynn Thomas, Watkins 'found release from [this sense of Englishness] by making contact [in his poetry] . . . with a great European tradition that included, in his eyes, [Friedrich] Hölderlin [1770–1843],[23] [Heinrich] Heine [1797–1856], Novalis [1772–1801], the French Symbolists, [Stefan] George [1868–1933] and [Rainer Maria] Rilke [1875–1926]'.[24] And he also entered what he described as 'the whole orbit' of each European poet's 'thought'[25] through translating their work. His *Selected Verse Translations*, published in 1977, for instance, includes English translations of works by all of the aforementioned poets, with the French

Symbolists represented by Charles Baudelaire, Jules Laforgue, Arthur Rimbaud and Paul Valéry. This collection also encompasses extracts from Homer's *Iliad* and Dante's *Purgatorio* from his *Divine Comedy*, and omits further translations of Hungarian and Spanish poetry.[26] The capacious range of European poetry that Watkins translated, however, as well as the concomitant cultural diversity of his own poetry, posits a more complex motive than the need to escape, or 'find release' from, his own 'Englishness'. Indeed, in a number of Watkins's poems, continental European and English culture appear to be deliberately synthesised. This is, arguably, most strikingly evident in 'Discoveries', a poem first published in Watkins's inaugural collection, *Ballad of the Mari Lwyd and Other Poems* (1941). As such, a substantial section of this chapter – what immediately follows – will be devoted to a detailed analysis of this text:

> Ptolemy's planets, playing fast and loose,
> Foretell the wisdom of Copernicus.
>
> Dante calls Primum Mobile, the First Cause:
> 'Love that moves the world and the other stars.'
>
> Great Galileo, twisted by the rack,
> Groans the bright sun from heaven, then breathes it back.
>
> Blake, on the world alighting, holds the skies,
> And all the stars shine down through human eyes.
>
> Donne sees those stars, yet will not let them lie:
> 'We're tapers, too, and at our own cost die.'
>
> The shroud-lamp catches. Lips are smiling there.
> 'Les flammes – déjà?' – The world dies, or Voltaire.
>
> Swift, a cold mourner at his burial-rite,
> Burns to the world's heart like a meteorite.
>
> Beethoven deaf, in deafness hearing all,
> Unwinds all music from sound's funeral.
>
> Three prophets fall, the litter of one night:
> Blind Milton gazes in fixed deeps of light.

Beggar of those Minute Particulars,
Yeats lights again the turmoil of the stars.

Motionless motion! Come, Tiresias,
The eternal flies, what's passing cannot pass.[27]

Both in terms of form and content, these stanzas resemble a chain of epitaphs – the use of the present tense and of direct quotation (from Dante in the second stanza cited above, from John Donne in the fourth, and from Voltaire, in the fifth) immortalising, in literary form, an array of deceased artists and thinkers from both English and European cultures. This epitaphic mode, which may owe something to the ancient Welsh *Engylion y Beddau*, or 'stanzas of the graves' – a collection of 'lyrical and elegiac' poems, 'which name the graves of heros'[28] – is underscored in the reference to the Anglo-Irish writer and political activist Jonathan 'Swift' (1667–1745) as 'a cold mourner at his burial-rite'. Here, Watkins alludes to the similarly immortalising, instructive words that Swift decreed should appear in Latin on his tombstone:

> Here lies the body of Jonathan Swift, Doctor of Divinity and Dean of this Cathedral Church, where savage indignation can no more lacerate his heart. Go, traveller, and imitate if you can one who strove with all his might to champion liberty.[29]

This sense of creative immortality is underscored in the final stanza cited above, through Watkins's reference to the blind soothsayer, Tiresias,[30] a figure from ancient Greek mythology (and also, famously, T. S. Eliot's *The Waste Land*), to whom the God, 'Zeus gave the privilege of retaining the gift of prophecy even after his death'.[31]

W. B. Yeats (1865–1939), whose name appears in the tenth stanza cited above, translated Swift's epitaph into an English poem, thereby, in a sense, allowing Swift to continue to speak vicariously to the world from beyond the grave and making him, in Watkins's words, 'a cold mourner at his burial-rite':

Swift has sailed into his rest;
Savage indignation there
Cannot lacerate his breast.
Imitate him if you dare,

World-besotted traveller; he
Served human liberty.[32]

And there are also echoes, in Watkins's description of Swift as 'a cold mourner', of Yeats's 1938 poem, 'Under Ben Bulben', the closing four lines of which Yeats selected as his own epitaph:

Under bare Ben Bulben's head
In Drumcliff churchyard Yeats is laid,
An ancestor was rector there
Long years ago; a church stands near,
By the road an ancient Cross.
No marble, no conventional phrase,
On limestone quarried near the spot
By his command these words are cut:

Cast a cold eye
On life, on death.
Horseman, pass by![33]

Indeed, Watkins forms an impression in 'Discoveries' of a timeless and sacred stratum of artists and thinkers, of intellectual visionaries, which he marks out through an intricate array of inter- and cross-cultural echoes, interactions and affinities. 'Dante calls Primum Mobile' is adapted from Dante's *Paradiso* – the third and final part of the medieval Italian poet's Christian epic poem, *The Divine Comedy*. Dante's poem, as Peter Armour notes, is 'structured on ancient Greek astronomy as systematized by Ptolemy',[34] and Watkins dramatises this connection through his reference to 'Ptolemy's planets' in the first stanza cited above. Watkins also appears to trace the origins of Ptolemy's celestial model back to Aristotle through the declarative 'Motionless motion!' in the eleventh cited stanza, which evokes Aristotle's proposition that 'the heavenly bodies revolve eternally in perfect circles, kept in steady motion (somehow) by an Unmoved Mover'[35] that European Christians presumed to be God.[36] Indeed, Aristotle, Ptolemy and Dante are placed within a kind of eternal order of creative thinkers in Watkins's poem. 'Ptolemy's planets, playing fast and loose' – a line which seems to draw on Ptolemy's argument that the planets 'travel with variable speeds'[37] and not in a 'uniform motion'[38] as Aristotle originally claimed – 'Foretell the wisdom' of the Polish cosmologist, Copernicus (1473–1543), who challenged Ptolemy's assumption that the earth is at the centre of the universe by claiming that, in contrast, the earth and the other planets in the solar system revolve around the sun.[39] The Italian astronomer, Galileo Galilei (1564–1642), who is also commemorated in Watkins's poem, corroborated and expanded on Copernicus's theories, but was prosecuted by the Catholic Inquisition for his views.[40] Watkins's description of Galileo as 'twisted by the rack' as he repositions 'the bright sun' in the heavens seems to act as a metaphor for the way in which Galileo was pulled in opposing directions by the pursuit of scientific knowledge and the Christian ideology of his day – a conflict which, later, Bertolt Brecht also explored in his 1943 play, *Leben des Galilei* or *The Life of Galileo*.

To return to the stanza of Watkins's poem that explicitly engages with the work of Dante, however: 'Dante calls Primum Mobile' is adapted from canto XXVIII of the *Paradiso*, in which the hero, accompanied by his love and guide, Beatrice, arrive at 'the ninth heavenly sphere or Primum Mobile' – a region 'moved by its love for God and . . . held [by Dante] to communicate motion to the rest of the universe'.[41] As Peter Armour explains,

> the earth [in Dante's poem] is stationary at the centre of the universe; around it revolve nine transparent circular spheres, bearing the visible heavenly bodies – the Moon, Mercury, Venus, the Sun, Mars, Jupiter, Saturn, and the Fixed stars – beyond which is the Primum Mobile (the First Moved Heaven or Crystalline Heaven), which exists in the Empyrean. Through these and their light, God's creative power and providence are transmitted down to earth.[42]

Dante references this deep structure at the close of the *Paradiso*, describing 'the Love that moves the sun and the other stars' (canto XXXIII, l. 145); and Watkins also assimilates this line from Dante's text into his poem. The 'First Cause' that Watkins refers to is God, who in canto XXVIII of the *Paradiso*, is manifested as 'an infinitesimal point of pure light, surrounded by nine revolving circles (the nine orders of the angels)'.[43] Dante initially sees this image of God glowing in the 'lovely eyes' (canto XXVIII, l. 11) of Beatrice, and Watkins imports this event into another stanza, which admits the English poet and visual artist, William Blake (1757–1827) into the poem's immortalising realm of visionaries. In *The Divine Comedy*, the stars or '*stelle*'[44] – with which Dante concludes all the three parts of his poem, the *Inferno*, *Purgatorio* and *Paradiso* – are 'blazing emblems of divinity'[45] and 'the highest heavenly spheres which humans can see in their aspiration to God'.[46] As Dante reveals, when he turns to face the divine light in canto XXVIII,

> I saw a point that sent forth so acute
> a light, that . . .
> . . . any star that, seen from earth, would seem
> to be smallest, set beside that point,
> as star conjoined with star, would seem a moon.[47]

In 'Blake . . . holds the skies / And all the stars shine down through human eyes', Watkins seems to be invoking the moment at which the divine light appears in Beatrice's eyes in canto XXVIII of the *Paradiso* and relating it to Blake's conception of God as the 'Divine Humanity'[48] – his notion of 'Humanity' or 'man' as 'the image of God in which he was created'[49]– and, in particular, to what Robert Ryan identifies as the 'unconventional theological conception that persists in Blake's work from first to last, the identification of God or Jesus with the human imagination'.[50] Blake gives poetic form to his theological vision in 'The Divine Image', from his 1789 collection, *Songs of Innocence*:

> Then every man of every clime,
> That prays in his distress,
> Prays to the human form divine
> Love Mercy Pity Peace.
>
> And all must love the human form,
> In heathen turk or jew.
> Where Mercy, Love & Pity dwell,
> There God is dwelling too.[51]

And these ideas find similar, though more ambiguous, expression in the final lines of 'Auguries of Innocence', from the *Pickering Manuscript*, published posthumously in 1863:

> God appears, and God is light,
> To those poor souls who dwell in night;
> But does a human form display
> To those who dwell in realms of day.[52]

Indeed, Watkins seems to be drawing directly on the opening lines of 'Auguries of Innocence' in his stanza on Blake. 'Blake, on the world alighting, holds the skies' evokes the opening lines of 'Auguries', while preserving the celestial imagery of the *Paradiso*:

> To see the world in a grain of sand,
> And heaven in a wild flower,
> Hold infinity in the palm of your hand,
> And eternity in an hour. (ll. 1–4)

The conceit of Blake 'alighting' on 'the world' and holding 'the skies' indicates the propinquity of earthly life to 'eternity', and the above lines from Blake's poem also create this impression. Indeed, 'Auguries of Innocence' pivots on this notion of terrestrial and metaphysical proximity – the speaker declaims, for example, that 'A robin redbreast in a cage / Puts all Heaven in a rage' (ll. 5–6) and 'Kill not the moth nor butterfly, / For the Last Judgement draweth nigh' (ll. 39–40), though Blake's main objective seems to be to criticise the psychological tyranny of the established Church in contemporary English society. Through subtly interweaving the work and thought of Blake and Dante in 'Discoveries', moreover, Watkins dramatises a genuine imaginative 'relationship', just as he illustrates the actual creative influence of Aristotle on Ptolemy and of Ptolemy on Dante elsewhere in the poem. For although Blake often found fault with Dante's writings,[53] he 'ranked . . . [the Italian Poet] with Shakespeare',[54] and 'in his old age began a vast project of illustrating the entire *Divine Comedy*', producing 102 water-colour paintings in all.[55]

The next stanza of 'Discoveries' focuses on the English Metaphysical poet, John Donne (1572–1631), whom Watkins integrates into his transcendental territory of artists and thinkers by extending the theme of stars, observed previously in the stanzas on Dante and Blake: 'Donne sees those stars, yet will not let them lie'. On one level, the stars appear to be figured here as deceptive markers of permanence in the eyes of the seventeenth-century beholder. For in 1572, shortly before Galileo (as Watkins's speaker recognises) began corroborating and developing Copernicus's revolutionary ideas about the structure of the cosmos, the Danish astronomer, Tycho Brahe (1546–1601), observed what appeared to be a new star in the night sky. The object, later identified as a supernova,[56] or an exploding, self-destructing star, emitted an unusually brilliant light before steadily diminishing and finally vanishing from sight in March 1574.[57] This event contradicted the astronomical configurations of Aristotle and Ptolemy, who had envisaged a distinct sphere of 'fixed stars', lying 'outside the [seven] planets'.[58] Indeed, as John Carey notes in his study, *John Donne: Life, Mind and Art*, 'the appearance and disappearance of new stars [at this time] shook the semi-mystic belief in the changelessness of the heavens',[59] and Donne himself criticised 'Aristotle's followers [in *Biathanatos. A declaration of that paradoxe, or thesis, that Self-homicide is not so Naturally Sinne, that it may never be otherwise* (1648)] because they insist[ed] on considering the heavens unalterable'.[60] In keeping with the central theme of astronomy in the poem – as well as with the poem's title, 'Discoveries' – Watkins seems to be articulating this contemporary realisation of the mutability of 'the skies' by suggesting that the stars, as conceptualised by Aristotle, Ptolemy and also Dante (whom Donne read in the original)[61] mislead or 'lie': they are, in actuality, not 'fixed' but protean and apparently subject to the same mortality as life on earth. Watkins makes this explicit in the following line, which he adapts from Donne's 1633 poem, 'The Canonization' ('We're tapers too, and at our own cost die').[62] In this context, Donne's words impress upon the reader that both stars and humans (a commonality that Watkins stresses by adding a comma before 'too' rather than quoting Donne verbatim) are cognate with 'tapers'– 'self-consuming candles',[63] whose very 'life' is, necessarily, also a process of material extinction. In this way, Watkins effectively develops or replies to his previous stanza on Blake by emphasising the fundamental difference between the 'humanity of man'[64] and the 'Divine Humanity' of God.

But Watkins also seems to be concerned – in his own words – with the wider 'orbit' of Donne's 'thought' in this stanza. The intimation that both stars and humans are 'self-consuming candles' calls to mind Donne's theory, expounded in *Paradoxes, Problems, Essayes, Characters* (1652), that 'all things kill themselves'[65] – Donne, in fact, as the full title of *Biathanatos* cited above suggests, studied and argued a case for the legitimacy of suicide[66] – and this theme of self-sabotage also finds expression in 'The Canonization' itself. In the original context of Donne's poem, the speaker's assertion that he and his mistress 'die' at their 'own cost' reflects the popular seventeenth-century credence that 'lovers shorten their lives by sexual emission'.[67] Broadly, moreover, Watkins seems to be attempting in these lines to epithetically represent Donne's well-known preoccupation with death as a philosophical and poetic theme, as evidenced, for instance, in the 'Holy Sonnets' (1633), and in love poems such as 'The Dissolution' (1633) and 'The Relic' (1633), which is centred on the seventeenth-century practice of reusing graves.[68] Another example is 'The Expiration' (1633), in which Donne hyperbolically invokes the theme of death in order to dramatise the parting of two lovers:

> 'Go.' And if that word have not quite kill'd thee,
> Ease me with death, by bidding me go too.
> Oh, if it have, let my word work on me,
> And a just office on a murderer do.
> Except it be too late, to kill me so,
> Being double dead, going, and bidding, 'Go.'[69]

Donne's suspicion of 'those stars' in 'Discoveries', however – which, as previously discussed, on one level, seems to index Watkins's continuing engagement with the great astronomical 'discoveries' of antiquity – could quite plausibly have another, parallel meaning. Indeed, the poem seems actively to invite plural readings and cultivate semantic instability: Watkins opens up and concatenates entire lifetimes of thought through cryptically terse and allusive two-line stanzas, encouraging the reader, in a sense, to assume the role of 'discoverer' or (to cite Yeats's translation of Swift's epitaph) 'world besotted traveller'. Indeed, the reader begins to resemble the speaker of John Keats's 1816 poem, 'On First Looking into Chapman's Homer': as we encounter each of Watkins's pedestalled poets and thinkers, just as Keats's speaker encountered George Chapman's translation of Homer's *Odyssey*, we are, in a sense, positioned as 'watcher[s] of the skies / When a new planet swims into [our] ken'.[70] Donne was born into a Roman Catholic family, but famously 'betrayed his Faith'[71] by converting to Anglicanism[72] – an apostasy that, arguably, finds expression in 'The Canonization', where the speaker invokes 'Catholic languages of ritual, miracle and transubstantiation'[73] in order to defend and exalt illicit sexual love. As Carey explains, seventeenth-century Protestant doctrine held that Christian

> faith meant belief in your own salvation. It necessitated a psychological belief by which you accepted Christ consciously as your personal saviour. But this psychological act could not come about by your own effort. Faith, the Protestant theologians believed, was wholly in God's gift. Man

> could do nothing to attain it. Nor was there any point in his trying to qualify for it by virtuous behaviour. God selected those whom He would save according to an inscrutable process, known only to Him.[74]

When this is taken into consideration, the stars, as Watkins presents them in his stanzas on Dante and Blake, inevitably 'lie' in his stanza on Donne because they attest to a knowable God and promise that all souls may aspire to heaven; and the emphasis on the inevitability and 'cost' of death in the second, ventriloquised line of this stanza pertains to a fear of damnation.[75] Indeed, Donne poeticises these very anxieties in the *Holy Sonnets*. In Sonnet 19, the speaker reveals that 'In prayers and flattering speeches I court God: / Tomorrow I quake with fear of his rod',[76] and in Sonnet 1, addressing God, Donne writes:

> Oh I shall soon despair, when I do see
> That thou lov'st mankind well, yet wilt not choose me,
> And Satan hates me, yet is loath to lose me.[77]

Regardless of how we read Watkins's richly suggestive stanza on John Donne, however, what is clear is that he uses its central theme of death as a means to link Donne with the French Enlightenment writer and philosopher, Voltaire (1694–1778), thereby introducing another eminent name into the poem's timeless fold of artists and thinkers. The opening clause of the next stanza, 'The shroud-lamp catches', records the moment at which a lamp next to Voltaire's deathbed is reputed to have caught fire.[78] Voltaire is thought to have reacted to this event by exclaiming '*Les flammes déjà?*' or 'The flames [that is, of Hell] already?',[79] a sardonic reference (which appears in Watkins's poem in the original French and is alleged to have been Voltaire's last utterance before he died[80]) to the liberal, controversial and, to many ecclesiastics, blasphemous writings about institutional religion that he produced throughout his lifetime.[81] As Voltaire wrote in his *Dictionnaire Philosophique* or *Philosophical Dictionary*, published in 1764, for instance:

> If I were permitted to reason consistently in religious matters, it would be clear that we all ought to become Jews, because Jesus Christ our Saviour was born a Jew, lived a Jew, died a Jew, and said expressly that he was accomplishing, that he was fulfilling the Jewish religion. But it is clearer

> still that we [people of different denominations and faiths] ought to be tolerant of one another, because we are all weak, inconsistent, liable to fickleness and error. Shall a reed laid low by the wind say to a fellow reed fallen in the opposite direction: 'Crawl! As I crawl, wretch, or I shall petition that you be torn up by the roots and burned'?[82]

Voltaire's closing rhetorical question in the above call for religious tolerance has a particular resonance in relation to John Donne – a writer who, as previously noted, experienced, on a deeply personal level, the historical division and hostilities between Anglicans and Catholics. Indeed, Donne and Voltaire (and also Galileo, 'twisted by the rack') found themselves in similarly vexed positions with regard to the religious institutions of their day; King Louis XV even banished Voltaire from Paris and Versailles for his writings.[83] Watkins appears to recognise this affinity and, as with Dante and Blake, unites these two figures in inventive and subtle ways. '*Les flammes déjà?*' seems to function in 'Discoveries' as both a wry counterpoint to – Watkins underscores Voltaire's grim humour by describing 'smiling' lips and by placing a dash each side of '*déjà?*' – and an ominous echo of Donne's terror of damnation, adumbrated in the previous stanza. The burning 'shroud-lamp', too, clearly reinscribes and reworks Donne's metaphor of the 'taper', associating 'self-consuming' light with human mortality, while 'The world dies, or Voltaire' is strikingly evocative of Donne's 'The Will' (1633), in which the speaker opines, in a similar way, that his own death will signify the demise of the world:

> Therefore I'll give no more, but I'll undo
> The world by dying, because love dies too.
> Then all your beauties will be no more worth
> Than gold in mines, where none doth draw it forth;
> And all your graces no more shall have,
> Than a sundial in a grave.[84]

Principally, as previously discussed, the opening line of Watkins's next stanza seems to be an allusion to Swift's famous epitaph to himself on his grave in Dublin. And Watkins may also be referring here to how, after Swift's death, 'his ghost was said to haunt the aisles of St Patrick's Cathedral . . . [where he was buried], complaining, "The Pamphlets wrote against me, would have form'd a Library."'[85] At the same time, however, as in Watkins's stanza on John Donne, the text proffers another meaning that creates a nexus between Swift, Voltaire and, by implication, the larger edifice of progressive minds that comprises 'Discoveries'. This is because, having proclaimed the 'death' of Voltaire at the end of the previous stanza, the speaker advances with 'Swift, a cold mourner *at his* burial-rite' (my emphasis), generating a sense of ambiguity regarding exactly whose 'burial-rite' the speaker is envisaging. Watkins also creates this effect in his next stanza on Beethoven – the account of 'Beethoven, in deafness hearing all' both honouring the composer's musical genius and intimating a kind of metaphysical communion between Beethoven and the other artists and thinkers of the poem. The reference to Swift as a 'cold' or lifeless 'mourner' sustains this dualism: not only did Swift die thirty-three years before Voltaire, but also the two men respected each other and corresponded during their lifetimes,[86] with Voltaire, at one point, hailing Swift as 'the English Rabelais'.[87] It was Swift's aptitude as a satirist that prompted Voltaire to draw this comparison, and the subject of satire adds further credence to this plural reading of Watkins's stanza. Swift and Voltaire are equally renowned for their controversial satires of seventeenth- and eighteenth-century society. Indeed, Swift's short story, *A Tale of a Tub* (1704) is, as Joseph McMinn notes, 'a satire on divisions within Christianity, written . . . in imitation of theological extremism'[88] and targeting both 'Catholicism and Puritanism'[89] – subjects which, as his novel, *Candide*[90] and the extract from his *Dictionnaire Philosophique* cited above attest, also preoccupied Voltaire. Watkins also unites the two writers, it seems, by playing on the notion, introduced in his stanza on Voltaire, of the individual artist's death as signifying the 'undoing' of the world: 'Swift . . . / Burns to the world's heart like a meteorite.' Again, Watkins may well be giving poetic expression to a genuine affinity here. In suggesting, like the egoistic speaker of Donne's 'The Will', discussed previously, that the world is afflicted by the event of a single individual's death, Watkins captures the 'new individualism'[91] of the Enlightenment age that Swift and Voltaire inhabited, a mood that is captured in Swift's immortal words: 'Go, traveller, and imitate if you can one who strove with all his might to champion liberty.'[92]

The next stanza enables John Milton (1608–74) to take his place alongside Swift and Voltaire in Watkins's holy order of minds. Here, Watkins seems to be drawing on *Paradise Lost* (1667), and, more specifically, on book three of Milton's poem in which the speaker addresses the Creator as follows:

. . . thee I revisit safe,
And feel thy sov'reign vital lamp; but thou
Revisit'st not these eyes, that roll in vain
To find thy piercing ray, and find no dawn;
So thick a drop serene hath quenched their orbs,
Or dim suffusion veiled. Yet not the more
Cease I to wander where the Muses haunt
Clear spring, or shady grove, or sunny hill,
Smit with the love of sacred song; but chief
Thee Sion and the flow'ry brooks beneath
That wash thy hallowed feet, and warbling flow,
Nightly I visit: nor sometimes forget
Those other two equalled with me in fate,
So were I equalled with them in renown,
Blind Thamyris and blind Maeonides,
And Tiresias and Phineus prophets old.[93]

Milton famously lost his sight (he is introduced as 'Blind Milton' in Watkins's poem) and hence the poet-speaker of the above lines can only sense God's presence – he can only 'gaze' at 'fixed deeps' and 'feel [his] sov'reign vital lamp' – and cannot perceive his divine light: 'thou / Revisit'st not these eyes, that roll in vain'. The 'fixed deeps' into which Milton stares emphasise the darkness of the poet's world because Milton, as John Leonard notes, 'repeatedly refers to the infinite space outside our universe as "the deep"'[94] in *Paradise Lost*; and whereas 'the interstellar space within Milton's universe is bright',[95] 'illumined by God's love'[96] (a conviction outlined previously with reference to Dante's *Divine Comedy*), 'outside [this domain] . . . is unremittingly dark'.[97] Milton's predicament causes his poetic persona in *Paradise Lost* to feel an affinity with Homer or 'Maeonides', who is also thought to have been blind; 'Thamyris', 'a legendary Thracian poet [who appears in Homer's *Iliad*], punished with blindness for boasting that he could outsing the Muses'; 'Tiresias', 'the blind Theban prophet' whom Watkins mentions earlier in his poem; and 'Phineus', 'a Thracian prophet, blinded by the Gods'.[98] Conceivably, Watkins may be referring to Thamyris, Tiresias and Phineus, as they appear in book three of Milton's poem, in his phrase, 'Three prophets fall'. But he also seems to be assimilating Milton's fatalistic lines, 'Those other two equalled with me in fate, / So were I equalled with them in renown, / Blind Thamyris and blind Maeonides'. From this perspective, Thamyris, Maeonides and Milton himself are the 'three prophets', and they 'fall' or die and are immortalised in Watkins's stanza because they are, as Milton proclaims, 'equalled with [him] in fate'. Milton is also 'equalled' in 'Discoveries' with other members of Watkins's sublimated constellation of artists and thinkers. His description of 'fixed deeps of light', for example, also evokes the language of William Blake's 1794 poem, 'The Tiger':

> Tiger tiger, burning bright,
> In the forests of the night;
>
> . . .
>
> In what distant deeps or skies,
> Burnt the fire of thine eyes?[99]

Indeed, a similar interplay between Milton and Blake is perceptible earlier in Watkins's poem. As well as echoing Blake's 'Auguries of Innocence', the phrase, 'Blake, on the world alighting' seems to allude, again, to book three of *Paradise Lost*, in which the poet-speaker explains that 'Satan alights upon the bare convex of this world's outermost orb . . . thence comes to the gate of Heaven' (iii. 20–4). In drawing a parallel between Blake and Milton's Satan, Watkins seems to be acknowledging Blake's irreverence towards the institutional religion of his day and alluding, in particular, to his infamous assertion in his prose piece, *The Marriage of Heaven and Hell* (1793), that 'the reason Milton wrote in fetters when he wrote of Angels and God, and at liberty when he wrote of Devils and Hell, is because he was a true Poet and of the Devil's party without knowing it'.[100] Moreover, again, as with Blake and Dante, and Swift and Voltaire, Watkins poeticises an historical artistic relationship in his poem; as S. Foster Damon notes, 'Milton . . . in Blake's opinion, was England's greatest poet',[101] and a considerable source of inspiration. Blake completed *Milton, a Poem in Two Books* (1804), for example, and he also illustrated many of Milton's poems, including *Paradise Lost*.[102]

If Milton had a profound influence on Blake's oeuvre, then Blake was equally influential in shaping the life and poetry of W. B. Yeats. As Keith Alldritt notes, Yeats co-wrote with E. J. Ellis 'a commentary on the mystical system of William Blake as articulated in his Prophetic Books',[103] which was published in 1893, and 'Blake's vision' formed 'an important part of Yeats's mystical understanding'[104] of art and the world. Watkins dramatises this creative bond in 'Discoveries' by hailing Yeats as a 'Beggar of those Minute Particulars' – 'Minute Particulars' being the term that Blake invented to denote

> the outward expression in this world of the eternal individualities of all things. God, 'the Divine-Humanity', is ultimately 'the only General and Universal form'; he contains all things, including the various Universal Forms, the sources of the Particulars. The Minute Particulars of God are men; of men, they are their children; of life, the joys of living, especially the embraces of love, of ethics, forgiveness instead of judgement; of art, the vision and the finished product; of science, the basic facts. In short, they are reality as we encounter it. They are not negligible aberrations from a Platonic norm, but are highly organised and direct expressions of their eternal and individual existences.[105]

There are also clear echoes of Blake in Watkins's subsequent account of how 'Yeats lights again the turmoil of the stars.' While the trope of the 'stars' again links Yeats with all of the aforementioned figures that define Watkins's transcendental realm, this line is especially evocative of Blake's poem 'The Tyger', discussed earlier vis-à-vis Watkins's stanza on Milton. In this poem, Blake writes:

> When the stars threw down their spears
> And water'd heaven with their tears:
> Did he smile his work to see?
> Did he who made the lamb make thee? (ll. 17–20)

The 'turmoil' that Watkins observes concords with Blake's representation of the stars in the above stanza, where they '[throw] down their spears' and cry 'their tears' on 'heaven'. Moreover, in declaring that 'Yeats lights again the turmoil of the stars', Watkins's speaker seems to be registering how Yeats revived and promoted the creative achievements of Blake, stimulating 'an enormous increase in interest' in the poet's work during the twentieth century.[106] Watkins may also be foregrounding and playing on a recursive motif in Yeats's own work here. The stars function as a kind of poetic muse in many of Yeats's poems – for example, in 'Brown Penny' (1910), 'When You are Old' (1895) and in 'The Song of Wandering Aengus' (1899):

> And when white moths were on the wing,
> And moth like stars were flickering out,

I dropped the berry in a stream
And caught a little silver trout.[107]

I have analysed 'Discoveries' in some detail in order to do justice to how Watkins embraces and utilises his 'deterritorialised' position as an 'Anglo-Welsh' writer; he develops a rootless, roving poetic voice – the experimental idiom (in Yeats's words) of 'a world-besotted traveller' – which acts as a 'verbal ikon' for his, and also, effectively, other contemporary Anglophone Welsh writers' experience of social and cultural dislocation. The semantic instability and plurality of this poetic mode – the manifold and labyrinthine interpretive paths that Watkins lays before the reader – reinforce this overall impression of homelessness and itinerancy. In 'Discoveries', Watkins wanders across an unbounded metaphysical, intellectual territory of his own making that is superficially and thus, perhaps, liberatingly divorced from the reality of Wales, both past and present, and yet ultimately formed and shaped by the force of his own socio-cultural, psychic and spiritual dissociation from his native country. Moreover, Watkins's socio-cultural position and poetic praxis link him with many other, canonical Modernist writers and artists. As Malcolm Bradbury argues,

> much Modernist art has taken its stance from, [and] gained its perspectives out of, a certain kind of distance, an exiled posture – a distance from local origins, class allegiances, the specific obligations and duties of those with an assigned role in a cohesive culture.[108]

Bradbury cites the work of T. S. Eliot as an outstanding example of this trend, but Watkins's 'Discoveries' is an equally apposite case in point. Indeed, we might say that Watkins makes use of his peripatetic cultural perspective, just as Eliot, an American who, Peter Ackroyd points out, 'was never completely at home anywhere and, even after he adopted British citizenship . . . would sometimes sign himself 'metoikos', the Greek for 'resident alien',[109] creatively utilised his position as 'wandering, culturally inquisitive'[110] émigré. Eliot's 'The Love Song of J. Alfred Prufrock', for example, interweaves references and allusions to Dante, Homer, Hesiod, Andrew Marvell, Shakespeare, Chaucer, Jules Laforgue and the French philosopher, Henri Bergson (1859-1941), among others, while in *The Waste Land* – Eliot's most densely intertextual poem – the voices of all of the aforementioned figures sound alongside those of Ovid, Virgil, Milton, St Augustine, the Buddha, Charles Baudelaire, Paul Verlaine, Joseph Conrad, the German composer, Richard Wagner (1813–83), the German novelist, Hermann Hesse (1877–1962), and many more besides.

The work of Watkins and Eliot, whose Faber and Faber Press published Watkins's poetry along with that of Lynette Roberts and David Jones, actually intersects at several points. Both in terms of its subject matter and its self-conscious connective and connotative strategies, 'Discoveries' accords with the distinctly Eliotic belief that creative progressiveness and ingenuity arise from engagement or dialogue with the past – from what Eliot calls in his influential essay of 1919, 'Tradition and the Individual Talent', a 'historical sense . . . that the whole literature of Europe from Homer . . . has a simultaneous existence and composes a simultaneous order'.[111] Eliot's essay points towards the innovatory potential of just the kind of cultural expansiveness and 'sense of the timeless as well as the temporal'[112] that we encounter in Watkins's poem. Both texts, in a sense, intimate that 'not only the best, but the most individual parts of his [the poet's] work may be those in which dead poets, his ancestors, assert their immortality most vigorously'.[113] Watkins posited a very similar outlook on poetry to that expressed by Eliot in 'Tradition and the Individual Talent' in a lecture which he presented at Swansea University in 1966. Here, he insisted that

> the perceptions of a poet must be composite, as he is a witness for the living and the dead at the same time. If he observes the two responsibilities, he will begin to see what is ancient in the contemporary scene and what is contemporary in the ancient; and his style will emerge from that collision . . .[114]

Watkins also seems to evoke the ideas that Eliot expressed in 'Tradition and the Individual Talent' in the following stanza from his later 'Ode: to T. S. Eliot' (1962):

> Art is various, verse develops unsearchably.
> See, from the mid-leaf born,
> Growth may copy the cactus
> Yet adhere to its ancient root.[115]

Here, Watkins suggests that 'art' in the modern world may advance and assume apparently divergent, unfamiliar forms, just as the cactus, which is 'without leaves . . . armed with curious clusters of spines . . . and . . . often of grotesque shape',[116] deviates from other plants, but it always 'adhere[s] to its ancient root', always grows out of and carries the trace of the art that has gone before. Echoing 'Discoveries', Watkins also seems to be directly assimilating Eliot's verse in this stanza; Eliot invokes the image of the cactus in 'The Hollow Men' (1925), where the speaker declares, 'This is the dead land / This is cactus land.'[117]

Moreover, again following Eliot – and also conforming to a pattern traced previously in the Welsh Modernist work of Gwyn Thomas, Glyn Jones and Idris Davies – Watkins's new mode of expression entails a process of Modernist *reterritorialisation*. However, whereas Thomas, Jones and Davies search for a foothold within an emerging territory of 'Anglo-Welsh' writing, and the early Eliot seeks a grounding, as Bradbury argues, within 'a [kind of] modern country of the arts', where 'the place of art's making . . . become[s] an ideal distant city',[118] Watkins employs a different strategy. Owing, perhaps, to the centrally religious nature of his detachment from his home culture – we recall that Watkins's Anglican religious education set him apart from his traditional Welsh Nonconformist family – he opts for 'a religious or spiritual reterritorialization'[119] within an elite, Christianised 'country of the arts', with 'its own [culturally expansive] society . . . [of thinkers and artists] from other countries, other languages, other ages'.[120] In this respect, Watkins, like Gwyn Thomas, Glyn Jones and Idris Davies, is surely negotiating his position as a 'post-Nonconformist, Anglo-Welsh writer'[121] (in M. Wynn Thomas's words), and his 'verbal ikon' therefore carries all the religious connotations of that label.

At the same time, Watkins's poem bears comparison with the later Eliot, in particular his *Four Quartets* (1935–42). Eliot locates each of the four poems that make up this collection in real, geographical places of personal significance to him – at 'Burnt Norton', a manor house that he encountered during a visit to Gloucestershire; 'East Coker', a village in Somerset where his family lived before they emigrated to America in the seventeenth century; 'The Dry Salvages', a cluster of rocks lying off the coast of Massachusetts, New England, where his ancestors had settled 'in the 1650s and . . . established themselves as social and cultural leaders';[122] and 'Little Gidding', a church in Cambridgeshire.[123] He is primarily concerned, however, with pursuing a kind of mystical absorption into a sacred, timeless state or imagined realm:

At the still point of the turning world. Neither flesh nor fleshless;
Neither from nor towards; at the still point, there the dance is,
But neither arrest nor movement. And do not call it fixity,
Where past and future are gathered. Neither movement from nor towards,
Neither ascent nor decline. Except for the point, the still point,
There would be no dance, and there is only the dance.
I can only say, *there*, we have been: but I cannot say where.
And I cannot say, how long, for that is to place it in time.
The inner freedom from the practical desire,
The release from action and suffering, release from the inner
And the outer compulsion, yet surrounded
By a grace of sense, a white light still and moving,
Erhebung without motion, concentration
Without elimination, both a new world
And the old made explicit, understood . . .[124]

F. O. Mathiessen has described the transcendental 'point' that the poet-speaker identifies above as 'Eliot's poetic equivalent in our cosmology for Dante's 'unmoved mover' [discussed earlier in this chapter], another way of symbolising a timeless release from the outer compulsions of the world';[125] and this imagined ground accrues a more overtly Christian significance in the third poem of the sequence, 'The Dry Salvages' (1941):

Men's curiosity searches past and future
And clings to that dimension. But to apprehend
The point of intersection of the timeless
With time, is an occupation for the saint –
No occupation either, but something given
And taken, in a lifetime's death in love,
Ardour and selflessness and self-surrender.
For most of us, there is only the unattended
Moment, the moment in and out of time,
The distraction fit, lost in a shaft of sunlight,
The wild thyme unseen, or the winter lightning
Or the waterfall, or music heard so deeply
That it is not heard at all, but you are the music
While the music lasts. These are only hints and guesses,
Hints followed by guesses; and the rest
Is prayer, observance, discipline, thought and action.
The hint half guessed, the gift half understood, is Incarnation.
Here the impossible union

> Of spheres of existence is actual,
> Here the past and future
> Are conquered, and reconciled.[126]

Furthermore, recalling Watkins's transcultural and transhistorical approach in 'Discoveries', in addition to Dante, Eliot incorporates the ideas of Bergson, and the ancient Greek philosopher, Heraclitus, in *Four Quartets*;[127] and, as in *The Waste Land*, he also looks beyond Western cultural tradition, to India and the Hindu scripture, the *Bhagavad-Gita*. Indeed, the format of 'Discoveries' seems almost to anticipate and actualise Eliot's assertion in the final poem of *Four Quartets*, 'Little Gidding' (1942), that 'Every phrase and every sentence is an end and a beginning, / Every poem an epitaph.'[128]

Watkins's wandering poetic idiom, which is the voice of Anglophone Welsh disorientation reoriented within an almost Eliotic 'modern country of the arts', is also evident in 'The Collier' (1941) – though here it has a different, ballad-like complexion:

> When I was born on Amman hill
> A dark bird crossed the sun.
> Sharp on the floor the shadow fell;
> I was the youngest son.
>
> And when I went to the County School
> I worked in a shaft of light.
> In the wood of the desk I cut my name:
> Dai for Dynamite.
>
> The tall black hills my brothers stood;
> Their lessons all were done.
> From the door of the school when I ran out
> They frowned to watch me run.
>
> The slow grey bells they rung a chime
> Surly with grief or age.
> Clever or clumsy, lad or lout,
> All would look for a wage.
>
> I learnt the valley flowers' names
> And the rough bark knew my knees.
> I brought home trout from the river
> And spotted eggs from the trees.

A coloured coat I was given to wear
Where the lights of the rough land shone.
Still jealous of my favour
The tall black hills looked on.

They dipped my coat in the blood of a kid
And they cast me down a pit,
And although I crossed with strangers
There was no way up from it.

Soon as I went from the County School
I worked in a shaft. Said Jim,
'You will get your chain of gold, my lad,
But not for a likely time.'

And one said, 'Jack was not raised up
When the wind blew out the light
Though he interpreted their dreams
And guessed their fears by night.'

And Tom, he shivered his leper's lamp
For the stain that round him grew;
And I heard mouths pray in the after-damp
When the picks would not break through.

They changed words there in darkness
And still through my head they run,
And white on my limbs is the linen sheet
And gold on my neck the sun.[129]

This poem differs from 'Discoveries' in that it is located within a real, earthly space: the industrialised south Wales Valleys of Watkins's birth. And yet, recalling Eliot's *Four Quartets*, the poetic voice is distanced from this geographical territory. Like the figures in 'Discoveries', the poetic voice is elevated, transmuted from the socio-political to the realm of the transcendent and timeless. The speaker looks down at his body covered with a 'white . . . linen sheet' and recalls the events of his life leading up to his death following an explosion in a coalmine; he and his co-workers, it seems, were unable to dig themselves to safety ('the picks would not break through'), and were suffocated by the 'after-damp', the noxious atmosphere generated when 'carbonic acid gas' rises and combines with 'nitrogen, steam, smoke and dust'.[130] Moreover, again recalling 'Discoveries', Watkins's speaker shares his transcendental territory with other voices that sound or, as Rowan Williams suggests, 'echo' within his own.[131] Most obviously, the poem is structured around the biblical story of Joseph. But, more specifically, as Richard Ramsbotham notes, Watkins is drawing here on Richard Strauss's dramatic adaptation of this narrative in his ballet, *Josephslegende* or *The Legend of Joseph* (1914).[132] Ramsbotham points out that Watkins attended a performance of *Josephslegende* in Nuremberg in 1930, and notes that he found it to be, in his own words,

> a work of immortal beauty and most wonderfully portrayed. It . . . shows the pagan rule of tyranny, savagery, lust and monarchical pride penetrated by the subtle spirit of free untamed aesthetic beauty evolved from innocent childhood in the figure of Joseph.[133]

In Watkins's poem, the 'pagan rule of tyranny, savagery, lust and monarchical pride', so vividly portrayed by Strauss, takes the form of industry in the south Wales Valleys, and this milieu threatens the young speaker's 'innocent' 'spirit of free untamed aesthetic beauty' – the spirit in which he 'learnt the valley flowers' names', felt 'rough bark' on his skin and 'brought home trout from the river / And spotted eggs from the trees'. This commercial menace is symbolised by the dark hills with their concealed networks of coal pits and shafts, which are likened to the grasping, envious brothers of the Joseph story. But Watkins is not only invoking Strauss's production here. Rather, in his initial portrayal of a solitary and sensitive child's uniquely intimate communion with nature, he also seems to be assimilating the themes of William Wordsworth's *The Prelude* (1805). As Wordsworth writes in book one of this text, in which he recalls his '*Childhood and School-Time*':[134]

> . . . I believe
> That Nature, oftentimes, when she would frame
> A favoured Being, from his earliest dawn
> Of infancy doth open out the clouds,
> As at the touch of lightning, seeking him
> With gentlest visitation
>
> (i. 362–7)

The young poet-speaker of Wordsworth's poem is constructed as such a 'favoured Being'. In the following passage, for example, it is as if 'Nature' itself is assisting him in his endeavours to observe the most sublime and inaccessible natural sights:

> . . . and when the Vales
> And woods were warm, was I a plunderer then
> In the high places, on the lonesome peaks
> Where'er, among the mountains and the winds,
> The Mother Bird had built her lodge. Though mean
> My object, and inglorious, yet the end
> Was not ignoble. Oh! When I have hung
> Above the raven's nest, by knots of grass
> And half-inch fissures in the slippery rock
> But ill sustained, and almost, as it seemed,
> Suspended by the blast which blew, amain,
> Shouldering the naked crag; Oh! At that time,
> While on the perilous ridge I hung alone,
> With what strange utterance did the loud dry wind
> Blow through my ears! The sky seemed not a sky
> Of earth, and with what motion moved the clouds! (i. 335–46)

Not only does Wordsworth's preoccupation with childhood 'favour' chime with Watkins's poem, Strauss's ballet, and the original biblical tale of Joseph, but the image of the young Wordsworth 'plundering' the treasures of the natural world manifestly finds an echo in 'The Collier' when the speaker scours the river for 'trout' and gathers birds' 'eggs from the trees'. Wordsworth also concedes that 'not the less, / . . ., / does it delight her [Nature] sometimes to employ / severer interventions' (i, 367–71); and, evoking Watkins's poem, this threatening quality is registered in the recurring image of the hills. The speaker in *The Prelude* describes how he 'heard among the hills / Low breathings coming after me' (i 329–30) and recalls how

> The leafless trees, and every icy crag
> Tinkled like iron; while the distant hills
> Into the tumult sent an alien sound
> Of melancholy, not unnoticed;
> (i. 468–71)

Watkins's allusions to *The Prelude* add further poignancy to the collier's narrative; for while Wordsworth's young poet-speaker proceeds on an artistic and spiritual journey of self-discovery, Watkins's speaker is unable to free himself, at least in his lifetime, from the constrictions of his social environment. As he ruefully suggests,

> They dipped my coat in the blood of a kid
> And they cast me down a pit,
> And although I crossed with strangers
> There was no way up from it.

Watkins also differs from Eliot, however, in his use of Romantic tropes and allusions. Whereas Eliot 'professed to despise' Romanticism,[135] and was able to repudiate the Romantics because he was incontrovertibly their heir, Watkins – like Idris Davies – with no 'Anglo-Welsh' Romanticism to rebel against, instead, seems to have approached the Romantic poets in the manner of 'culturally inquisitive' outsiders within the English poetic tradition.

Also perceptible in 'The Collier' is the voice of W. B. Yeats, a poet who, we have seen, features prominently in 'Discoveries', and for whom Watkins reserved particular admiration. 'But Yeats, Yeats the poet / Under Dublin skies', he wrote in his 1945 poem 'Yeats in Dublin' after meeting the Irish poet for the first time,

> After ten years' journey . . .
> After the waves of silence
> I look him in the eyes.[136]

Yeats's presence is felt, specifically, in the rhyme and rhythm of 'The Collier', which call to mind 'The Song of Wandering Aengus', quoted earlier, from Yeats's 1899 collection *The Wind Among the Reeds*. The opening lines of this poem, in which Yeats's speaker utilizes the bounties of the natural world, also overlap thematically with stanza five of 'The Collier', where the young collier catches 'trout from the river' and plucks 'spotted eggs from the trees'.

In 'The Collier', then, as in 'Discoveries', Watkins grounds his deracinated poetic voice within a kind of transcendental, sacred territory of art, constructing a 'new verbal ikon' that functions, as Rowan Williams argues, 'not by simple imitation', but through what might be described as 'the semi-ventriloquism of allusion and delicate pastiche', through, to cite Williams again, 'a sort of transmutation [of other voices] into a slightly but significantly different medium'.[137]

Another of Watkins's poems in which this particular Welsh Modernist process of reterritorialisation is especially palpable is 'Ophelia' (1948) – a poem which takes as its subject the fate of the tragic character of Ophelia in Shakespeare's 1604 play, *Hamlet*:

> Stunned in the stone light, laid among the lilies,
> Still the green wave, graven in the reed-bed,
> Lip-read by clouds in the language of the shallows,
> Lie there, reflected.
>
> Soft come the eddies, cold between your fingers.
> Rippling through cresses, willow-trunk and reed-root,
> Gropes the grey water; there the resting mayfly
> Burns like an emerald.
>
> Haunting the path, Laertes falls to Hamlet;
> He, the young Dane, the mover of your mountains,
> Sees the locked lids, your nunnery of sorrows,
> Drowned in oblivion.
>
> Dense was your last night, thick with stars unnumbered.
> Bruised, the reeds parted. Under them the mud slipped,
> Yielding. Scuttling and terrified, the moorhen
> Left you to sink there.
>
> . . .
>
> Bride-veils of mist fall, brilliant are the sunbeams,
> Open the great leaves, all the birds are singing.
> Still unawake in purity of darkness
> Whiter than daylight
>
> Dream the soft lids, the white, the deathly sleeping;
> Closed are the lashes: day is there a legend.
> Rise from the fair flesh, from the midnight water,
> Child too soon buried.[138]

In Shakespeare's play, Ophelia is sent mad with grief when Hamlet mistakenly kills her father, Polonius. Ophelia, while distractedly picking flowers, falls into a river and drowns. In the above lines, Watkins envisages the scene of her death, combining his 'Shakespearean subject with a Ruskinian intensity of natural observation':[139] the speaker perceives a 'resting' 'emerald' 'mayfly', for example, and observes water 'Rippling through cresses, willow-trunk and reed-root' in a kind of poetic rendering of the Pre-Raphaelite visual artist Sir John Everett Millais's famous 1852 painting *Ophelia*, Watkins was, after all, as Ian Hilton notes, always 'concern[ed] with the links created between poetry, music and the visual arts, and [with] the possession of the imagination by a melody, painting or carving'.[140] There are not only echoes, or touches, of Millais here, however: the language of Shakespeare's play itself is woven into the poem. The reference to Ophelia's 'nunnery of sorrows', for example, assimilates Hamlet's acerbic remark in act three scene one, 'Get thee to a nunnery',[141] and 'Lie there, reflected' seems to adapt Queen Gertrude's recollection, in act four scene seven, of 'the glassy stream' (l. 165) in which Ophelia's body is discovered. Moreover, the form and content of the poem is redolent of Arthur Rimbaud's representation of the same event in his 1870 poem, 'Ophélie':

I

In the calm black stream where stars sleep,
White Ophelia floats like a great lily,
Very slowly floats, lying in long veils …
– Up in the woods, dogs bark, men shout.

For a thousand years or more, sad white phantom
Ophelia has moved down the long black river.
A thousand years or more her sweet song
Of madness has charmed the evening air.

The wind kisses her breasts and like a flower opens
Her long veils gently moving with the water.
On her shoulder willows weep and shiver,
Over her wide dreaming face rushes lean.

Around her, jostling water-lilies sigh;
In a drowsy alder, when sometimes she disturbs
A nest, there's a quick flurry of wings
– Mysterious music tumbles from the golden stars.

II

O pale Ophelia, beautiful as snow!
Yes, poor child, downstream you died.

> – Because great Norway mountain winds
> Moaned their message of harsh freedom
>
> . . .
>
> III
>
> – The Poet says that when the stars come out
> You come looking for flowers you picked;
> He says he's seen, lying in her long veils,
> White Ophelia, like some great lily, float by.[142]

Like the stream in which Ophelia floats, the surface of Watkins's poem ripples with the imagery of Rimbaud's 'Ophélie'. In Watkins's text, the speaker imagines Ophelia as 'Whiter than daylight' and states, 'Dream the soft lids, the white, the deathly sleeping', while in Rimbaud's poem we also encounter a 'White Ophelia', like a 'sad white phantom', whose death is figured as a kind of sleep or dream: 'Over her wide dreaming face rushes lean.' Similarly, just as Watkins's Ophelia is 'laid among the lilies', around the Ophelia of Rimbaud's poem 'jostling water-lilies sigh'; and in the same way that the Ophelia of Watkins's poem alarms a 'moorhen', sending it 'Scuttling' into the undergrowth, the Ophelia of Rimbaud's poem 'sometimes . . . disturbs / A nest, [and] there's a quick flurry of wings'. In both poems, too, Ophelia is identified as a child: in Watkins's poem she is a 'Child too soon buried', while Rimbaud's speaker avers, 'Yes, poor child, downstream you died'. But most significantly, in the context of Watkins's impulse towards reterritorialisation within a transcendental, sacred realm of art or, in M. Wynn Thomas's words, 'a spiritual refuge beyond the flux of things',[143] both poems also effectively immortalise Ophelia, securing and celebrating her afterlife as an artistic muse. Watkins encourages Ophelia to 'Rise from the fair flesh, from the midnight water, / Child too soon buried'; and indeed in making her the subject of his poem he poetically enacts this resurrection. Ophelia is artistically revivified in a comparable way in Rimbaud's text; indeed, in the final stanza she is observed by 'The Poet', alive, and 'looking for the flowers [that she] picked'.

According to James A. Davies, 'in . . . Watkins's intertextual procedure . . . we . . . encounter a modernist flourish',[144] and this 'intertextuality is [also] a potent reminder that Watkins is another poet of the interstice in which geographical Welshness meets English literature'.[145] This chapter has aimed to explore and elucidate the relationship between these qualities in some of Watkins's poems: between the intertextual 'collision' (to use Watkins's term) of his poetic idiom, his firmly 'interstitial' position as an Anglophone Welsh writer, and his particular form of Modernism. That Watkins's Modernism is rarefied, resolutely internationalist and aestheticist, and often intensely spiritual in nature – quite different, often, from that of his Anglo-Welsh contemporaries, Gwyn Thomas, Glyn Jones and Idris Davies – seems to reflect his more complex and deep-rooted feelings of detachment from his home culture and perhaps from any firm sense of social and cultural belonging in the physical, contemporary world. Instead, like the similarly nomadic T. S. Eliot, Watkins cultivates a sense of rootedness and stability from his own timeless society of fellow writers and intellectuals – his own, self-made 'modern country of the arts'.

4

Cadaqués and Carmarthenshire: The Modernist 'Heterotopias' of Salvador Dalí and Dylan Thomas

In contrast to Vernon Watkins, who is generally labelled simply as a metaphysical, religious or romantic poet, Dylan Thomas (1914–53) has been readily accepted and widely regarded as a creator of Welsh Modernism. As I suggested in chapter one, this is due, in part, to Thomas's radically inventive approach to language in his early work. But another reason for Thomas's comparatively easy admission into the canon of 'British' Modernism, aside from his enduring popular and critical appeal, seems to be his well-documented involvement and interest in the European avant-garde. Not only was Thomas, as Christopher Wigginton points out, 'an avid reader of and contributor to [the Paris-based avant-garde journal] *transition*',[1] but he also famously

> attended the 1936 International Surrealist Exhibition at the New Burlington Galleries in London . . . which played host to, amongst others, green-haired André Breton, Paul Éluard and Herbert Read, who delivered their lecture on 'Art and the Unconscious' . . . and Salvador Dalí, who was almost asphyxiated after giving his paper clad in a diving suit, whose helmet became stuck. (Thomas offered visitors cups of boiled string, asking 'weak or strong?' and later read his work at one of the evening events . . .)[2]

This anecdote reveals that, although Thomas often dismissed Surrealism – in a letter written in the same year, he identifies it as among 'the clever things one (me) doesn't want to understand'[3] – he was, in reality, obviously attracted to the movement, particularly to its element of humour and its principle of irrationality. His critically neglected friend and contemporary, Glyn Jones, by contrast – whose early work, as previously discussed, is often no less surreal in its effects than Thomas's – assumes a more detached position, and takes a more measured approach, writing in 'Notes on Surrealism': 'And here, as far as I can see it, is one of the main weaknesses of the Surrealists; they are trying to base their art, as it were, on one element, the element of incongruity, shutting out important and fruitful experience.'[4]

The relationship between Dylan Thomas's work and European Surrealism has been theorised by Christopher Wigginton in *Modernism from the Margins*. Referring to Thomas's 1936 poem, 'Altarwise by owl-light', Wigginton argues that Thomas

> guys and mimics the attributes of a European metropolitan style [that is, Surrealism] where it can be made to coincide with his own contexts and tactics of estrangement. In both embracing and rejecting surrealism . . . he creates a provincial simulacrum of surrealism ('surrealist imitations'), or what might thus be called *surregionalism*.[5]

More recently, John Goodby has expanded this argument, suggesting that

> Thomas's surre(region)al surrealism . . . availed itself of the materials available from his hybrid Anglo-Welsh origins, linking these to the dream, madness and visionary aspects of surrealism, as he discovered in *transition* and elsewhere . . .[6]

The distinction between 'Surrealism' and 'regionalism', however, implicit in this new term 'surregionalism', is problematic. This is because in fact the term 'surregionalism', which Wigginton and Goodby coin to *distinguish* Dylan Thomas's style from European Surrealism, could be just as easily applied to the work of many of the practitioners of the movement, including perhaps the most well-known and influential European Surrealist artist of all, Salvador Dalí. Dalí may have been based in Paris and, therefore, ostensibly, a creator of 'a European metropolitan style', but many of his paintings are inspired by an alternative, regional or provincial location – 'the coastline of Cadaqués in north-east Spain'.[7] Dalí was born and grew up in Figueras – a town on the Empordà (also known as the Ampurdán) plain, separated from Cadaqués by mountains.[8] He spent his summer holidays, however, at Cadaqués, and this location, as Ian Gibson notes, became his 'childhood paradise'.[9] Indeed, according to Jonathan Jones, 'it is the persistent reappearance, endlessly metamorphosed, of the rocks and cliffs of this unique coast that anchors his [Dalí's] art in a real, physical context of memory and longing'.[10] As Dalí once admitted:

> This is the spot which all my life I have adored with a fanatical fidelity which grows with each passing day. I can say without fear of falling into the slightest exaggeration that I know by heart each contour of the rocks and beaches of Cadaqués, each geological anomaly of its unique landscape and light, for in the course of my wandering solitudes these outlines of rocks and these flashes of light clinging to the structure and the aesthetic substance of the landscape were the unique protagonists on whose mineral impassiveness, day after day, I projected all the accumulated and chronically unsatisfied tension of my erotic and sentimental life.[11]

Cadaqués is indeed the subject of many of Dalí's early paintings, even before the advent of Surrealism. The Impressionistic *View of Cadaqués from Playa Poal* (1920) is a notable example, as is *View of Cadaqués from Mount Pani* (1921). But this regional location also seems to reappear, 'metamorphosed', as Jonathan Jones suggests, in many of Dalí's Surrealist paintings – in *The Persistence of Memory (Soft Watches)* (1931), for example, which depicts three watches melting, and another crawling with ants, on a still seashore where a rocky promontory is bathed in a distinct golden 'light' also seen in the earlier *View of Cadaqués from Mount Pani*. However unfamiliar, bizarre and removed from the recognisable external world Dalí's work appears, then, he can also be seen as invoking and engaging with a regional space outside the metropolitan centre, by means of a European metropolitan style.

This calls into question Christopher Wigginton's analysis of Dylan Thomas's style as simply 'a provincial simulacrum of surrealism', which reflects a more general critical inclination towards viewing Welsh writers only as marginal and even inferior 'imitators' and adapters, rather than as active creators of European Modernism. Indeed, the previous chapters, in viewing the work of Welsh writers as a product of the distinct social and cultural conditions of Wales in the early twentieth century, have also challenged this tendency. The kind of critical perspective that Wigginton adopts might, contrastingly, be compared in principle, with some theoretical paradigms of modernity in Ireland. As Joe Cleary points out,

> Any account that describes Irish [or, I would add, Welsh] modernisation primarily in terms of local reactions to wider tendencies leaves itself vulnerable to the objection that in such accounts modernity is always one-way traffic, with the modern inevitably disseminated outwards from a given centre . . . to the retarded margins. In such paradigms, marginal cultures (like Ireland [and Wales]), reduced to the status of the recipients of modernity, can only progress to the extent that they imitate the centre . . . the marginal culture's destiny is to emulate; it does not inaugurate, initiate or invent.[12]

The present chapter does not aim to refute the idea that Welsh writers were importing, adapting and even, as John Goodby has observed in Dylan Thomas's work, parodying Modernist styles.[13] In the previous chapter I demonstrated how Vernon Watkins delineates his own 'modern country of the arts' in his work in a manner reminiscent of T. S. Eliot, and Watkins acknowledges his creative affinity with Eliot in his 'Ode' to the poet. However, in the current chapter I aim to go beyond this approach and suggest that Dylan Thomas, like the other writers considered so far in this book, can be seen as engaged in Modernist experimentation that is not necessarily and straightforwardly influenced by, but independently comparable and often concurrent with, other European Modernisms, such as the Surrealism, or surregionalism, of Dalí.

The comparability of Dalí's 'surregionalist' paintings and Dylan Thomas's short stories from the 1930s comes sharply into focus when these works are viewed through a particular theoretical lens – that is, when they are considered in the context of Michel Foucault's essay, 'Different Spaces'.[14] In this essay, Foucault discusses his concept of 'heterotopia', which Andrew Thacker, in *Moving through Modernity: Space and Geography in Modernism*, summarises as follows:

> A heterotopia . . . is a real space that acts as a counter-site . . . It is a place that is outside all places, but which can be located in reality, unlike a utopia. Foucault cites the mirror as an instance of heterotopia. The mirror is actually located in reality; but the image of myself I see within it is located nowhere, in a virtual space. The mirror functions heterotopically because it contains both the real space and the unreal space simultaneously; or more precisely, it functions as a kind of 'counteraction' upon the person who gazes at the mirror . . . The important point is that heterotopia involves a sense of *movement* between the real and the unreal; it is thus a site defined by a process, the stress being upon the fact that it contests another site.[15]

'Heterotopia' is a term that we might use to describe the 'surregional' spaces of Dalí's paintings, because they convey, as Thacker explains, 'a sense of *movement* between the real and the unreal' – between the real, regional space of Cadaqués, and the 'unreal', 'virtual' space of the unconscious mind. In *The Persistence of Memory*, for instance, our eyes wander from the solid, recognisable coastline of Cadaqués to the strange drooping shapes of giant watches and a distorted, disembodied face slumbering in the sand. Significantly, this 'movement' or 'process' registers Dalí's paintings as 'sites of contestation'[16] – as spaces that invert, challenge and resist, in André Breton's words, the oppressive 'control exercised [both] by reason' and by 'aesthetic or moral concern'[17] in the conscious, social world. In *Vertigo – Tower of Pleasure* (1930), for example, the familiar, rocky coast of Cadaqués forms a backdrop to an imposing, square tower. On the roof of the tower is an arbitrary blue sphere; what appears to be a cartoon-like head of a lion; and a long, formless shadow. Accompanying these images is that of a naked man and woman in a simultaneously, and explicitly, erotic and violent embrace. The woman is sitting on the floor facing the man and holding a knife, as if about to stab him; the man, on the other hand, is standing over her in a position suggestive of oral sex. Although the man is depicted with one hand over his face, seemingly expressing his anguish or shame (a theme which this chapter will return to), this painting manifestly constructs a space in which moral propriety is transgressed and questioned – where, to cite Dalí, 'the chronically unsatisfied tension of . . . erotic and sentimental life' finds a release. Clearly, logicality and reason in the external, social world are also interrogated here, and we can see this again in Dalí's 1934 painting, *The Spectre of Sex Appeal* (1934), in which a young boy is confronted, in a sandy cove – again, unmistakably, the landscape of Cadaqués – by a grotesque, phallic apparition. Male sexuality is similarly, though more explicitly, manifested in Dalí's work in his 1933 untitled representation of William Tell and Gradiva. In this painting, Dalí depicts William Tell on the Cadaqués shoreline, grasping Gradiva[18] by the hair and masturbating. Indeed, 'Dalí was', as Gibson points out, 'the first serious artist in history to make onanism one of the principal themes of his work.'[19] To varying degrees, then, the spaces of all the paintings mentioned can be further delineated as what Foucault calls 'heterotopias of deviation', or 'those in which . . . behaviour' – such as the artistic representation of masturbation and its apparent location in a public place – is [in some way] deviant with respect to the required norm'.[20]

In a letter to John Goodland in 1938, Thomas is as dismissive of Salvador Dalí as he often is of the Surrealist movement as a whole, identifying him, along with the poet Edmund Blunden, as a 'popular-at-the-time dud'.[21] Yet the heterotopic spaces of Dalí's paintings can be compared to the locations of many of Dylan Thomas's short stories from the 1930s. The foundations of this comparison lie in Dalí and Thomas's shared childhood fascination with a particular regional space, and their use of that space as a locus of Modernist possibility. Just as the young Dalí, as previously noted, spent his holidays exploring the rock pools of Cadaqués, Thomas, who was born and brought up in suburban Swansea, spent his summers in rural Carmarthenshire, playing on his aunt's farm, Fernhill – a location that, Paul Ferris suggests, 'became fixed in his imagination'.[22] Thomas invokes this particular psycho-geographical space in his semi-autobiographical short story, 'The Peaches' (first published in 1938 and reprinted in the collection, *Portrait of the Artist as a Young Dog*, in 1940), replacing 'Fernhill' with the fictional name, 'Gorsehill':

> Down the thick dingle Jack [Williams] and I ran shouting, scalping the brambles with our thin stick-hatchets, dancing, hallooing. We skidded to a stop and prowled on the bushy banks of the stream . . . We crawled and rat-tatted through the bushes, hid at a whistled signal, in the deep grass, and crouched there, waiting for the crack of a twig or the secret breaking of boughs. On my haunches, eager and alone, casting an ebony shadow, with the Gorsehill jungle swarming, the violent, impossible birds and fishes leaping, hidden under four-stemmed flowers the height of horses, in the early evening in a dingle near Carmarthen . . .[23]

Here, Fernhill is nostalgically configured as an enchanting, exhilarating childhood paradise. Like Dalí, Thomas 'anchors his art in a real, physical context of memory and longing' that seems to encompass not only Fernhill itself, but also the surrounding area – the narrator consciously identifying his temporal and geographical position as 'in the early evening in a dingle near Carmarthen'.

Thomas's representation of Carmarthenshire in this extract seems more comparable with Dalí's early, Renoir-esque depictions of the landscape of Cadaqués, than with the heterotopic spaces of his Surrealist paintings, evoking what Dalí once described as 'the instantaneous, luminous moment'[24] of the Impressionist painting.

Yet, Dalí-like tensions between the real and the unreal are plain to see; this 'dingle near Carmarthen' is a 'swarming' 'jungle', where 'impossible' fishes leap and flowers are 'the height of horses'. Indeed, fundamentally, 'The Peaches' does function heterotopically. As previously mentioned, the location of this story, 'Gorsehill', is both existent and fictitious, necessitating '*movement* between the real and the unreal';[25] the setting is 'located in reality' and yet, at the same time, 'located nowhere, in a virtual space', like a reflection in a mirror. Indeed, crucially, there is also evidence in Thomas's story of the kind of contestation that characterises the heterotopic space. The narrator, playing on the farm, for example, watches his friend Jack climb a tree and reveals:

> I climbed too, and we clung to the top branches and stared down at the lavatory in the corner of the field. Gwilym was sitting on the seat with his trousers down. He looked small and black. He was reading a book and moving his hands.
>
> 'We can see you!' we shouted.
>
> He snatched his trousers up and put the book in his pocket. (p. 133)

This 'vignette', which, as Ferris notes, 'somehow slipped past the publishers in 1940',[26] sees the narrator's God-fearing older cousin, Gwilym, masturbating – 'reading a book and moving his hands' – in the lavatory in the corner of a field. Perhaps one of the reasons why this passage escaped censorship was because here, masturbation (that most Dalí-esque of themes, and an activity that 'English dictionaries were calling 'self-abuse' up to the 1960s'[27]) is encoded in language – and in the nostalgically childlike register seen earlier in Thomas's description of 'the dingle near Carmarthen'[28] – that simultaneously suggests that Gwilym is engaged in an innocent, and characteristically eccentric, act of religious devotion. Gwilym is described as looking 'small and black', reminding the reader of his habit of dressing in 'minister's black' (p. 126), even on 'a weekday morning' (p. 126). This description, in turn, underscores and destabilises the meaning of the already ambiguously worded 'reading a book and moving his hands' – a phrase that equally calls to mind a 'minister' reading fervently and expressively from a Bible or prayer book. Indeed, the idea that Gwilym could be simply preaching to himself in the lavatory is not so surprising given that he regularly delivers sermons to whoever will listen in an 'old barn' (p. 128) – which he identifies as his 'chapel'

(p. 128) – on a 'mucky hill' (p. 128) using a 'broken' cart (p. 128) for a pulpit. The narrator witnesses this routine, recalling:

> I sat on the hay and stared at Gwilym preaching, and heard his voice rise and crack and sink to a whisper and break into singing and Welsh and ring triumphantly and be wild and meek. The sun through a hole, shone on his praying shoulders, and he said: 'O God, Thou art everywhere all the time, in the dew of the morning, in the frost of the evening, in the field and the town, in the preacher and the sinner . . . Thou canst see us when the sun is gone; Thou canst see us when there aren't any stars, in the gravy blackness . . . Thou canst see and spy and watch us all the time, in the little back corners . . . Thou canst see everything we do, in the night and day, in the day and the night, everything, everything . . . (p. 128)

Thomas's account of Gwilym's activities in the 'Gorsehill' lavatory of 'The Peaches' can be seen to contest '[an]other site[s]' in a manner characteristic of the heterotopic space; taboo sexual behaviour and religious piety appear momentarily indistinguishable, contesting what Thomas appears to view as the oppressive moral respectability both of Anglophone literary culture – his publishers often censored his work, and several critics 'charged him . . . with sexual immaturity'[29] – and of the 'Welsh way of life' or '*buchedd*', discussed in chapter one, with its doctrine of self-denial and sexual shame expressed in Gwilym's tortured prayer. In this respect, Thomas's work clearly bears the mark of Caradoc Evans – particularly his infamous short story collection, *My People* – and he again subversively portrays lust and devoutness as interchangeable when the narrator reveals: 'I found a lot of poems in his [Gwilym's] bedroom once. They were all written to girls. And he showed them to me afterwards, and he'd changed all the girls' names to God.' (p. 135)

As Conran notes, 'the *buchedd* represented . . . an alliance between the peasantry, the respectable working class and the petty [sic] bourgeoisie',[30] and the heterotopic space of 'The Peaches' seems, particularly, to 'counteract' the respectable suburban Swansea in which Thomas grew up: what Ferris describes as the 'society of teachers and shopkeepers – Welsh nonconformity still lapping at its feet, easily scandalised and quick to condemn deviants'.[31] Indeed, the story hinges on a visit that Mrs Williams 'from Swansea' (p. 129), a representative of this society, makes to Gorsehill in her 'motor car' (p. 129). Significantly, when Mrs Williams arrives, Annie, the narrator's aunt, is seen fretfully 'upsetting the [family] Bible on the floor, picking it up, [and] dusting it hurriedly with her sleeve' (p. 131). While 'The Peaches' clearly lacks the formal experimentation and overt shock-tactics of paintings such as Dalí's *William Tell and Gradiva* and *Vertigo – Tower of Pleasure*, then, the space that Thomas creates can, nevertheless, be analysed, in the same Foucauldian terms: as a heterotopic space of Modernist 'deviation' from the respectable social world.

The devout and sexually prohibitive 'Welsh way of life' from which Thomas deviates in 'The Peaches' might, in fact, be compared with certain aspects of the social and cultural climate of Dalí's Spain in the early twentieth century. The action of Dalí's close friend, Federico García Lorca's *La Casa de Bernarda Alba*, or *The House of Bernarda Alba: A Drama about Women in the Villages of Spain* (1936), for instance, is centred on a sexually repressed and oppressively religious, traditionalist and class-conscious Spanish household, presided over by the uncompromising matriarch, Bernarda. The latter's world view is encapsulated in the following exchange from act one:

> BERNARDA Women in church shouldn't look at any man but the priest – and him only because he wears skirts. To turn your head is to be looking for the warmth of corduroy.
> FIRST WOMAN Sanctimonious old snake!
> PONCIA [THE MAID], *between her teeth* Itching for a man's warmth.
> BERNARDA, *beating with her cane on the floor* Blesséd be God!
> ALL, *crossing themselves* For ever blessed and praised.[32]

Bernarda's expectations, and those of the culture that she represents, weigh particularly heavily on her five daughters, frustrating their desire for emotional and sexual fulfilment, a sentiment that is echoed in Dalí and Luis Buñuel's film, *Un Chien Andalou*. In one scene of Dalí and Buñuel's film, a man is sexually aroused by a woman, but finds that he cannot physically reach her because he is tied with ropes to 'two Marist brothers',[33] two grand pianos, and the corpses of two donkeys; he is literally impeded both by the religious establishment and by middle-class values (as symbolised by the grand pianos), which are, in turn, suggestively associated with decay. This symbolism is particularly telling, given that the young Dalí, reflecting a popular trend in Spanish middle-class families, was sent to both the state school in Figueras and a private school – the Marist Brothers' College – where, as Gibson notes, there was 'religious instruction, with early morning masses, the rosary and improving homilies'.[34] Buñuel's 1930 film, *L'Age d'or*, in which Dalí was also initially involved,[35] poses a similar, though more overt, challenge to the Catholic Church's attitude to sexuality, and features a scene in which a sexually exasperated man pushes a priest out of his bedroom window.

The man's sexual frustration in *L'Age d'or* is, essentially, comparable with that of Gwilym in 'The Peaches', except that in Buñuel's film it has, of course, escalated to the point of frenzy and violence. Indeed, Thomas's reconfiguration of Carmarthenshire as a 'heterotopia of deviation' from sexually repressive social and cultural ideals of morality and respectability is not confined to this story; on the contrary, it can be traced back to Thomas's earliest writings – to the opening of the first poem in his first collection, *18 Poems* (1934), 'I see the boys of summer':

> I see the boys of summer in their ruin
> Lay the gold tithings barren,
> Setting no store by harvest, freeze the soils;
> There in their heat the winter floods
> Of frozen loves they fetch their girls,
> And drown the cargoed apples in their tides.
>
> These boys of light are curdlers in their folly,
> Sour the boiling honey;
> The jacks of frost they finger in the hives;
> There in the sun the frigid threads
> Of doubt and dark they feed their nerves;
> The signal moon is zero in their voids.[36]

The 'boys of summer' in these stanzas are, effectively, prototypes of Gwilym: sexually inhibited and unenlightened – in 'doubt and dark' – they simply 'feed their nerves', or amplify the guilt and anxiety that they associate with their sexual urges through masturbation. In this respect, the boys, or 'dark deniers' (p. 8) as they are later called, are reminiscent of the central figure in Dalí's 1930 painting, *The Hand – Remorse* (1930), who looks down morosely from a remote, shadowy seat at people walking and playing below, while holding out a grossly exaggerated hand – a symbol, surely, of his own excessive, debilitating and remorseful 'solitary pleasure'.[37] Indeed, Dalí's painting and Thomas's poem are, essentially, comparable in that they both audaciously voice the 'unmentionable' issue of masturbation, while, appealing to contemporary views of masturbation as 'self-abuse', employing this theme as a means to question intransigent social attitudes towards supposedly 'normal' sexual behaviour: the man in Dalí's painting has become a pitiful grotesquery, segregated from 'normal' society – one figure standing below, for example, is pointing at 'the hand', while looking down at a child as if to warn him of what he might become. Similarly, in the first stanzas of Thomas's poem, the boys are portrayed as sabotaging the relationship between humanity and nature. They are 'curdlers' (connoting, simultaneously, the spoiling and wasting of semen and milk), who 'Lay the gold tithings barren, / Setting no store by harvest', 'freeze the soils', 'sour the . . . honey' and 'drown the cargoed apples in their tides'. What is particularly striking about these lines, however, is the way in which Thomas repeatedly couches – or locates – the act of masturbation in an explicitly rural and agricultural linguistic landscape; it is almost as if, just as the sands at Cadaqués transmute into an unsettling, otherworldly environment – a heterotopic 'place that is outside all places' – in Dalí's *The Hand – Remorse*, the psycho-geographical space of Thomas's Carmarthenshire summer holidays is similarly invoked, embellished and metamorphosed in 'I see the boys of summer' to form a comparable, poetic 'counter-site'.

As previously inferred, the 'counter-sites' that Dalí and Thomas construct in *The Hand – Remorse* and 'I see the boys of summer' are, as this term suggests, 'defined by a process' – by a progression, not just from the real to the unreal, but towards the Modernist articulation of sexual taboo, and contestation of, or movement away from, repressive social codes; and, as if to prolong and reinforce this effect, Thomas situates the third stanza of his poem in the womb:

> I see the summer children in their mothers
> Split up the brawned womb's weathers,
> Divide the night and day with fairy thumbs;
> There in the deep with quartered shades
> Of sun and moon they paint their dams
> As sunlight paints the shelling of their heads. (p. 7)

John Goodby and Christopher Wigginton argue that 'in pushing back to pre-natal origins' the speaker of this poem is 'attempting to reach the point at which [he] can [both] escape [and "exorcise"] the anxieties of sexual maturity facing Thomas himself'.[38] Yet the womb is not just a space of 'origin' but precisely 'a space defined by a process' – a site of change, growth and development, of 'splitting', 'dividing' and proliferating cells. Indeed, as Walford Davies argues, '"Process", organic, emotional, physical, sexual, etc., is perhaps the commonest theme in Thomas's early, notebook-derived poetry', and this, he contends, is exemplified in the 1934 poem, 'A process in the weather of the heart',[39] to which this chapter will return. Furthermore, the womb is resistant to the social and sexual limitations of the outside world; in Thomas's poem, it is a space in which the individual is empowered, as the babies creatively separate night from day and 'paint' their maternal, watery world. Contrastingly, when they are born, it is the sunlight – the external world – that 'paints the shelling of their heads', branding them with the mark of conformity or 'sameness'.[40] In essence the womb seems to act, here, almost as an allegory of the heterotopic process observed in stanzas one and two; and, moreover, like Dalí in *The Hand – Remorse*, Thomas does not just seem to be expressing 'anxieties of sexual maturity', but also pointing out and contesting their underlying social cause.

The short stories that Thomas wrote around the time of the publication of 'I see the boys of summer' can certainly be interpreted in this way. Whereas in 'The Peaches', the Carmarthenshire of Thomas's boyhood becomes the fictionalised 'Gorsehill', in many of the early short stories – in 'The Enemies' (1934), for example – this region is recast as 'the Jarvis hills'[41] and 'the green acres of the Jarvis valley' (p. 16).[42] This poses a challenge to the tenacious critical view, discussed by Jeni Williams, that 'Dylan Thomas wrote two distinct kinds of stories'.[43] The early stories, Williams notes, are generally regarded as 'bizarre allegories, often brutal and surreal', while the later stories, such as those collected in *Portrait of the Artist as a Young Dog*, are seen as more 'realist' and autobiographical. Williams goes on to dispute this reading and suggests that 'in their focus on excess, his [Thomas's] later short stories are as selectively 'unreal' as his early ones'.[44] The mutually real yet unreal 'Gorsehill' and 'Jarvis Valley' reinforce Williams's argument; and these two locations are also linked through their functioning as sites that enervate the values of 'respectable' society. In 'The Enemies', for instance, 'the Reverend Mr Davies' (p. 18), whom the narrator identifies as 'the rector of a village some ten miles away' (p. 18), becomes lost while walking on the Jarvis hills and is taken into the home of a Mr and Mrs Owen:

> Soon the meal was ready, and Mr Owen came in unwashed from the garden.
>
> 'Shall I say grace?' asked Mr Davies when all three were seated around the table.
>
> Mrs Owen nodded.
>
> 'O Lord God Almighty, bless this our meal,' said Mr Davies. Looking up as he continued his prayer, he saw that Mr and Mrs Owen had closed their eyes. 'We thank Thee for the bounties that Thou hast given us.' And he saw that the lips of Mr and Mrs Owen were moving softly. He could not hear what they said, but he knew that the prayers they spoke were not his prayers.
>
> 'Amen', said all three together.
>
> Mr Owen, proud in his eating, bent over his plate . . . Outside the window was the brown body of the earth, the green skin of the grass, and the breasts of the Jarvis hills . . . there was creation sweating out of the pores of the trees . . . He saw, with a sudden satisfaction, that Mrs Owen's throat was bare. (p. 19)

In this passage – which, in some ways, evokes 'the Respected [minister,] Josiah Bryn-Bevan's' (p. 109) visit to old Nanni's cottage in Caradoc Evans's short story, 'Be This Her Memorial' (1915) – an agent of 'respectable' society strays into a highly sensual, fecund and eroticised space that again seems at once real and dream-like, even nightmarish. Mr and Mrs Owen's behaviour reflects the character of their environment, as Mr Owen gazes with lustful 'satisfaction' at Mrs Owen's 'bare' throat, and instructs the worms that he unearths in his garden to 'Multiply, multiply' (p. 18). Indeed, the Jarvis Valley appears even more sexually intoxicating in 'The Holy Six' (1937), Thomas's sequel to 'The Enemies', in which 'The Holy Six of Wales'[45] – six clergymen, for whom, 'the holy life', Thomas provocatively writes, is 'a constant erection' (p. 95) – venture, with the clerical Miss Myfanwy, into the Jarvis Valley to rescue Mr Davies. Here again, Thomas images the Jarvis Valley through language that is loaded with erotic meaning: the 'moist' Jarvis fields, below the 'bedded' hills, 'groan' and the trees stand 'erect' beside 'half-parting blooms' (pp. 97–8). This creates a sexually symbolic topography reminiscent of Dalí's *The Red Tower (Anthropomorphic Tower)* (1930), where an aqueous image of sexual fantasy rises out of the sea, while on the distant shore, a wood and tower with a gateway also represent the male genitalia. The narrator's account of how 'the early light [was] lying under the wind as the south-west opened', and how the branches of the phallic Jarvis trees 'spouted up to the summits of the hills' and 'angelically down through ribbed throats of flowers' (p. 98) is also intensely erotic. Thomas's ironic use of the adverb 'angelically' in conjunction with this second example is especially inflammatory; and the irreverent tone of the story is maintained as the 'pious' Holy Six are, like the 'unrespectable' Mr Owen, with 'open trousers' and 'wagging' (p. 98) phallic beard, assimilated into their profligate surroundings – the grass beneath their feet assuming 'a woman's stillness under the thrust of man'.

Thomas, in fact, often constructs a kind of mythology of dissoluteness around the Jarvis Valley in his early stories. In 'A Prospect of the Sea' (1937), its hills and trees are said to be 'as Jarvis had known them when he walked there with his lovers and horses for half a century, a century ago'.[46] Similarly, in 'The Map of Love' (1937) – in which two children embark on a hallucinatory journey across what Annis Pratt has theorised is 'the map . . . of sexual intercourse'[47] – the narrator identifies 'The first field wherein mad Jarvis, a hundred years before, had sown his seed in the belly of a bald-headed girl who had wandered out of a distant county and lain with him in the pains of love' (p. 110). Later in the narrative, the children run 'down the Jarvis flank' (p. 112) and into this infamous field, where they are confronted by the voice of 'mad Jarvis' himself:

> Said a voice, Hold hard, the children of love.
>
> Where are you?
>
> I am Jarvis.
>
> Who are you?
>
> Here, here, lying with a virgin from Dolgelley.
>
> In the third field the man of Jarvis lay loving a green girl, and, as he called them the children of love, lay loving her ghost and the smell of buttermilk on her breath. He loved a cripple in the fourth field, for the twist in her limbs made loving longer, and he cursed the straight children who found him with a straight-limbed lover in the fifth field marking the quarter.
>
> A girl from Tiger Bay held Jarvis close, and her lips marked a red cracked heart upon her throat; this was the sixth and the weather-tracked field. My rose, said Jarvis, but the seventh love smelt in his hands, his fingering hands that held Glamorgan's canker under the eighth hedge. From the convent of Bethel's Heart, a holy woman served him the ninth time. (pp. 112–13)

Like the young boy gazing timidly up at the grotesque 'spectre of sex appeal' in Dalí's painting of that name, the children in Thomas's story are both intrigued and terrified by the elusive, intangible and hyperbolic sexual force that is 'Jarvis'. In both painting and story, sexuality and sexual desire are viewed from the perspective of the child, as at once alarming and captivating, reflecting the particular psycho-geographical spaces – the childhood 'adventure playgrounds' of Cadaqués and Carmarthenshire – from which Dalí and Thomas's 'counter-site[s]' are derived.

Yet, at the same time, in juxtaposing sexual desire with the child in such an obvious way, it seems likely that both Dalí and Thomas are consciously drawing on Sigmund Freud's controversial and, as Jerome Neu notes, often very 'unpopular ideas . . . involving the postulation of infantile sexuality and so the denial of the presumed innocence of childhood'.[48] Dalí revered Freud to the point of considering him a 'father figure',[49] and the influence of Freud's writings on his work is similarly evident in *The Enigma of Desire – My Mother, My Mother, My Mother* (1929), where the sands of Cadaqués shift to form a heterotopic landscape of the unconscious in which Freud's theory of the Oedipus complex,[50] or the male child's sexual desire for his mother and jealous resentment of his father, is visualised. Similarly, Thomas, who, as previously noted in the discussion of his relationship with Surrealism, was notoriously reluctant to reveal his literary influences, responded in 1934 in the 'Answers to an Enquiry' section of *New Verse* to the question, 'Have you been influenced by Freud and how do you regard him', with 'Yes' – 'whatever is hidden should be made naked. To be stripped of darkness is to be clean'.[51] In 'The Map of Love', Thomas seems to be undermining Welsh society's particularly unshakeable faith in the 'innocence of childhood' – a tradition to which Glyn Jones also responds in his novel, *The Valley, the City, the Village*. As the narrator of Jones's novel reveals

> The generations of my grandmother and my uncle, faithful to the reticent and fastidious Puritanism in which they were nurtured, saw childhood as symbolic of some Edenish innocence and so cherished it, accepting regretfully the signs of its departure. (p. 34)

Thomas seems to uphold his Freudian proposal in *New Verse* that 'whatever is hidden should be made naked. To be stripped of darkness is to be clean' in 'The Map of Love'. According to Freud, the 'superego' or 'agency of morality',[52] which is responsible for 'hiding' or banishing the unruly desires of the unconscious to the 'dark' recesses of the psyche, is formed during childhood, when adult, and particularly parental intervention – intervention that concentrates on 'sexual' and 'aggressive desires' – is internalised and exerts 'power over the child's ego or self'.[53] In Thomas's story, however, the adult/parent figure, Sam Rib, intervenes, it appears, in order to elucidate and endorse sexual desire, rather than to curb or conceal it:

> Here dwell, said Sam Rib, the first beasts of love. In the cool of a new morning the children listened, too frightened to touch hands. He touched again the sagging hill [on the map] above the island, and pointed the progression of the skeleton channels linking mud with mud, green sea with darker, and all love hills and islands into one territory. In the cool the grass mates, the green mates, the grains, said Sam Rib, and the dividing waters mate and are mated for the bearing and fostering of the globe. Sam Rib had mated with a green woman, as Great-Uncle Jarvis with his bald girl; he had mated with a womanly water for the bearing and fostering of the child who blushed by him. (p. 111)

Similarly, 'Great-Uncle Jarvis' (p. 111), as he is sometimes referred to in this story – another authoritative familial figure – openly displays a 'superhuman promiscuity'[54] that is felt across Wales, from 'Dolgelley' to 'Glamorgan', undermining the collective 'moral conscience'[55] of respectable society. More specifically, Jarvis's sexual voraciousness and pervasiveness seem to constitute both an ironic comment on contemporary English views, inherited from the 1847 'Blue Books' report on education in Wales, of the Welsh as 'lax in their sexual habits',[56] and a theme intended to rile those in Wales who defined Welsh society as intrinsically moral, pious and temperate.[57] In stark contrast to this ideology, Jarvis's 'fingering hands' seduce 'a holy woman' and 'a girl from Tiger Bay' (a playful allusion, perhaps, to 'the popular image of [Cardiff's] Tiger bay' as a 'lascivious hotbed of prostitution'[58]). His other sexual conquests include a 'wandering', 'bald-headed girl'– a description that hints at her insanity – and 'a cripple' because 'the twist in her limbs made loving longer'. These last two examples seem particularly calculated to unsettle and offend, as Jarvis appears to seek out both vulnerable and marginalised members of society in his pursuit of sexual pleasure.

The ensuing passage from 'The Map of Love', in which Thomas's 'children of love' swim naked in a river, also seems to draw on the Freudian sense of conflict between unruly, unconscious sexual urges and the proscriptive superego or 'moral conscience', and further undermines what Mark Spilka has called, in his discussion of Henry James's proto-Freudian short story, *The Turn of the Screw* (1898), as middle-class society's 'cult of childhood innocence':[59]

> . . . as Beth [Rib] swam, the water tickled her; the water pressed on her side.
>
> My love, cried Reuben, excited by the tickling water and the hands of the weeds.
>
> And, as they stood naked on the twentieth field, My love, she whispered.
>
> First fear shot them back. Wet as they were, they pulled their clothes on them. (p. 111)

Like the terrain of Dalí's *The Enigma of Desire*, the Jarvis Valley acts almost as a landscape of the unconscious here, as the children are sexually 'excited' and drawn to each other by 'the tickling water and the hands of the weeds' before being 'corrected' by fear. Moreover, to expand on the initial parallel drawn between 'The Map of Love' and *The Turn of the Screw*, Thomas's 'mad Jarvis', and indeed Dalí's 'spectre of sex appeal', might arguably be viewed as modern, more extreme versions of what Spilka describes as the 'sex-ghosts',[60] Peter Quint and Miss Jessel, in James's story – reputed transgressors of Victorian sexual and class boundaries in life, who, in death, have returned, according to James's unreliable governess-narrator, to collaborate with two ostensibly innocent children. More specifically, Thomas's 'mad Jarvis' and Dalí's 'spectre' might be viewed as, to borrow James's term, erotic 'horrors':[61] as 'monstrous outgrowth[s] of mental sexuality,[62] or grotesque materializations of 'accumulated and chronically unsatisfied', unresolved and unarticulated sexual 'tension', present since early childhood, which, in the real space of polite society, are repressed or 'hidden'. Indeed, Thomas denudes society's mask of respectability in a similar way in the following extract from a letter written to Pamela Hansford Johnson in 1934, in which he expresses his impatience with Welsh bourgeois morality:

> I wish I could see these passing men and women in the sun as the motes of virtues, this little fellow as a sunny Fidelity, this corseted hank as Mother-Love, this abusing lout as the Spirit of Youth, and this eminently beatable child in what was once a party frock as the walking embodiment of Innocence. But I can't. The passers are dreadful. I see all their little horrors.[63]

In the case of Dalí's 'spectre', sexual repression is given a physical form: the 'erotic' apparition is maimed and subjugated – there are what appear to be sacks or pillow-cases pulled over its two heads – and supported by crutches. While Thomas's notably similar conflation of eroticism and disfigurement – as previously mentioned, Jarvis loves 'a cripple' in 'the fourth field' – seems more a representation of the 'unrespectable' nature of repressed unconscious desires, these apparitions, nevertheless, each manifest what Katie Gramich terms both artists' 'wilful' or 'perverse' 'focus on the unspeakable'.[64] Thomas's Jarvis can, effectively, be viewed in the same light as Dalí viewed the 'spectre of sex appeal' in his painting – as 'an erotic bogie [sic] of the first order'.[65]

Dalí's words also resonate strongly with Thomas's 'A Prospect of the Sea', in which another less-than-innocent child, 'a boy on a holiday' (p. 89) in the Jarvis Valley, encounters a 'girl', described in markedly erotic terms, with 'bare brown legs' (p. 88) and wearing a 'torn cotton frock' (p. 88). Here, growing yet unspoken and unfulfilled sexual desire, evocatively conveyed through the image of the girl moving and causing the grass to rise and bend between her 'brown legs', again assumes 'terrifying', monstrous proportions; the girl's lips become stained with blood and her nails sharpen into 'scissor-blades', poised – reinforcing the theme of sexual desire as 'unspeakable' – to cut off the boy's 'tongue' (p. 89). The girl's scissor-hands also echo the children's story of 'Little Suck-a-Thumb' by Heinrich Hoffman, which Thomas read as a child. In this story, contained in the collection *Struwwelpeter* (1845), a young boy's thumbs are severed by a castigating tailor with giant scissors.[66] As Ferris notes, Freud thought that Hoffman's stories 'touch[ed] on childhood complexes',[67] and both 'Little Suck-a-Thumb' and Thomas's story itself seem to engage, in particular, with the Freudian 'fear of castration as a motive for repression'.[68] Perhaps unsurprisingly, given that, according to Freud, 'people threaten him [the child] . . . with cutting off his penis during the phallic phase, at the time of his early masturbation, and hints at that punishment . . . regularly find a phylogenetic reinforcement in him',[69] the symbolism that Thomas employs here also, in many ways, echoes that used by Dalí in his 1929 painting, *The Great Masturbator* (1929). In this work, an enormous, grossly misshapen head, containing many other images, including an overtly sexual one of a man's lower body and 'a woman positioned [as in *Vertigo – Tower of Pleasure*] for fellatio',[70] rests on the Cadaqués sands, which have been transformed into an apparently unbounded environment. Dalí provides further analysis of the painting in his autobiography, *The Secret Life of Salvador Dalí* (1942), recalling that the

> face had no mouth, and in its place was stuck an enormous grasshopper. The grasshopper's belly was decomposed, and full of ants. Several of the ants scurried across the space that should have been filled by the non-existent mouth of the great anguishing face, whose head terminated in architecture and ornamentations of the style of 1900.[71]

In this work, then, as in Thomas's story, unrealised and unvoiced desire – the former captured in the themes of sexual fantasy and, as in *The Hand – Remorse*, 'anguished' masturbation, and the latter symbolised by the absence of a mouth and the presence, in its place, of a huge rotting insect – assumes a shape. The presence of an image of a lion's head, with a suggestively elongated tongue, within the grotesque face – a motif observed previously in *Vertigo – Tower of Pleasure*, which, as Ian Gibson notes, 'in Dali's paintings of this period tend[s] to symbolize raging and terrifying desires'[72] – enhances its meaning and also comports with the boy's fear in 'A Prospect of the Sea' that the girl will 'beckon Carmarthen tigers out of the mile-away wood to jump around him and bite his hands' (p. 89). Indeed, the girl in Thomas's story becomes more and more frightening until the boy's sexuality is finally expressed:

> This is death, said the boy to himself, consumption and whooping-cough and the stones inside you ... and the way your face stays if you make too many faces in the looking-glass. Her mouth was an inch from his. Her long forefingers touched his eyelids. This is a story, he said to himself, about a boy on holiday kissed by a broom rider . . . she stroked his eyes and put her chest against him; and when she had loved him until he died she carried him off inside her to a den in a wood. But the story, like all stories, was killed as she kissed him; now he was a boy in a girl's arms, and the hill stood above a true river, and the peaks and their trees towards England were as Jarvis had known them when he walked there with . . . his lovers . . . (pp. 89–90)

The boy's description of the girl here as 'the way your face stays if you make too many faces in the looking-glass' further suggests that her appalling transformation is, in fact, a manifestation of his own frustrated desires, of the sexually repressed self or ego.

While, on one level, the 'death' that the boy initially associates with his desire in this story seems to allude to the idea, derived from the French '*la petite mort*', of orgasm as 'the little death', this juxtaposition of the erotic with the morbid and macabre also again connects Thomas's story with Freud's writings, and, more specifically, with his theory of the coexistence of 'life [or "sexual"] instincts'[73] and the 'death instinct' or 'drive' [74]– that is, 'the urge inherent in life to restore an earlier state of things'.[75] Indeed, Dalí's 1933 painting, *Average Atmospherocephalic Bureaucrat in the Act of Milking a Cranial Harp*, in which a figure is 'milking' an exaggeratedly phallic skull, also seems to have this double meaning. It is precisely this Freudian notion of a natural world motivated by conflicting yet inextricable death and life 'drives', that Thomas seems to be exploring in his well-known 1934 poem, 'The force that through the green fuse':

> The force that through the green fuse drives the flower
> Drives my green age; that blasts the roots of trees
> Is my destroyer.
> And I am dumb to tell the crooked rose
> My youth is bent by the same wintry fever.[76]

The boy's association of his repressed sexuality with violence and death in 'A Prospect of the Sea', however, might, more specifically, be said to dramatise what Ivan Phillips identifies as 'Freud's notion of . . . death as the ego's ultimate escape from contradiction and frustration',[77] an idea that Dalí and Buñuel also seem to dramatise in *Un Chien Andalou*, when the sexually frustrated male cyclist imagines touching the naked body of the woman he desires and subsequently assumes a deathly appearance, with rolled-back eyes and blood trickling from his mouth.[78]

A sense of the interrelatedness of sex and death also dominates Thomas's 'The Enemies'. In this story, Mrs Owen gazes into 'the depths of her crystal' (p. 16) ball, which, the narrator reveals, 'like an open grave, gave up its dead to . . . [her]. She stared on the lips of women and the hairs of men that wound into a pattern on the face of the crystal world' (p. 17). Here, as Mrs Owen 'stares' fetishistically at 'the lips' and 'hairs' of the dead, sensuality and morbidity, life and death, once again coalesce. And the way in which her husband 'cut[s] the brown worms' that he unearths in his garden 'in half, so that they might breed and spread their life over the garden and go out contaminating into the fields and the bellies of the cattle' (p. 18) also has this effect – as does the narrator's account of how Mr Owen 'patiently strangled the weeds' (p. 16) along the path, while 'each weed [he] . . . pulled out of the ground screamed like a baby' (p. 17). The language of this second quotation evokes the moment of birth, and calls to mind another of Thomas's poetic meditations on the interconnected life and death instincts, 'A process in the weather of the heart' (1934):

> A process in the eye forwarns
> The bones of blindness; and the womb
> Drives in a death as life leaks out.[79]

The 'process' referred to here seems to be the formation of the 'death drive' within the developing foetus or new 'life', with 'forwarns the bones of blindness' connoting decomposition and the darkness of burial. In particular, Mr Owen's actions in 'The Enemies' call to mind Freud's theory that

> instincts are readily modified and, in particular, readily take on new objects. Thus, though originally directed onto oneself, the death instinct can be easily turned around and directed outwardly onto others. When this happens, the instinct takes the form of an outwardly destructive or aggressive instinct.[80]

As John Deigh notes, Freud identified 'sadism' as 'an instance of the transformation of the death instinct into an aggressive instinct, an instant whose manifest erotic component is explained by the fusion of the sexual instinct with the aggressive instinct'.[81] Thomas joked about this aspect of Freud's work a year before the publication of 'The Enemies', writing in a letter to Trevor Hughes in 1933: 'Are you playing Freud to me as I tell you that . . . I . . . cut a pigeon's throat as I copulate?'[82] Yet he clearly exploits the transgressive impetus of Freud's theory in 'The Enemies' – in the image, for example, of Mr Owen gazing with 'satisfaction' on his wife's 'bare throat' as if he were fantasising about 'strangling' her. Moreover, this, in turn, once again connects the Jarvis Valley with Dalí's paintings. As previously noted, the interfacing sexual and aggressive instinct is a salient theme in Dalí's *Vertigo – Tower of Pleasure*, and it also finds expression in *Illuminated Pleasures* (1929). In this painting, Dalí places an array of images – many of them recognisable from his other works, including the 'grasshopper', the dumb or 'mouthless' face (seen previously in *The Great Masturbator*) and the sexually symbolic lion's head – in a defamiliarised yet also of course, for Dalí, intimately familiar landscape of rocks, sand and sea. In the foreground there is an image of a man who has his arm around a woman's waist, his hand apparently edging upwards towards her semi-naked breasts, while his other hand is clasping her throat. The woman's hands, too, are covered with blood, and draw the spectator's eyes across to a separate image of a hand holding a blood-stained knife aloft, and another clasped around its wrist. In *Illuminated Pleasures* (1929), as in Thomas's 'The Enemies' – and as in much of the work of these two artists from the 1930s – society's veneer of respectability is stripped away to reveal an alternative, distinctly Freudian reality of anarchic unconscious drives, processes and conflicts.

Thus, the origins of the alternative reality that Dalí and Thomas construct are entrenched in a very specific location. Both artists repeatedly invoke particular regional sites, and reconstruct and reimagine those sites as heterotopias of Modernist deviation – spaces in which repressive, traditionalist social and cultural mores are variously dramatised, transgressed and contested. In this respect, both Dalí and Thomas can be seen as 'surregionalists' or as 'geomodernists', like all of the Welsh writers considered so far, writers whose Modernism is a direct product of their acute 'self-consciousness about positionality'.[83] In addition, Thomas's surregionalism can be viewed as independently comparable with that of Dalí, thus presenting a challenge to the similarly reductive view of Modernism in Wales as inevitably derivative in nature, as simply 'belated encounter[s] between modernist techniques and "the matter of Wales"'.[84] In this comparative context, moreover, Thomas's surregionalism emerges as an example, in Joe Cleary's words, of the 'marginal culture's' capacity to 'invent', and not be just a peripheral, Welsh imitation or 'simulacrum' of a more prominent, canonical Modernist style. Moreover, the heterotopia – 'a place that is outside all places, but which can be located in reality' – can be seen as an analogue and outgrowth of the Anglophone Welsh writer's deterritoriaised position, contestation of the cultural establishment, and movement towards reterirritorialisation in the early twentieth century.

5

'Hellish Funny': The Grotesque Modernism of Gwyn Thomas and Rhys Davies

All of the chapters in this book have, in their own ways, resisted the critical tendency to view Welsh Modernist writing as purely derivative: as simply a collection of belated, peripheral imitations and appropriations of a more genuinely innovative, authentically Modernist body of work. Moreover, I would argue that Welsh Modernism should not necessarily be regarded in the same way that Tyrus Miller, for instance, views other manifestations of so-called 'late Modernism': 'in the empty spaces left by modernism's dissolution, late modernists reassembled fragments into disfigured likenesses of modernist masterpieces: the unlovely allegories of a world's end'.[1] To apply Miller's analysis to Welsh Modernism is to overlook the specifics, the individuality and, in particular, the novelty of the cultural and societal conditions in which Anglophone Welsh writers were operating in the 1930s and 1940s. Indeed if, as Terence Brown argues, the combination of the publication of Joyce's *Ulysses* and the formation of the Irish Free State invites us to regard 1922 as a Modernist moment in Ireland in both an artistic and a social sense,[2] then Welsh writers can also be seen as witnesses to, and participants in, a comparable (albeit more protracted) Modernist moment or 'event'[3] in Wales, where an unprecedented process of, or 'experiment'[4] in, linguistic, cultural and social change was taking place. This mood was captured by Glyn Jones who, writing in 1980, revealed: 'in the Thirties, I was . . . conscious . . . of being in at the beginning as it were, of being part of something quite new in Wales'.[5]

As I stressed in the previous chapter, to view Welsh Modernism from this perspective is not to refute the idea that Welsh writers were, to some extent, importing and adapting or 'reassembling' aspects of established 'Modernist masterpieces' in their work. On the contrary: as Pascale Casanova has suggested, it might be argued that

> authors living . . . on the edge of the literary world [such as those of Anglophone Wales during this period], who . . . [have] learned to confront the laws and forces that sustain the unequal structure of this world and who are keenly aware that they must be recognised in their respective centres in order to have any chance of surviving as writers . . . [are likely to be] the most sensitive to the newest aesthetic inventions of international literature [and art]. . .[6]

My aim, rather, has been to propose a less restricted and more searching critical understanding of the relationship between Modernism and Welsh writing, and Modernism and marginal literatures more generally. Welsh Modernism, as Tony Conran suggests, is potentially both 'home-grown' and 'part of an international climate',[7] and this more open, inclusive approach will continue to frame my analysis in this final chapter, on the role of the grotesque in the Modernism of Gwyn Thomas and Rhys Davies.

I

According to Tony Conran, 'modernism in Wales is most at home with the grotesque. It is there', he contends,

> that modernism characteristically shows itself, in Saunders Lewis as much as in Caradoc Evans or Dylan Thomas. The nightmare of monstrosity underlies the middle-class rejection of the *buchedd* [or 'Welsh way of life'], the sense of being suffocated by its hypocrisy and narrowness.[8]

Conran bases this theory both on the thematic preoccupations of Welsh Modernist literature and on what he calls 'the grotesquerie of [its] language'[9] – a feature which he traces back to Caradoc Evans's *My People*. Other Welsh writers whose modes of expression possess a grotesque or incongruous quality are Glyn Jones, Rhys Davies and Gwyn Thomas; but the motivation behind the 'new verbal ikons' of Jones, Davies and Thomas is not estrangement from *buchedd* values in any straightforward sense. The grotesque plays an altogether more complex role in the work of these writers, as M. Wynn Thomas has argued.[10] And in the case of Gwyn Thomas, this is especially apparent in the experimental novella, *Oscar*.

At the centre of this text, which, like all of Thomas's early works, is set in the industrialised south Wales Valleys during the 1930s, is the figure of Oscar, whom we see through the eyes of Thomas's narrator, Lewis. A wealthy industrialist and landowner, Oscar is repeatedly dehumanised: he is identified as 'a great, busy ram',[11] a 'goat' (p. 6) and, most frequently and evocatively, 'a hog'. Lewis reasons that 'for a hog, Oscar did very well out of being a man' (p. 6), and remarks that, since he had started working for Oscar, 'lads who . . . would always say, "Hullo, Lewis" . . . in a very friendly way, grew either to saying just "Hullo", or nothing at all . . . All because Oscar was a hog and owned a mountain' (p. 6). Oscar's behaviour is also more like that of a pig than a human. The narrator observes how he 'shook his great fat head stupidly from side to side' (p. 25), and states: 'I wiped Oscar's mouth and eyes with my sleeve, which was thick and rough and made him grunt' (p. 19). From one perspective, we might see Oscar as a capitalist counterpart to the tyrannical pig Napoleon in George Orwell's famous satire of Stalinism, *Animal Farm* (1945). Indeed, the subtitle of the volume in which *Oscar* was first published, *Folk Tales from the Modern Welsh*, also calls to mind Orwell's text, which is subtitled 'A Fairy Story'. Thomas's narrative does not operate in the same way as Orwell's, however. *Animal Farm* is, fundamentally, an allegorical fairytale, which relies on 'the active participation of the reader'[12] in its generation of socio-political meaning. Thomas, by contrast, is concerned with 'maintaining . . . the primacy of the *social image* [my emphasis] through its subjective expression',[13] and presents the reader with a distorted yet, at the same time, pellucid and instructive social reality. More specifically, Oscar represents a point in the narrative at which the 'objective representation of reality disappears behind [a subjective] vision, which is called upon to express a deeper truth, a more essential insight'.[14] Thomas's portrayal of Oscar is not simply grotesque, but also Expressionistic, evoking the European Expressionist premise that

> if the creative individual is a conscious and active participant in the structure of the reality of which he forms a part, then his will manifests itself by representing, criticising and changing that structure by means of self-expression, since his subject, in an aesthetic sense, represents objective reality. Therefore objective reality emerges through his subject, and the objective social goal through his art.[15]

The 'more essential insight' that Thomas's 'Rhondda Expressionist style of writing'[16] elicits is that of Oscar's inhumanity – a 'truth' which is conveyed in a more conventionally realist way in, for example, the image of Oscar's destitute employees 'waiting to pick up . . . scraps of coal that went to fill Oscar's bags and Oscar's pockets' (p. 28). The Expressionist presentation of Oscar as 'a hog' and his hoggish behaviour also conveys his greed and corruption, as does Lewis's account of how his employer's 'huge, fat body poured over the sides of the chair on which he sat' (p. 15). Moreover, through his Expressionistic approach, Thomas achieves his 'objective social goal': the exaggerated, distorted and grotesque[17] Oscar is clearly an expression – or, as Raymond Williams suggests, a 'cry'[18] – of outrage at the capitalist system and its consequences in industrial south Wales.[19] Expressionism, Williams writes, is 'the language of the cry, the exclamation', which 'in some later Expressionist work . . . is a consciously liberating, indeed revolutionary moment . . . that cry which fights to be heard above the news bulletins, the headlines, the false political speeches of a world in crisis'.[20] This invites us to view Oscar not only as a 'modern version of a native [Welsh] unfriendly giant fable, with some resemblance to "Culhwch ac Olwen"',[21] as Stephen Knight suggests, but also as a figure akin to the grotesques that populate German Expressionist visual art. He recalls the monstrous characters in Otto Dix's paintings, for example, whom the artist deployed to rail against German militarism and expose the corruption of the Weimar Republic. And he would also merge seamlessly into what George Grosz referred to as the 'hellish procession of dehumanised figures'[22] in his appalled visualisation of modern urban society, *Dedicated to Oskar Panizza* (1917–18) – a scene which he claimed he 'painted . . . [in] protest against a humanity that had gone insane'.[23]

In resorting to the grotesque, then, Gwyn Thomas does not, primarily, seem to be reacting to the suffocating 'hypocrisy' and 'narrowness' of the 'Welsh way of life' in the same way as Dylan Thomas and Caradoc Evans, but articulating and criticising the mercenary exploitation of working-class communities in industrialised south Wales during the first half of the twentieth century – exploitation which he witnessed first hand. As Glyn Jones points out,

> when short working and unemployment first began to be felt in the valleys in 1923, [Thomas] was ten years of age; when prosperity was restored with the outbreak of the Second World War, he was twenty-six; so that

> part of his childhood and the whole of his young manhood were lived in a period of crippling poverty, emigration and unprecedented unemployment, and the widespread frustration, bitterness, suffering and despair that inevitably followed.[24]

If Thomas's use of the grotesque does also pertain to his 'rejection' of the *buchedd*, then it might be interpreted as a challenge to its Liberal politics – a manifestation, in Conran's words, of 'a genuinely proletarian consciousness . . . in the south Wales mining valleys'.[25] Moreover, the grotesque effects of capitalism and social inequality on a particular community are externalised in this way in other Modernist works – in the German visual artist, Conrad Felixmüller's emotively distorted representations of workers and families in the industrialised Ruhr area of Germany, such as *Industrie-Regenlandschaft* (1922) and *Ruhrrevier I* (1920); and in the plays of the Spanish dramatist Ramón del Valle-Inclán, which Thomas, a competent and enthusiastic reader of Spanish, may well have encountered.[26] Valle-Inclán's 1920 play, *Luces de Bohemia* or *Bohemian Lights*, for instance, is an Expressionistic representation of

> Madrid and Barcelona, between 1917 and 1922: the long smouldering industrial strife, the strikes and demonstrations, clashes with the police, political assassinations, the right-wing backlash in the form of vigilante groups like the Acción ciudadana, the impact of Lenin and the Bolshevik revolution, workers' meetings in the Casa del pueblo.[27]

Valle-Inclán's poet-protagonist and anti-hero in *Bohemian Lights*, Max Estrella, defines this turbulent socio-political milieu as 'a grotesque deformation of European civilisation',[28] and opines that, by extension, all 'forms of expression' should be distorted 'in the same mirror that . . . contorts the whole miserable life of Spain' (p. 161). These lines are, in fact, self-conscious references to Valle-Inclán's own aesthetic in the play. The world of *Bohemian Lights* is indeed 'systematically deformed' (p. 160), or 'reflected in concave mirrors' (p. 160), and Valle-Inclán calls his particular 'version of the Expressionist grotesque'[29] '*esperpento*', meaning literally a frightful 'sight' or 'piece of nonsense'.[30]

Valle-Inclán's *esperpento* aesthetic and Gwyn Thomas's grotesque narrative in *Oscar* actually overlap in a number of ways. In scene two of *Bohemian Lights*, we are introduced to a bookseller, Zarathustra:

> ZARATHUSTRA's cave-like bookshop along Calle Consegos. Randomly stacked piles of books litter the floor and cover the walls. Four sordid illustrations from a serialized story are pasted over the glass plates of the door. In the 'cave' the cat, the parrot, the dog and the bookseller are having a literary gathering. The repellent puppet-like ZARATHUSTRA, a hunched figure with a face reminiscent of rancid bacon and with a green, serpent-like scarf wrapped around his neck, is at once sharply distant and painfully immediate. Enveloped in the torn stuffing of a tiny chair, his feet buried in rags and wrapped in vines around the brazier stand, he minds the shop. A mouse sticks his prying snout through a hole. (p. 100)

Zarathustra is a nonsensical 'sight', distorted and exaggerated in the concave mirror of contemporary Spanish society. Hunched and 'puppet-like', he is expressly dehumanised. Indeed, he appears overtly animalistic, lurking in a 'cave' with a cat, a parrot and a dog, and attracting the attention of a prying mouse. The 'green, serpent-like scarf wrapped around his neck' and the macabre comparison of his face to 'rancid bacon' reinforce this effect, as does his name, which alludes to Friedrich Nietzsche's philosophical work, *Thus Spake Zarathustra* (1883–4), in which humanity is identified as 'a rope suspended between animal and Superman'.[31] What is most arresting about Zarathustra, however, is his similarity to Oscar. He and Oscar are each repellently materialistic representatives of an entrepreneurial middle class,[32] who have been rendered (in Valle-Inclán's words) 'at once sharply distant and painfully immediate'. They are Expressionist grotesques, dehumanised and disfigured in a manner reminiscent of the work of the Spanish painter Francisco Goya (1746–1828)[33] – Max Estrella actually claims in Valle-Inclán's play that 'it was Goya who invented the Grotesque' (p. 160)[34] – and starkly emblematic of an abhorrent, modern capitalist reality. Indeed, both Valle-Inclán and Thomas seem to invoke the grotesque 'as a reaction against the constraints of capitalist society at its ugliest and most mediocre';[35] and this is reinforced when, just as Oscar employs the impoverished people of the valley to pick coal 'at fivepence a bag' (p. 23), and then sells 'each bag for one and sevenpence' (p. 23), Zarathustra defrauds the blind and penniless Max by purchasing his books from his associate, Don Latino, for 'three measly pesetas' (p. 98). When, outraged, Max visits Zarathustra's shop in person to demand that the transaction be reversed, Zarathustra tells him that he has already sold the books on, while, at the same time, hastily secreting them in 'a murky backroom' (p. 101).

Zarathustra and Oscar do not just incite feelings of revulsion, however. They have been 'transformed', in Mikhail Bakhtin's words, 'into . . . funny monster[s]':[36] both Valle-Inclán and Thomas use 'the grotesque and its corresponding sense of interchange and disorder'[37] to blur the distinction between amusement and disgust, comedy and tragedy. This is evident in *Bohemian Lights* when Valle-Inclán indicates that 'only half of [Zarathustra's] face can be seen: the rest remains in shadow, giving the appearance that his nose is folded over one ear' (p. 102), and in Thomas's novella following Oscar's confession, 'I'd like to kill somebody, Lewis. That's the thing to make you tingle I bet' (p. 48):

> I [Lewis] jumped to my feet thinking he was going to pass into a fit. I moved back a little from the bed and looked at the door. I did not wish to be in that room if Oscar was going to be taken in such a fashion. I did not know how I would handle a man with a body shaped so much like a whale, and a mind shaped so much like another man's rear. (p. 48)

The passage in which Lewis attends to Oscar in his bedroom provides another memorable example:

> I found him . . . sitting in . . . bed with his legs drawn up and, between his vast gut and his legs, look[ing] as if he had taken another bed into bed with him to start some new fashion that only landowners could afford. The colour had drained from his face. It might have gone lower down his body for a change, being sick of Oscar's face as I sometimes got, but his face was like the fine ash when the cinders have been riddled away. His lower lip was hanging down over his chin like a pale red sunshade . . . He did not stop gazing at himself in the huge mirror on the wall opposite. He seemed afraid that his reflection would vanish and never return if he turned his eyes away from it for a second. (p. 44)

Oscar almost seems to enact the reader or spectator's reaction to the grotesque here; he appears startled, horrified, repulsed, but at the same time, enthralled, entertained, unable to 'turn his eyes away'. Indeed, again evoking *esperpento* theatre in particular, he stares at his own reflection – at what should be a recognisable and commonplace sight – with the same puzzled intensity as someone contemplating the bizarre, unfamiliar image looking back at them from a fairground mirror. It is almost as if, like Valle-Inclán, Thomas is self-reflexively drawing attention to his own distorting aesthetic.

The unsettling tragicomedy that infuses *Oscar* itself assumes grotesque shapes in Thomas's Expressionistic fairground mirror, swelling and contorting into a 'gallows-humour',[38] which finds expression, for example, when Lewis observes 'the people who stood waiting to pick up the scraps of coal' (p. 28) from Oscar's tip:

> I had seen the same look on all their faces, the look of people who are being fed in parts through a mangle. And at the handle of the mangle, turning away like blue hell in case anybody should have a little less pain than he paid rent on, stood Oscar. (p. 28)

Lewis evaluates his own job, on the other hand, in the following terms:

> All I had to do was to stand there, far enough away from the tipping machine to be out of the dust, and count the number of elements who had turned up to do the picking and count the number of sacks picked. Then I had to see that these sacks were picked up in the proper order to be taken away by the cart that came for them at the end of the afternoon. Any job connected with counting I consider to be very easy, especially when you are in hearing and seeing distance of other elements whose jobs cause them to be scratching about bent up like monkeys for bits of coal, getting their guts turned half solid with coal dust and their limbs occasionally knocked inside out by those small rocks that came flying down from the trains emptied by the tipping machine. (p. 51)

In the first extract cited above, the narrator combines an image of human cruelty with overt, sardonic humour. Indeed this scene calls to mind Kafka's Expressionist short story, 'In the Penal Colony' (1919), in which a machine comprising a Bed, a Designer and a Harrow, subjects prisoners to a protracted and excruciating death. In the second quotation from Thomas's novella, on the other hand, injury in the coalfield is depicted in the form of a gruesome, but also comically understated and slapstick – a 'Hellish funny'[39] (to borrow Thomas's phrase) – account of workers' limbs being 'occasionally knocked inside out'. Once again, these passages resonate with *Bohemian Lights*, which is pervaded with an equally macabre humour, exemplified in Valle-Inclán's portrayal of the Home Secretary, whose 'glasses hang from the end of a string like two absurd eyeballs dancing on his belly' (p. 139), and through his attention to the journalist Don Filiberto's 'yellow, ink-stained hands – the hands', he writes, 'of a diligent skeleton on the biblical Day of Judgement!' (p. 135). Fittingly, however,

Valle-Inclán reserves his most outrageously warped comedy for the disorientating climax of the scene in which Max expounds the concept of *esperpento*:

> MAX Latino, I think I'm beginning to see again. How did we get to this funeral? . . . Latino, how did we come to preside over such an affair?
> DON LATINO Stop hallucinating, Max. . . .
> MAX The sun's shining so brightly on the funeral hearse!
> DON LATINO If everything you say wasn't one big joke it would have some theosophical significance. . . .If I presided over a funeral, I would be the corpse. All these wreaths seem to suggest that you must be the corpse.
> MAX Allow me to oblige. To calm your fear, let me lie here in wait. I am the corpse! . . .
>
> MÁXIMO ESTRELLA lies down against the door. A stray dog, running in a zig-zag, crosses the steep, narrow street. He stops in the middle, lifts a hind leg and urinates. His bleary eyes, like those of a poet, are raised up to the sky's remaining star.
>
> MAX Latino, prepare for the Gloria.
> DON LATINO If you don't put a stop to this macabre joke, I am leaving.
> MAX I'm the one who's leaving. Forever!
> DON LATINO Get up Max. Let's move on.
> MAX I'm dead.
> DON LATINO You're frightening me! Max, let's go. Stand up and stop twitching you silly bastard! Max! Max! Damned fool! Say something!
> MAX Dead people can't talk.
> DON LATINO I'm definitely leaving.
> MAX Goodnight! (pp. 162–3)

This exchange is made all the more disconcerting when a neighbour, 'lean[ing] over [Max] to peer at the half-open eyes, beneath his pale forehead' (p. 165), makes the horrific discovery that he is, in fact, dead; and the whole 'macabre joke' takes another grotesque turn when the people at his funeral begin to suspect that Max has been alive all along:

> BASILIO SOULINAKE My dear concierge, please inform the funeral service coachman that the burial has been postponed . . .
> MADAME COLLET Ask him to wait! . . . You could be mistaken, Basilio . . .
> MADAME COLLET Oh, Jesus! I don't know what to do.

SEÑORA FLORA THE CONCIERGE It'll cost you double. Is it really worth keeping the corpse in the house for a couple more hours. Let them take him away, Madame Collet!

MADAME COLLET What if he's not dead?

SEÑORA FLORA THE CONCIERGE Not dead! You haven't left the room So you don't notice the stench.

BASILIO SOULINAKE Señora, would you be so kind as to tell me whether you have ever studied medicine at a university? If you have I will shut my mouth and say nothing more. But if you have not, then I will refrain from entering into an argument and simply state that he is not dead but merely cataleptic.

SEÑORA FLORA THE CONCIERGE Not dead? He's dead and rotting! . . .

THE FUNERAL SERVICE COACHMAN Just put a lit match to his thumb. If it burns to the end, he's as dead as my grandfather. (pp. 170–2)

The mourners' crass approach to Max Extrella's death in this scene calls to mind Lewis's comically unfeeling attitude towards his uncle at the beginning of Oscar: 'I wore a waterproof jacket [which] . . . had belonged to an uncle of mine. I took it from his house without telling anybody, just after he died. The rain did not bother him anymore. It bothered me' (p. 3). Furthermore, like the description in Oscar mentioned earlier of workers' limbs 'getting occasionally knocked inside out' by falling debris, the scene has a farcical, slapstick quality, which chimes with Valle-Inclán's portrayal of The Porter in scene seven as 'a stumpy, sour-faced man with a moustache and a beer gut, looking like one of those dashing colonels who always manage to fall off their horses during a parade' (p. 129), and his image of the Home Secretary in scene eight, emerging from his office with 'his flies . . . undone' (p. 139). We recall that Valle-Inclán emphasised the bookseller Zarathustra's grotesqueness by identifying him as 'puppet-like',[40] and the often farcical tenor of *Bohemian Lights* is an extension of this theme, echoing and alluding to the Spanish tradition of puppet-theatre.[41] Whether or not Gwyn Thomas was drawing on *esperpento* theatre during the writing of Oscar, or indeed whether, like Valle-Inclán, he was independently invoking and experimenting with Spanish puppet theatre, or even the British 'Punch and Judy' show[42] in this text, his prose certainly has the air of a puppet-play; and this is exemplified in the following scuffle which breaks out between Lewis and Oscar:

> He [Oscar] rolled like a flash on to his side and shot his hand beneath the bed. His hand swung wildly back and fore in search of the chamber.

> For a second I couldn't see what was meant by all this activity. Then I saw he had a notion of swinging this article up from under the bed and breaking it over my head. I kicked his hand as hard as I could. The vessel shot from his grasp and landed with cracking force against a farther wall.
>
> 'You'd better not try any of those tricks with me, Oscar.'
>
> I pushed him back into the bed. He was weak as a baby now and crying and sucking his hand where I had kicked it, sucking it slowly as if he liked it, as if it were a toffee apple. (p. 49)

This passage clearly displays the grotesquely exaggerated, ungainly physical action and comical violence that are the hallmarks of Spanish puppet theatre (as well as Punch and Judy), and Thomas creates a similar atmosphere when Lewis reacts to a comment made by the fruit and vegetable seller, Waldo Williamson, about his position as 'Oscar's boy' (p. 4):

> I drove my open hand into his face and he went down into a puddle. He laughed at that too . . . He looked altogether like a duck as he sat there, his lips stuck outwards like the beginnings of a beak, and wondering how the hell he got down there so near the ground with waves all around him. (p. 8)

Indeed, these passages also evoke the Modernist puppet-plays of another Spanish dramatist, and contemporary of Valle-Inclán, Federico García Lorca – particularly Lorca's *Tragedia de Don Cristóbal y la señá Rosita*, or the *Tragicomedy of Don Cristóbal and Miss Rosita* (1922–5), in which the puppet, Mosquito (another grotesque, described as 'part ghost, part leprechaun, part insect'[43]) 'strikes [the sleeping] Cristobita a sharp blow on the head with [a] trumpet and wakes him up' (p. 115).[44] Thomas's vignette of Oscar 'crying and sucking his hand . . . slowly . . . as if it were a toffee apple', at the same time, calls to mind the infantile behaviour of Rosita and Cocoliche in scene two of Lorca's play:

> *Pause, during which Rosita, gasping for breath, sobs comically.*
>
> I can't marry you!
>
> COCOLICHE Rosita!
> ROSITA You're the apple of my eye, but I can't marry you!
>
> *She sobs.*

COCOLICHE Are you going to act as balky as a nun now? Have I done anything wrong? Oh, oh, oh!

His weeping is halfway between childish and comic.

ROSITA You'll find out all about it later. But now, goodbye.
COCOLICHE, *shouting and stamping his feet* Oh, no, no, no, no, no! (p. 89)

Additionally, Oscar's absurdly childlike and melodramatic stance is cognate with the exaggerated, clownish poses assumed by Charlie Chaplin in his comic films; after all, Thomas was, as Parnell notes, 'always a great devotee of the cinema'.[45] This again invites us to compare his narrative style with the grotesque Modernism of Lorca and Valle-Inclán, which was inspired, in part, by the silent comedies of Chaplin, Buster Keaton and Harold Lloyd.[46] As G. G. Brown points out, 'several of the techniques of the esperpento [in particular] clearly derive from [their] silent comedies'.[47]

One of the ways in which Valle-Inclán educes the puppet-like essence of his characters in his *esperpento*s is by emulating what Gwynne Edwards terms the puppet-theatre's 'simplification and undermining of the complexity and dignity of human behaviour' and "emotions"[48] – its reduction of human nature to a comically 'simple, spontaneous level'.[49] This is evidenced in the figure of the 'dirty tramp' (p. 109) in scene three of *Bohemian Lights*, who 'begins maniacally shaking his shoulders', 'like a dog who is trying to rid itself of fleas' (p. 109), and it is also a feature of Lorca's *La zapatera prodigiosa* or *The Shoemaker's Prodigious Wife* (1930). A human puppet-play which shares many similarities with Valle-Inclán's *esperpento* theatre, *The Shoemaker's Prodigious Wife* features a Shoemaker who is 'constantly swallowing',[50] and a character called Don Blackbird, who 'moves his head like a wire doll' (p. 141).[51] The childlike behaviour of Rosita and Cocoliche in Lorca's *Tragicomedy of Don Cristóbal and Miss Rosita* and, significantly, the image of Oscar 'crying' and 'sucking his hand . . . slowly . . . as if it were a toffee apple' also register this process. It is when, having finished his own dinner, Oscar grabs Lewis's plate of 'bacon and kidneys' (p. 72) and eats them, shouting '"More for me. More for me More for me," . . . in a high, childish voice' (p. 73), however – an outburst that additionally recalls the 'vigorous, repeated [verbal] patterns'[52] of puppet-theatre – that Thomas's use of this technique is most obvious; as well as at the novella's brutal climax:

> We [Lewis and Oscar] came to the fence that had been put up to keep people away from the quarry, the fence that various voters had made it their business to kick down. I told Oscar to lift his legs to keep them free of the tangled tracks of wood and wire which were all that was left of the fence. He did that. He lifted his legs up a lot higher than was necessary and he screamed that the movement made him feel like a bloody woman.
>
> 'That's right, Oscar,' I said. 'Like a woman. Go on, boy.'
>
> And on he went, right over the quarry. (p. 99)

Indeed, it is not only Oscar who is characterised in this way. The other figures in Thomas's novella are similarly distorted and dehumanised, and they too register a puppet-theatre-esque flattening or caricaturing of human behaviour and emotions. There is Waldo Williamson, mentioned earlier, whose 'lips [stick] outwards like the beginnings of a beak', and who wears multiple layers of clothing all year round in order to ward off rheumatism, only to visit 'every pub he [passes] to get cool from all the heat he [works] up from wearing such a load of leggings and capes' (p. 7); there is Clarisse, who has 'lips . . . like good chops of meat' (p. 9) and who makes a 'glugging sound' (p. 11) which, the narrator decides, she 'must have picked up from the pictures or the chickens' (p. 11); and then there is Macnaffy – a woman described as 'tired, thin and savage (p. 14), and looking 'as if she were going to rip you open' (p. 15) – who incessantly caresses 'her right leg . . . as if', Thomas writes, her 'bulging calf were a good friend' (p. 14). Perhaps the most memorable example, however, is No Doubt, who wears 'a fisherman's hat . . . pulled down towards his neck' (p. 40), giving him 'the look of something growing out of the earth' (p. 40), and who responds to whatever anyone says to him with the phrase, 'No doubt', in order to avoid being 'fined or put in jail' (p. 40). In essence, No Doubt's identity, emotions and behaviour condense into one simplistic, perfunctory phrase, as the following exchange illustrates:

> 'God, it's a lovely morning,' I [Lewis] said.
>
> 'No doubt,' said No Doubt, taken aback a bit, because he must have thought I was addressing him as God, which he was not, being little, grey, overworked and limping.
>
> 'What are you doing up here so early?' I asked.
>
> 'No doubt', said No Doubt, cautiously. (p. 41)

Lewis subsequently remarks that No Doubt

> was like Meg [Oscar's housekeeper] and Danny and Hannah [Lewis's friends in the Terraces] because they, too, seemed to be going round with a rope on their necks jerking them to a halt every time they tried moving forward. (p. 42)

And this idea of people in the valley being 'jerked' into life by some higher, controlling force, while echoing Caradoc Evans's infamous short story, 'Lamentations' (1919), in which Evan Rhiw leads his daughter Matilda by a rope to the 'madhouse' in Carmarthen,[53] reinforces their marionette-like actions. Lewis seems to resist his own puppet-like status, boasting, 'I could not see the moon and had no wish to jerk my head round looking for it' (p. 28), yet, seeing Oscar approach Danny on the coal tip, he reveals:

> I turned my head towards Oscar. He was standing beside his horse, his gun levelled at Danny.
>
> 'Watch out Danny,' I shouted and I did not feel I could do any more than that. I fixed my eyes on the ground, expecting a great noise when the gun went off. It went off. The noise of it was not as great as my promise of it. The zip of it passing dragged my eyes to the tip. I saw the earth a yard to the right of Danny shoot up. Startled, Danny swung round, his arms above him in the air, off balance. His legs shot from beneath him and he came plunging down, somersaulting. He slithered the last two feet and his head came to a stop against one of the large stones that littered the tip. (pp. 59–60)

Something prevents Lewis from intervening here; as if held in suspension by a rope or strings, he does not feel that he can do any more than shout, 'Watch out Danny', and then 'fix his eyes on the ground', anticipating the inevitable gunshot. The way in which Danny is said to have 'swung round, his arms above him in the air', also evokes the limp, involuntary movement of a string-puppet, as do Lewis's glimpses of how Danny's 'legs shot from beneath him', and how he came 'plunging down' and 'slither[ing] . . . to a stop'. Indeed, the action and overall mood of this scene is redolent of Valle-Inclán's *Esperpento de Los cuernos de Don Friolera* or *Esperpento of The Horns of Don Friolera* (1921):

> Don Friolera, tripping over himself, rushes into the garden . . . He fires the pistol, and with a yell the moonlit puppets climbing the wall tumble into the next-door garden. Doña Loreta reappears, her hair standing on end, her arms extended.[54]

According to John Lyon, Valle-Inclán's first *esperpento* play, *Bohemian Lights*, documents 'the metamorphosis of the heroic into the absurd under the influence of a trivialised and grotesque social context',[55] which, as previously noted, is an expression, or distorted reflection, of contemporary Spanish socio-political reality; as Max Estrella avers in scene twelve of that play, 'classical heroes reflected in concave mirrors give us the Grotesque or Esperpento' (p. 160).[56] In other words, the grotesque world of *Bohemian Lights* (and the 'deformed' Spanish society that it represents) elicits 'an atmosphere in which the hero can no longer breathe', in which 'collective social pressures and circumstances have become the controlling agents over the life of the individual'.[57] To cite Gwynne Edwards, 'the viewpoint of the esperpento . . . sees [man] as a tragic puppet, his humanity glimpsed still but rendered farcical and futile'.[58] Lyon's exegesis seems equally appropriate to Gwyn Thomas's *Oscar*. That is, within the grotesque social context of this novella – a context distorted so as to convey more effectively a social reality where, to cite Thomas, 'lunacy [is] established . . . as an apparently normal stable companion'[59] – individuals metamorphose into absurdities or *esperpentos*; the contemporary socio-political climate reduces them, like the people of Madrid and Barcelona in *Bohemian Lights*, to tragicomic, puppet-like figures.

Indeed, this notion of transmutation from the heroic to the grotesque is echoed in Thomas's own theories about humour, which he explicated in an interview with Glyn Jones in 1950. Here, he divulged:

> people tell me there are comic undertones in even my most sombre imagery. I can quite believe it. Humour is a sense of the incongruous or absurd, an aggravated contrast between man's divine promise and his shambling, shabby reality.[60]

This 'aggravated contrast' is perceptible throughout *Oscar*, in Thomas's panoply of strangely vital characters. Even the novella's apparently debonair and streetwise narrator, Lewis, as Victor Golightly observes, effectively embodies a conflict between 'the Hero'[61] and 'the murdering buffoon'.[62] Moreover, while we might detect in many of Thomas's characters a Dickensian comedic energy and a Caradoc Evans-like hyperreality – we might view the rural Welsh community of Manteg in Caradoc Evans's *My People* as 'a model of a real without origin or reality: a hyperreal'[63] – they most strongly evoke the citizens of Madrid and Barcelona in *Bohemian Lights* and the urbanites in Grosz's *Dedicated to Oscar Panizza*. Lewis, Oscar, No Doubt, Waldo Williamson, Macnaffy and Clarisse, to name a few, are all ultimately cast as 'shambling' figures, analogous with '*the row of puppets [or characters] pinned to the wall*' (p. 168) in scene thirteen of *Bohemian Lights* – as tragicomic grotesques, defined, degraded and manipulated by modern socio-political forces beyond their individual control.[64]

II

While in *Oscar*, the grotesque principally marks the dehumanising and demoralising effects of industrial capitalism and its collapse on the people of the south Wales Valleys, in Rhys Davies's 1931 short story, 'Arfon', it is more ingrained in the fabric of the community. This is certainly not to imply that Davies overlooked the effects of industrialisation and economic collapse in south Wales in his work. On the contrary, like Gwyn Thomas, Davies was born and raised in the Rhondda Valley, and 'was in the first half of his writing career', as Stephen Knight points out, 'substantially committed to considering the condition and plight of the people among whom he grew up'.[65] In 'Arfon', however, he seems to have a different objective, and this becomes apparent in the story's opening:

> Mr. and Mrs. Edwards did not deserve such a child. There was nothing peculiar about them, they were chapel people and a respected business couple, he selling oil, soap, candles, and oddments from a cart in the streets, and she, a thin staid woman, making savoury pasties on Tuesdays and Fridays, eight for sixpence and very delicious. So no one could understand why such a funny little boy was born to them.
>
> Odd he was to look at, too. He never grew beyond the stature of a small boy of ten, but his head was ridiculously large, and the expression on his heavy grey face was of such gravity that no one felt at ease in his presence . . . His mother and father were convinced he was of idiotic tendencies. Mrs. Edwards never forgave him for appearing in a deformed state. So silly he looked, her only child, with his paltry thin body and massive head, she shut herself away from him in resentment and became angry at the continual ache in her heart when she looked at him. His father roared at him, protruding his thick lips and rolling his violent eyes, beating him for the sulky gravity of his face.[66]

Arfon, with his 'ridiculously large head', 'paltry thin body' and disconcerting 'heavy grey face', instantly calls to mind the characters in Thomas's *Oscar* and Valle-Inclán's *esperpento* theatre; and he, too, would not be out of place among the grotesques of German Expressionist art – his 'heavy-fleshed head' (p. 18) and brooding expression evoking, in particular, the distorted figure in Erich Heckel's painting, *Portrait of a Man (Self-Portrait)* (1919). Indeed, it seems likely that Davies would have been aware of the aesthetics of European Expressionism, and of the European avant-garde in general. He records in his autobiography, *Print of a Hare's Foot* (1969), how he 'dream[t] of becoming a painter'[67] in his youth; moved in artistic circles in London (where, he later revealed, 'he felt . . . more en rapport with European exiles . . . than English people'[68]); and first published his work in the avant-garde magazine, *The Coterie*, edited by the German bookseller, Charles Lahr.[69] He also travelled in Germany and France,[70] and read and admired a variety of European literary works.[71]

Moreover, recalling Tony Conran's comments concerning the origins of the grotesque in Welsh Modernist literature, Arfon is the product of parents who are firmly entrenched in what remains of the *buchedd* or 'Welsh way of life' in the Rhondda. 'Chapel people and a respected business couple', Mr and Mrs Edwards are the epitome of Welsh 'respectability', and they also embody the 'alliance between the peasantry, the respectable working class and the petty [sic] bourgeoisie';[72] Davies writes that Mrs Edwards 'had her own little pasties business before she married [Mr. Edwards]' (p. 17), who 'had come to the valley from another [probably a rural] part of Wales' (p. 17).[73] Mrs Edwards later tells her husband: 'You got funny blood in your family . . . blood that's mad and bad. Found out I have that your aunt was put away in an asylum and your grandfather in jail for whatnot. Gipsy blood is in you. (p. 17) And this again implicitly associates Mr Edwards with the rural Welsh peasantry, who are portrayed as similarly 'mad and bad' or 'non-respectable' in other Anglophone Welsh writing at this time – most notably, in the work of Caradoc Evans and, as demonstrated in the preceding chapter, Dylan Thomas. Davies's account of how, together, Mr and Mrs Edwards 'became of similar temperament, thrifty and mean in the house, regular chapel-goers . . . nicely prosperous' (p. 18) and 'of that simple class that respects school masters and learning' (p. 19) emphasises their allegiance to the 'Welsh way of life'. As the ironic tone of this narrative voice intimates, however, the text builds up an impression of the stifling conservatism and double standards of *buchedd* ideology, and this is particularly apparent in Mr and Mrs Edwards's attitude towards Arfon. Calling to mind Evan Rhiw's treatment of his daughter in Caradoc Evans's 'Lamentations', Mr and Mrs Edwards ostracise and brutalise their son in a decidedly unchristian way for deviating from what they consider to be the 'respectable' norm. This sense of hypocrisy is underscored through the figure of Mr Jeb Watkin-Watkins, the local chapel minister, who, like Mr Edwards, shouts at Arfon and beats him, accusing him of being 'possessed with a devil' (p. 20), even after he has displayed an ability to 'recite from the Book, without discrimination, including a great many verses from the Old Testament' (p. 19):

> Rising, the minister, who had begun to heave with anger . . . told him [Arfon] to take off his clothes. Arfon did so and looked down with meek, silent resignation at his frail body.
>
> 'You lie on that mat,' said the minister sternly. 'And don't you cry out. The hand of God is in this. A sacred task it is for your benefit. You be grateful now for what I am doing to you . . .
>
> Arfon waited, lying on his stomach. The minister took a long cane from a cupboard and, muttering imprecations and curses, began to beat Arfon.
>
> 'Out devil, out!' rose Mr. Watkin-Watkin's voice.
>
> Arfon had never endured such pain . . . He almost swooned away. (pp. 20–1)

Thomas's narrative appears more and more grimly ironic as Davies portrays those members of 'respectable' Rhondda society who chastise Arfon for his grotesqueness as far from 'Normal' (p. 19). The narrator's pointed insistence that Mr and Mrs Edwards 'did not deserve such a child', that 'there was nothing peculiar about them', and that 'no one could understand why such a funny little boy was born to them' has the effect of ironically gesturing towards the 'peculiarity' of their 'way of life' and of the wider community that upholds it. Furthermore, they too are distinctly 'odd . . . to look at': Mr Edwards has a 'mottled blue' (p. 36) face and is seen 'protruding his thick lips and rolling his violent eyes' at his son – an image that is not only grotesque but also has a malevolently carnivalesque quality. Mrs Edwards, on the other hand, has 'worn, dried cheeks'

(p. 23), 'thin, spotted hand[s]' (p. 23) and a 'brow' that is 'brownish and spotted like an old lemon' (p. 29), while Mr Jeb Watkin-Watkins – recalling Gwyn Thomas's portrayal of Oscar – is figured as 'an ugly fat shape, heaving and snorting' (p. 21), with 'small elephant's eyes' (p. 19) that turn 'red, like an infuriated boar's' (p. 19). Ironically, then, Arfon does not seem especially out of place in *buchedd* society; on the contrary, as the 'sulky gravity of his face' suggests, he seems to be, in Valle-Inclán's words, 'distorted in the same mirror that distorts' what Davies appears to view in this text as 'the whole miserable ['Welsh way of'] life' in the Rhondda.

A number of Davies's narratives, in fact, feature characters that appear to have been warped in the 'concave mirror' of *buchedd* society. Another example is the 1936 short story, 'Resurrection', which begins:

> Half a day before the lid was to be screwed down on her, Meg rose in her coffin and faintly asked for a glass of water. Her two sisters were bustling about the room, tidying and dusting the flowers, and both, after a few moments of terrified shock, looked at the recently deceased with a bitter anger. Once again she was doing something improper.
>
> 'Water!' stuttered Bertha. 'Go on with you now. What you want with water?' Gathering strength at the sound of her own voice, she went on sternly as if speaking to a nuisance: 'Lie back thee [sic], lie back. Dead you are.'
>
> 'Yes, indeed,' breathed Ellen, 'dead these four days and the mourning ordered.'[74]

This morbidly farcical opening clearly has much in common with Valle-Inclán's *esperpento* theatre – the sisters' crass response to Meg's 'resurrection' evoking, in particular, the mourners' treatment of Max Estrella's death and funeral in *Bohemian Lights*. Moreover, Bertha and Ellen's absurd preoccupation with the 'impropriety' and, later, the financial cost of their sister's 'recovery' – Bertha complains that they had to 'spend money on mourning and that five-guinea coffin' (p. 166) – aligns them with the respectable, 'thrifty and mean' Mr and Mrs Edwards in 'Arfon'. Their *buchedd* principles are subsequently confirmed as the narrator tells how,

> Bleak and raddled and wintry, the sisters, who were in the [sic] fifties, pursed their lips. They were twins. Both wore a piled-up mass of coarse, dour hair in which was jabbed small combs and tortoise-shell prongs. Their faces were puckered in, secretive, and proud. In chapel and street

> they liked to swank: they liked people to think they were well off and to treat them with ceremony. They were daughters of a semi-successful builder, and in a hole behind some loose bricks in the cellar was the money he had made, for he trusted no bank; his daughters thought likewise. (p. 167)

With their 'raddled', 'puckered in' faces and 'coarse', 'piled-up' hair 'jabbed' with 'combs and . . . prongs', the sisters are also, like Mr and Mrs Edwards and Mr Jeb Watkin-Watkins, physically 'peculiar' – external projections of a grotesque socio-cultural climate.

In their different ways, then, both Rhys Davies and Gwyn Thomas use the grotesque as a means to, in José Ortega y Gasset's words, Expressionistically 'objectify the subjective' or "worldify" the immanent'.[75] Yet Arfon's grotesqueness is also more complex than this. More specifically, it not only reflects and criticises a particular social situation, but also actively subverts it, as the following passage from Davies's story evinces:

> He [Arfon] wouldn't grow beyond the stature of a young boy. Mr. and Mrs. Edwards continued to lament their lot; they didn't know what to do with Arfon, now he had left school. He was too fragile for the mines, and because of his strange look no tradesman would employ him.
>
> 'What you want to do?' bellowed his father. 'What d'you think you've got talent for?'
>
> 'I want to make drawings,' sulked Arfon.
>
> 'What d'you want to work at?' continued his father impatiently. 'To earn money. Think we're going to keep you? And dead we'll be soon. What'll you do then?'
>
> Arfon wished his father would die. 'Draw pictures for papers I can,' he muttered.
>
> 'The only thing left,' moaned his mother, who would have liked him to be a preacher, if there had been money for his training, 'is for him to help you sell your things in the streets. A hawker he must be, like you.'
>
> 'Don't you call me a hawker, Mrs. Edwards,' snapped her husband. 'I am a respectable tradesman of twenty years standing.' (p. 22)

The way in which Arfon will not 'grow beyond the stature of a young boy' might be said to anticipate Günter Grass's 1959 novel, *Die Blechtrommel* or *The Tin Drum,* where the narrator and protagonist, Oskar Matzerath, elects to remain 'the three-year old, the gnome, the Tom Thumb, the pigmy, the Lilliputian, the midget, whom no one could persuade to grow'[76] throughout his life, in an expression of, and a form of protest against, the stunted, warped nature of German society during the first half of the twentieth century. Arfon's comparably 'deformed state' means that 'he can't go out into the world and work like ordinary well-grown chaps' (p. 24), and this prompts an exchange that reveals the fault-lines in *buchedd* ideology. Class division and conflict surface when Mrs Edwards suggests that Arfon must become 'a hawker' like her husband, and the way in which she blames Mr Edwards's 'funny blood' (p. 17) for 'her son's oddness' (p. 17) at the beginning of the narrative also has this effect.[77] Furthermore, Arfon's grotesqueness destabilises the traditional gender roles that act as a strengthening framework for this 'respectable' society. He is 'too fragile for the mines' and too strange-looking to be employed as a 'tradesman'. Indeed, he tells his father that he only wants to 'make' drawings, appropriating the tradesman's vocabulary in order to justify an occupation that is other than that expected of 'ordinary . . . chaps' in the community.

Arfon's difference from quintessential images of masculinity is, in fact, crucial to his grotesqueness. The narrator tells how, undermining his parents' ethos of upward mobility, Arfon

> followed his father and the cart in the streets and sold oil and oddments. He did his work with the uncomplaining delicacy of a saintly martyr; he deftly measured out the oil with his thin fingers and counted threepennyworth of clothes pegs in a manner that made the transaction memorable to the women customers. His old-world courtesy, his large eyes slowly looking at them, his darling small body, tickled the women and girls. Sometimes they did their best to flirt with him.
>
> But Arfon became a very grave youth. His mind was always occupied with visions. He still imagined a different race of beings in the world. These fanciful persons were always tall, vigorous, and gentle in a proud way. He made pictures of them: walking, sitting, lying, naked or draped idly; and though their behaviour was earthly, their beauty was not of this world as we know it. (p. 22)

Arfon's 'large eyes' contrast sharply with Mr Jeb Watkin-Watkins's 'small elephant's eyes', and his 'thin fingers' echo the 'thin, spotted hand[s]' of his mother. His grotesqueness endows him, on one level, with a childlike, but also with an effeminate or androgynous quality, which is underscored through the 'delicacy' of his movements, through the description of his 'darling small body', and in his unusual affinity with 'the women customers'. This sense of gender ambiguity is also distilled through Davies's account of how Arfon 'almost swooned away' after his punishment at the hands of Mr Jeb Watkin-Watkins – a reaction normally associated with women in literature – and it is also manifested in the 'tall, vigorous, and gentle' 'persons' that Arfon depicts in his drawings, and in Mrs Edwards's apparent inability to classify them:

> Once, his [Arfon's] mother, who sat watching him for some time, got up and began to examine the drawing on the table . . .
>
> 'What are these, boy?' she cried shrilly.
>
> 'Men and women,' he said, without raising his head.
>
> He saw her . . . snatch up the drawings . . .
>
> 'You do pictures,' she cried, dropping them, 'like that in my house!'
>
> 'They are good,' he cried indignantly . . .
>
> 'Good! She muttered, moving away. 'There's awful your mind must be.' She crouched over the fire. There was no doubt he was daft. She had never seen such evil things put on paper. His mind was horrible. (p. 23)

Arfon only identifies the figures in his drawings as 'men and women' for the benefit of his mother and the 'Normal' society that she represents, and even when he does this, he appears reluctant and non-committal, saying 'men and women' 'without raising his head'. Moreover, just as another of his drawings, of 'a shirt dripping over the fireplace' (p. 22), seems to be a subjective representation of his domestic unhappiness – the narrator observes how the image of the shirt 'seemed to brood in such dejection that it wept' (p. 22) – these figures are clearly projections of Arfon's 'androgynous imagination',[78] of a 'mind' that is not conventionally masculine or gendered and, therefore, that is (in the eyes of 'Normal' Rhondda society) 'awful' and 'daft', or grotesque.

Arfon's 'grotesque' imagination, as manifested in his drawings, might also reflect what M. Wynn Thomas has expressed as 'Welsh Nonconformity's mistrustful highlighting of the artfulness of art' and, in particular, its 'stress on the dangers of the unregulated [artistic] imagination to the actual possessor of it'.[79] Glyn Jones also seems to be touching on this issue in his novel, *The Valley, the City, the Village*, when Trystan, an aspiring painter and aesthete, is not permitted to go to 'art school', and encouraged instead to attend university and 'qualify as a teacher' – a route which, his staunchly Nonconformist grandmother and guardian hopes, may eventually lead to 'the ministry or mission field' (p. 99). From this perspective, Arfon's otherness appears to be symbolic of his incongruous and disconcerting would-be artist status within *buchedd* society. Equally, in rendering the figure of the artist as a grotesque outcast, Davies might be Expressionistically reflecting both 'the middlebrow character of ageing establishment Nonconformity' and 'the aggressive anti-intellectualism of proletarian valleys society'.[80] The distinctively androgynous image of Arfon that repeatedly appears in the 'concave mirror' of Davies's text, however, also has more profoundly transgressive implications. For Arfon's 'grotesque' androgyny might additionally be said to allow Davies to recall, in literary form, his own emerging consciousness of homosexual feelings – his 'early, bewildered sense', to cite M. Wynn Thomas again, 'of difference, of not being as other men were, or at least of not being as other men seemed to be in the "heavily masculine" Rhondda of his youth'.[81] Indeed, Arfon's marginal status as artist might be viewed as complicit with – or as masking and, therefore, enabling – this articulation of homosexual experience. Davies can be seen (as Joseph Allen Boone has said of some American Modernist writers) to

> presage the contemporary understanding of queer subjectivity as the assumption of a defiantly non-normative identity that defines itself primarily in terms of its opposition to the status quo rather than [just] in terms of an opposition between heterosexual and homosexual categories.[82]

There are, in fact, many instances where Arfon's 'queerness' might be construed as a tacit acknowledgment of homosexuality. Davies writes, for example:

> Other youths would have no truck with him [Arfon] because of his queer look and reputation, and though there were girls who were ready enough to be approached, interested in his oddness, he was at the age when, to some sensitive natures, living young women were more fearsome than horned and tailed devils that have brimstone shining under their skin. (p. 23)

Arfon's 'oddness' is explicitly connected with sexuality here: it intrigues young women and, therefore, attracts them to him. This association, in turn, draws out the latent double meaning in the narrator's reference to Arfon's 'queer look and reputation'; that is, the word 'queer' appears to be potentially 'coded'[83] – to denote both 'grotesque' and, covertly, 'gay'. Indeed, the word 'queer' is etymologically linked with the grotesque; as Simon Baker and Joanna Furber point out, it is related to the 'Latin torquere (to twist [or contort])'.[84] Arfon's effeminate or androgynous physical features and demeanour discussed earlier, then, though appertaining to stereotypical images of male homosexuality, may also point towards the subversive duality of his 'queerness', as may his initial indifference to, and extreme sense of alienation from women as sexual beings.[85]

Arfon's 'horrible' drawings also have these sexually transgressive overtones. 'Vigorous', 'proud' and depicted 'naked or draped idly', his 'men and women' are collectively eroticised, and exude a decadence redolent of the illustrations of Aubrey Beardsley. Sexually ambiguous during his life and famous for depicting 'fanciful', androgynous figures in his work,[86] Beardsley became publicly connected with homosexuality when he illustrated Oscar Wilde's play, *Salome*[87] – a text which Davies knew well, and which he discusses at length in *Print of a Hare's Foot*:

> I was surly when I arrived home. But in my overcoat I had a thin book, bought that afternoon . . . After examining its illuminations in startled consternation I had left the shop, taken a walk, and returned to buy it. Random little bombs go off inside one with secret detonations. I took the book up to bed. It was an edition of Salome with the Beardsley drawings. Delight restored my nerves. I kept absorbing the drawings in my feather bed . . . Beardsley taught me that I couldn't draw.[88]

Davies's account of how the figures in Arfon's drawings possessed a 'beauty [that] was not of this world' and his revelation that Arfon also drew 'fanciful things out of the Bible – the tablets of Moses, the doses of Solomon, and the strange beasts of St. John the Divine' (p. 22) – in a way that 'made people either laugh or ill-tempered' (p. 22), reinforce this connection with Beardsley's often grotesque and also, at times, extremely sexually explicit drawings – the latter, in particular, echoing Beardsley's depiction of biblical characters in *Salome*. Arfon's impression of young women as 'fearsome' devils, in fact, recalls the figure of Salome in Wilde's play, who demands that the head of Iokanaan be presented to her on a plate after he resists her sexual advances.

'At last,' Davies finally writes,

> late, he [Arfon] began to long for girls, being seventeen. He forced himself to court one or two in the traditional manner: winking at the favoured across the gallery of the chapel and approaching them after the service for a walk. Some went with him. But he did not like their amusement. They seemed to treat him as a joke and he suffered deeply when they tittered at his high, romantic love-making, that was courteous and poetic. (p. 24)

Yet, even at this point, there is a sense that Arfon has merely learned to accept and conform to an intransigent social code. The way in which Arfon 'at last' becomes sexually curious about women recalls the ironic narrative voice of the story's opening ('Mr. and Mrs. Edwards did not deserve such a child. There was nothing peculiar about them'), and shows how Davies uses free indirect discourse in order to convey the superficial perceptions of an anxiously relieved, 'normal' society. Davies's account of how Arfon belatedly 'forced' himself to 'court one or two [girls] in the traditional manner' is equally suggestive. Indeed, it almost seems, from the way in which he winks 'at the favoured' across the chapel gallery and from his 'courteous and poetic' 'high, romantic love-making', that Arfon is simply impersonating or dramatising what Judith Butler refers to in her essay, 'Imitation and Gender Insubordination' (1991), as 'hegemonic heterosexual norms'.[89] Arfon almost seems to become a kind of grotesque parody of both the typical Rhondda male and the 'gentleman' intellectual – particularly the male 'artist'.

While the girls laugh and joke about this tragicomic posturing, Arfon's behaviour might actually be seen to interrogate and deconstruct both their own, and society's, conception of normality. More specifically, it might be argued that Arfon's behaviour produces what Butler identifies as a 'parodic or imitative effect' akin to that created by 'gay identities', which in turn, like those identities, 'works not to copy or emulate heterosexuality, but rather, to expose heterosexuality as an incessant and panicked imitation of its own naturalized idealization'.[90] As Butler affirms,

> heterosexuality is always in the process of imitating and approximating its own phantasmatic idealization of itself – and failing. Precisely because it is bound to fail, and yet endeavours to succeed, the project of heterosexual identity is propelled into an endless repetition of itself.[91]

Moreover, in portraying heterosexuality as imitative and grotesque in this way, Davies effectively denaturalises it, contravening its perpetual, idealised construction of itself as 'the original, the true, the authentic'[92] and, therefore, as 'the normative measure of the real'.[93]

Indeed, heterosexual relationships in Davies's narratives, far from seeming authentic, normal and ideal, often appear fraudulent, deranged and absurd. The narrator of 'Arfon' reports:

> the day after . . . [Mr. and Mrs. Edwards] married, Mr. Edwards took thirty pounds of . . . [Mrs. Edwards's] money and bought a new horse and cart for his hawking, replacing the old donkey he possessed. He brought her nothing but himself. He bossed her into continuing her pasties business too. Gradually, especially over their mutual disgust for their son, they became of similar temperament . . . (p. 17)

And the relationship that Arfon eventually forges with Dilys is similarly warped – founded on, and sustained by, greed, deceit, frustration and disgust:

> She [Dilys] often kissed Arfon in a sweet, delicious way. Within a month she had received from him the amber beads, a gold-plated watch, and some ear-rings. He cunningly cheated his customers and stole out of the takings and lied to his father about the value of the goods that remained in stock. Nothing mattered but Dilys's pleasure.
>
> But there came a time when he could steal and cheat no more and was left with only a few shillings of pocket money. October came, and Dilys was fancying a little fur to put round her neck . . .
>
> 'A darling little fur I saw in Lewis's window,' she said, 'just like a real fox it looked.'
>
> 'How much was it?' he asked, beginning to be angry.
>
> 'Only forty-five shillings.' She sighed again. 'I wish I wasn't so poor. I don't get a chance to save a shilling a week. My aunt is so miserly.'
>
> He felt, like a mutter deep within him, a revulsion from her rise up, dark and strange. And he thought how mean she was with herself. (pp. 31–2)

The grotesque dynamics of Arfon's relationship with Dilys are also laid bare in his drawings. Like the child in Katherine Mansfield's Modernist short story, 'The Woman at the Store' (1912), whose series of 'repulsively vulgar'[94] drawings culminates in a picture of her mother murdering her negligent, apparently estranged husband 'with a rook rifle and then digging a hole to bury him in' (p. 19), Arfon seems to function as artist truth-teller, revealing the 'ugly' (p. 18) reality underlying a supposedly normal and natural relationship:

> And with a fierce spurt of inspiration he began some new drawings. Of Dilys, clothed and unclothed, as he imagined her. He worked with quick, nervous energy, a heat in his limbs, his mind warmed through. It was as though he was possessing her as he drew.
>
> His inflamed vision did not see what came through in the drawings. In spite of the untamed beauty of his line there was a sinister ugliness in the portraiture of the young girl. A cruel meanness hovered in her face. Had he been aloof from his personal reactions to the living girl he would have seen the masterly vulgarity his strange talent had worked into the drawings. The cruelty of that ugliness emerged in a desperately triumphant way from the luminous beauty of her physical form. (p. 29)

This relationship takes an even more grotesque turn at the end of the story when Arfon lures Dilys onto a mountain and strangles her with the fur from 'Lewis's window':

> He gripped each end of the fur and, crossing them, pulled them tight, at the same moment rising to his feet and thrusting her on her back. He knelt over her, never losing his firm grip of the fur. Her choking cries were strange and awful. He had never heard the like. His own voice uttered quick, deep sighs, that were like groans, while his chest heaved and sank. Tighter and tighter he pulled the fur. And she went silent, though her body continued to throb beneath his legs. (pp. 41–2)

The sexual connotations of Davies's language in this passage – Linden Peach even goes as far as to suggest that the murder is 'redolent of intercourse'[95] – makes the event that it depicts all the more disturbing; and this ending also again foregrounds a connection between Davies's narrative and the fiction of Katherine Mansfield. As Andrew Bennett notes, 'an enduring feature of Mansfield's writing is her analysis of the way that both psychological and physical violence – violent, forced sexuality, in particular – underlie relationships between men and women'.[96] In Mansfield's 1910 short story, 'Frau Brechenmacher Attends a Wedding', for example, the narrator observes how Frau Brechenmacher 'lay down on the bed and put her arm across her face like a child who expected to be hurt as [her drunken husband] Herr Brechenmacher lurched in'.[97] Davies's particular association of heterosexual desire with the macabre, however, is perhaps most reminiscent of *Salome*, calling to mind the closing scene of Wilde's play, in which the heroine eroticises the severed head of Iokannan:

> THE VOICE OF SALOME Ah! I have kissed thy mouth, Iokannan, I have kissed thy mouth. There was a bitter taste on thy lips. Was it the taste of blood? . . . Nay; but perchance it was the taste of love . . . They say that love hath a bitter taste . . . But what matter? what matter? I have kissed thy mouth, Iokannan, I have kissed thy mouth.[98]

Through portraying sexual attraction and interaction between men and women as grotesque, Davies, Wilde, Beardsley and even Mansfield, who, as Bennett points out, was 'fascinated by Wilde'[99] and herself had several lesbian relationships,[100] might be seen as engaged in a similar, Modernist project to denaturalise 'compulsory heterosexuality',[101] as Adrienne Rich calls it, and invert its repeated 'idealization' in society.

Both Gwyn Thomas and Rhys Davies, then, invoke Modernist techniques of the grotesque in their work in order to challenge the contemporary socio-political status quo. In *Oscar*, Thomas develops a narrative style that replicates many of the techniques of European Expressionist art – particularly the *esperpento* plays of Valle-Inclán and the avant-garde puppet-theatre of Lorca – in order to represent and condemn the capitalist exploitation of people in the industrialised south Wales Valleys in the 1930s and 1940s. Rhys Davies's grotesque narratives, on the other hand, expose the inner workings of this society, Expressionistically manifesting what Davies appears to see as its endemic, suffocating 'hypocrisy and narrowness'. Just as Thomas's distortive narrative in *Oscar*, however, can also be interpreted more broadly, as a critique of the capitalist system as a whole, the grotesque also has a more expansive role in Davies's work. Through portraying the relationships that are formed between men and women in his narratives as disturbingly and often outrageously grotesque, Davies effectively denaturalises 'compulsory heterosexuality' and creates a progressive textual space in which there is apparently no 'normal' sexuality – a territory in which, moreover, homosexuality cannot legitimately be singled out, or comparatively defined and dismissed as warped, unnatural and perverse. In essence, the Modernism of Thomas and Davies is politically ambitious and concerned with representing and commenting on social reality – often, specifically, working-class or as Daniel G. Williams has described in his analysis of the 'three strains' of Welsh Modernism, 'proletarian' reality[102] – in a way that challenges narrow literary histories that polarise 'aesthetics and politics',[103] and define Modernism as inherently detached and rarefied in nature and bourgeois in origin. This includes studies such as Kristin Bluemel's *George Orwell and the Radical Eccentrics: Intermodernism in Literary London*, in which Bluemel feels it necessary to coin a new term for politically committed writing of this kind. 'In contrast to modernist writers', she argues, 'intermodern writers tend to have their origins in or maintain contacts with working- or lower-class cultures', have a propensity to 'attend to politics, especially politics that may improve working conditions', and 'pursue narrative strategies that are intellectually and culturally available to ordinary, non-elite, working English men and women'.[104] As her reference to 'ordinary, non-elite, working *English* men and women' suggests, Bluemel does not take into account in her study what I have shown in this book to be the distinct, Modernist socio-cultural conditions of Wales during the first half of the twentieth century. To view Thomas and Davies not as creators of Welsh Modernism, but as British 'intermodernists', moreover, would, effectively, be to continue to overlook and marginalise an important facet of literary Modernism in Wales.

Conclusion

In *On the Margins of Modernism: Decentering Literary Dynamics*, Chana Kronfeld suggests that 'Modernism, with its disruptions of bipolarities and its valorization of the marginal and the eccentric, could train us to look at the old question of literary periodization and typology with a more nuanced, kaleidoscopic gaze.'[1] I have aimed in this book to view the 'periodization' and 'typology' of Modernism with just the kind of searching, 'kaleidoscopic gaze' that Kronfeld advocates. Deleuze and Guattari's *Kafka: Toward a Minor Literature* and Kronfeld's appraisal and expansion of this study have illuminated the Modernist potentiality of a marginal or 'minor' literature such as that of Anglophone Wales. Moreover, Kronfeld's approach, along with the work of Laura Doyle and Laura Winkiel in *Geomodernisms: Race, Modernism, Modernity*, which see Modernism not as a fixed or 'solid thing' (to adapt David Jones's phrase), but as a phenomenon inflected by particulars of time and location, has helped to uncover a distinctive and diverse Anglophone Welsh Modernism in the 1930s and 1940s. I have shown how in the work of a number of writers, this was born of an awareness of a singular modern 'crisis of language' in Wales in the first half of the twentieth century. Occupying an effectively 'deterritorialised' position, set apart from the established domains of English and Welsh-language culture, these writers were effectively engaged in a Modernistic process of linguistic reterritorialisation – in the identification of a voice and a literature representative of modern Anglophone Welsh experience. And yet there is a sense that deterritorialization, dissociation, apartness, is itself a fundamental feature of that experience and of

Anglophone Welsh identity, as these writers' various attractions to intertextuality or textual instability, to the transcendental or other-wordly, the heterotopia and to the distorting mirror of the grotesque, suggest. In this respect, Anglophone Welsh Modernism has much in common with many other Modernist responses to the modern world. What is clear is that if Modernism indeed valorises the 'marginal and the eccentric' then Anglophone Welsh writing deserves further critical scrutiny. There is still much scope for the continued study of Welsh Modernism alongside other international Modernisms – both canonical and non-canonical. This study only constitutes an initial inquiry into the subject of Modernism in Wales: there are many more areas to investigate, including the role of women writers in the creation of a Welsh Modernism – not to mention the nature and significance of Modernism in the Welsh language and its relationship with its Anglophone counterpart.[2] There are earlier writers, such as Caradoc Evans, and later writers such as Tony Conran, whose role in the production of Welsh Modernism could be explored more fully. So Glyn Jones's words, which I cited in chapter four, have, we might say, come full circle: there is, once again, a palpable sense of something 'beginning', 'of something quite new in Wales'. But equally, in turn, there is also a sense that we are venturing deeper into new territory in Modernism studies – a sense (to reinvoke Gwyn Jones's rallying editorial from *The Welsh Review*) that Anglophone Welsh writers could, in this, another 'new age', yet 'shake with new impulse the weary body of English Literature.'

NOTES

Introduction

1. Raymond Williams, 'When Was Modernism?', in *Politics of Modernism: Against the New Conformists*, ed. Tony Pinkney (London and New York: Verso, 2007), pp. 31–5 (p. 34).
2. Raymond Williams, 'When Was Modernism?', pp. 34–5.
3. Daniel G. Williams, for example, discusses Caradoc Evans as a Modernist in his essay, 'Welsh Modernism', in *The Oxford Handbook of Modernisms*, ed. Peter Brooker, Andrzej Gasiorek, Deborah Longworth and Andrew Thacker (Oxford and New York: Oxford University Press, 2010), pp. 797–816. Williams argues that Evans's '*My People* may be best viewed as a distinctively modernist, inherently reflexive collection of stories' in which the author's 'fabricated Welsh vernacular functioned surrealistically to distort and to critique a rural reality'; see Daniel G. Williams, 'Welsh Modernism', p. 803.
4. Christopher Wigginton, *Modernism from the Margins: The 1930s Poetry of Louis MacNeice and Dylan Thomas* (Cardiff: University of Wales Press, 2007), p. 111.
5. John Goodby and Chris Wigginton, 'Welsh Modernist Poetry: Dylan Thomas, David Jones and Lynette Roberts', in *Regional Modernisms*, ed. Neal Alexander and James Moran (Edinburgh: Edinburgh University Press, 2013), pp. 160–83 (p. 163).
6. Daniel G. Williams, *Black Skin, Blue Books: African Americans and Wales, 1845–1945* (Cardiff: University of Wales Press, 2012), p. 140. See also Daniel G. Williams, 'Welsh Modernism', in *The Oxford Handbook of Modernisms*, pp. 797–816.
7. Daniel G. Williams, *Black Skin Blue Books*, p. 87.
8. Malcolm Bradbury, 'The Cities of Modernism', in *Modernism: A Guide to European Literature 1890–1930*, ed. Malcolm Bradbury and James McFarlane (London: Penguin, 1976), pp. 96–104 (p. 96).
9. See Alexander and Moran (eds), *Regional Modernisms*.
10. Laura Doyle and Laura Winkiel, 'Introduction', in Doyle and Winkiel

(eds), *Geomodernisms: Race, Modernism, Modernity* (Bloomington and Indianapolis: Indiana University Press, 2005), p. 3.

11 Doyle and Winkiel, 'Introduction', in *Geomodernisms*, p. 3.

12 Doyle and Winkiel, 'Introduction', in *Geomodernisms*, p. 3.

13 Gilles Deleuze and Félix Guattari, *Kafka: Toward a Minor Literature*, translated from the French by Dana Polan (Minneapolis: University of Minnesota Press, 1986), p. 18.

14 I thank Daniel G. Williams for drawing my attention to this book.

15 Richard Sheppard, 'The Crisis of Language', in *Modernism: A Guide to European Literature 1890–1930*, ed. Malcolm Bradbury and James McFarlane, pp. 323–36 (p. 323).

16 Tony Conran, *Frontiers in Anglo-Welsh Poetry* (Cardiff: University of Wales Press, 1997), p. 113.

1: 'The dissolving and splitting of solid things': Welsh Modernism's 'crisis of language'

1 Sheppard, 'The Crisis of Language', p. 323.

2 Elizabeth McCombie, 'Introduction', in *Stéphane Mallarmé: Collected Poems and Other Verse*, translated from the French by E. H. and A. M. Blackmore (Oxford and New York: Oxford University Press, 2006), pp. ix–xxvii (p. xiv).

3 As Clive Scott suggests, 'most fundamentally [Symbolism] . . . awakened an acute consciousness of language. Language was no longer treated as a natural outcrop of the person but as a material with its own laws and its own peculiar forms of life'; Clive Scott, 'Symbolism, Decadence and Impressionism', in *Modernism: A Guide to European Literature 1890–1930*, ed. Malcolm Bradbury and James McFarlane, pp. 206–27 (p. 212).

4 Arthur Rimbaud, *A Season in Hell*, in *Arthur Rimbaud: Collected Poems*, translated from the French by Martin Sorrell (Oxford and New York: Oxford University Press, 2001), p. 235. All further references to Rimbaud's poems are to this edition and are given in the text.

5 McCombie, 'Introduction', in *Stéphane Mallarmé: Collected Poems and Other Verse*, p. xvii.

6 Ferdinand de Saussure, *Course in General Linguistics*, ed. Charles Bally and Albert Sechehaye, translated from the French by Wade Baskin (New York: McGraw-Hill, 1966), pp. 67–9. Saussure suggests that the linguistic sign 'unites, not a thing and a name, but a concept [a signified] and a sound image [a signifier]. The latter is not a material sound, a purely physical thing, but the psychological imprint of the sound, the impression that it makes on our senses . . . The linguistic sign is then a two-sided psychological entity'; Saussure, *Course in General Linguistics*, p. 66. Saussure's ideas were published posthumously as *Cours de linguistique générale* (1916).

7 Saussure, *Course in General Linguistics*, p. 120.

8 Saussure, *Course in General Linguistics*, p. 120.

9 T. S. Eliot, 'The Love Song of J. Alfred Prufrock', in *T. S. Eliot: Collected Poems 1909–1962* (London: Faber and Faber, 1974), p. 6. All further references to Eliot's poems are to this edition and are given in the text.

[10] T.S. Eliot, *The Waste Land*, p. 54, ll. 37–41.
[11] Eliot, *The Waste Land*, p. 69, ll. 424–31.
[12] T. S. Eliot, 'East Coker', p. 190.
[13] Franz Kafka, 'The Metamorphosis', in *The Complete Short Stories of Franz Kafka*, ed. Nahum N. Glatzer, translated from the German by Willa and Edwin Muir (London: Vintage, 1999), pp. 89–139 (p. 89). All further references to Kafka's stories are to this edition and are given in the text.
[14] Filippo Tommaso Marinetti, 'The Founding and Manifesto of Futurism', translated from the French by R. W. Flint, in *Modernism: An Anthology of Sources and Documents*, ed. Vassiliki Kolocotroni, Jane Goldman and Olga Taxidou (Edinburgh: Edinburgh University Press, 1998), pp. 249–53 (p. 251).
[15] Marinetti, 'The Founding and Manifesto of Futurism', p. 251.
[16] Filippo Tommaso Marinetti, 'Technical Manifesto of Futurist Literature', in *Marinetti: Selected Writings*, translated from the Italian by R. W. Flint and Arthur A. Coppotelli (New York: Farrar, Straus and Giroux, 1972), pp. 84–93 (p. 89).
[17] André Breton, 'First Manifesto of Surrealism', translated from the French by Richard Seaver and Helen R. Lane, in *Modernism: An Anthology of Sources and Documents*, ed. Vassiliki Kolocotroni, Jane Goldman and Olga Taxidou, pp. 307–11 (p. 308).
[18] Breton, 'The First Manifesto of Surrealism', p. 309.
[19] Sheppard, 'The Crisis of Language', p. 328.
[20] Sheppard, 'The Crisis of Language', p. 328. Sheppard's argument is adapted from Roland Barthes's study of modern poetic writing, *Writing Degree Zero* (1953).
[21] Sylvia Martin, *Futurism* (Cologne: Taschen, 2006), p. 66.
[22] Andzej Gasiorek, *Wyndham Lewis and Modernism* (Tavistock: Northcote House, 2004), p. 17.
[23] Walter Benjamin, 'Surrealism: The Last Snapshot of the European Intelligentsia', in *Walter Benjamin: Selected Writings 1927–1934*, ed. Michael W. Jennings, Howard Eiland, and Gary Smith (Cambridge, MA, and London: Harvard University Press, 1999), II. 206–21 (p. 212). Benjamin's essay was first published in 1929.
[24] Conran, *Frontiers in Anglo-Welsh Poetry*, p. 1.
[25] Saunders Lewis, *Is there an Anglo-Welsh Literature? Being the Annual Lecture Delivered to the Branch on December 10th, 1938* (Cardiff: Urdd Graddedigion Prifysgol Cymru, 1939), p. 3.
[26] Deleuze and Guattari, *Kafka*, p. 18.
[27] Peter Elfed Lewis, 'Poetry in the Thirties: A View of the "First Flowering"', *The Anglo-Welsh Review*, n.s. 71 (1982), 50–74 (p. 50). It should be noted, however, that this 'first flowering' did not signify the beginning of Welsh writing in English. A number of writers, notably Allen Raine (Anne Adaliza Puddicombe née Evans), Amy Dillwyn and Bertha Thomas, were publishing works in English at the end of the nineteenth and beginning of the twentieth centuries.
[28] M. Wynn Thomas, *Internal Difference: Literature in Twentieth-Century Wales* (Cardiff: University of Wales Press, 1992), p. 26.
[29] Conran, *Frontiers in Anglo-Welsh Poetry*, p. 52.

[30] Conran, *Frontiers in Anglo-Welsh Poetry*, p. 51.
[31] Deleuze and Guattari, *Kafka*, p. 18.
[32] Deleuze and Guattari, *Kafka*, p. 18.
[33] Deleuze and Guattari, *Kafka*, p. 18.
[34] Deleuze and Guattari, *Kafka*, p. 18. 'Minor', in this context, does not of course mean 'inferior' or 'unimportant', but simply refers to Anglophone Welsh literature's minority-position within a dominant language and culture.
[35] Deleuze and Guattari, *Kafka*, p. 19.
[36] Chana Kronfeld, *On the Margins of Modernism: Decentering Literary Dynamics* (Berkeley and London: University of California Press, 1996), p. 8.
[37] Kronfeld, *On the Margins of Modernism*, p. 8.
[38] Kronfeld, *On the Margins of Modernism*, p. 12.
[39] Glyn Jones, 'Gwyn Thomas', in *The Dragon has Two Tongues: Essays on Anglo-Welsh Writers and Writing*, ed. Tony Brown, 2nd edn (Cardiff: University of Wales Press, 2001), pp. 100–16 (p. 102).
[40] Glyn Jones, 'Gwyn Thomas', p. 106.
[41] Glyn Jones, 'Gwyn Thomas', p. 116.
[42] Stephen Knight, *A Hundred Years of Fiction: Writing Wales in English* (Cardiff: University of Wales Press, 2004), p. 93.
[43] Knight, *A Hundred Years of Fiction*, p. 93.
[44] Walford Davies, 'The Poetry of Dylan Thomas: Welsh Contexts, Narrative and the Language of Modernism', in *Dylan Thomas: Contemporary Critical Essays*, ed. John Goodby and Chris Wigginton (Basingstoke: Palgrave, 2001), pp. 106–23 (p. 110).
[45] Walford Davies, 'The Poetry of Dylan Thomas', p. 110.
[46] Michael Parnell, *Laughter from the Dark: A Life of Gwyn Thomas* (London: John Murray, 1988), p. 8.
[47] John Davies explains how the Welsh Intermediate Education Act of 1889 saw the establishment of 'county schools' in Wales that 'slavishly imitated the ethos and curriculum of the English grammar schools…'. Davies notes that 'many of the early headteachers [at these schools] came from England and the atmosphere of the schools was completely English; in 1907, only forty-seven of the county schools offered Welsh lessons, and nobody suggested that the language should be used as a medium of instruction'; see John Davies, *A History of Wales* (London: Penguin, 1994), pp. 458–9.
[48] As Parnell notes, 'South Wales, and especially the Rhondda, had during the nineteenth century seen a huge influx of workers from Cornwall, the west Country, Yorkshire, and Ireland, as well as numerous others from Italy and Spain, and all these brought English either as their own language or as a lingua franca, and none of them understood Welsh at all. At another level, the education system was in various ways promoting English in preference to Welsh, it being far more 'convenient' to deal in one language only, and English, as they saw it, with its worldwide importance and its great heritage of literature to recommend it, was obviously more "desirable"'; *Laughter in the Dark*, pp. 8–9.
[49] Parnell, *Laughter in the Dark*, p. 9.
[50] Gwyn Thomas cited in Parnell, *Laughter in the* Dark, p. 9.
[51] Glyn Jones, 'Gwyn Thomas', p. 102.

[52] Gwyn Thomas, *Sorrow for thy Sons* (London: Lawrence and Wishart, 1986), p. 23. All further references are to this edition and are given in the text.

[53] Gwyn Thomas, 'Myself My Desert', in *Where did I put Pity?: Folk Tales from the Modern Welsh* (London: Progress Publishing, 1946), pp. 183–93 (p. 185). All further references are to this edition and are given in the text.

[54] Gwyn Thomas, *Oscar*, in *The Dark Philosophers* (Cardigan: Parthian, Library of Wales Series, 2006), pp. 3–101 (p. 3). All further references are to this edition and are given in the text.

[55] Tony Conran, *The Cost of Strangeness: Essays on the English Poets of Wales* (Llandysul: Gomer, 1982), p. 27.

[56] M. Wynn Thomas, *Corresponding Cultures: The Two Literatures of Wales* (Cardiff: University of Wales Press, 1999), p. 61.

[57] Wynn Thomas, *Corresponding Cultures*, p. 61.

[58] Parnell, *Laughter in the Dark*, p. 8.

[59] Stephen Knight discusses Thomas's 'capacity . . . for writing the hybrid stories characteristic of colonized writers, where some aspects of native tradition are interwoven with the modern situation of the society, in the language and the techniques – with some appropriate hybridizing revisions – of the colonizing culture'; *A Hundred Years of Fiction*, p. 97.

[60] Deleuze and Guattari, *Kafka*, p. 22.

[61] Deleuze and Guattari, *Kafka*, p. 22. Deleuze and Guatarri use Prague German as an example of this, noting its 'incorrect use of prepositions' and its 'employment of malleable verbs' (p. 23).

[62] It should be noted that Thomas's frequent emulation of the dialect of the south Wales Valleys also has this effect; for example, the narrator describes how, when Alf gave Annie a newspaper, 'she called him a bloody cleversticks of hell, rolled the paper into a tight tampy ball and flung it in Alf's face' (p. 16).

[63] Glyn Jones, 'Gwyn Thomas', p. 116.

[64] Bertolt Brecht, 'A Short Organum for the Theatre', in *Brecht on Theatre: The Development of an Aesthetic*, translated from the German by John Willet (London: Methuen, 1964), pp. 179–205 (p. 192).

[65] Bertolt Brecht, 'Short Description of a New Technique of Acting which Produces an Alienation Effect', in *Brecht on Theatre: The Development of an Aesthetic*, pp. 136–47 (p. 144–5). Gwyn Thomas wrote several plays later in his literary career.

[66] Wynn Thomas, *Corresponding Cultures*, p. 61.

[67] T. S. Eliot, 'The Metaphysical Poets', in *T. S. Eliot: Selected Essays*, 2nd edn (London: Faber and Faber, 1934), pp. 281–91 (p. 289).

[68] Thomas's use of the word 'plumb' is also unusual. Here, 'out of plumb' is interpreted as 'inexact'.

[69] James Joyce, *Ulysses* (London: Minerva, 1992), p. 177.

[70] I look more closely at the role of the grotesque in Thomas's work in chapter five.

[71] Deleuze and Guattari, *Kafka*, p. 19.

[72] Deleuze and Guattari, *Kafka*, p. 19.

[73] As Ian Gregson observes, Deleuze and Guattari 'celebrate minority status for being seized upon by . . . writers (who include, they say, [Kafka] Joyce and

Beckett) as a powerful opportunity to evolve a literature which undermines the stale authority of the major culture'; *The New Poetry in Wales* (Cardiff: University of Wales Press, 2007), p. 2.

74 M. Wynn Thomas, *In the Shadow of the Pulpit: Literature and Nonconformist Wales* (Cardiff: University of Wales Press, 2010), pp. 149, 156, 155.

75 Gwyn Thomas, 'Dust in the Lonely Wind', in *Where did I put Pity?*, pp. 148–70 (p. 154).

76 Glyn Jones, 'Gwyn Thomas', p. 116.

77 Gwyn Thomas, 'And a Spoonful of Grief to Taste', in *Where did I put Pity?*, pp. 171–82 (p. 171).

78 Glyn Jones, '18 Poems Again', *Poetry Wales*, n.s. 9 (1973–4), 22–6 (24).

79 Wynn Thomas, *Internal Difference*, p. 26.

80 Breton, 'First Manifesto of Surrealism', p. 309.

81 Dylan Thomas, 'The Lemon', in *Dylan Thomas: The Collected Stories* (London: J. M. Dent, 1984), pp. 54–8 (p. 55).

82 Wynn Thomas, *In the Shadow of the Pulpit*, p. 235.

83 Wynn Thomas, *In the Shadow of the Pulpit*, p. 251.

84 Deleuze and Guatarri, *Kafka*, p. 27.

85 Deleuze and Guatarri, *Kafka*, p. 24. Deleuze and Guattari use this phrase in their discussion of 'the breakdown and fall of the [Habsburg] empire', which they suggest 'accentuates everywhere movements of deterritorialization, and invites all sorts of complex reterritorializations' (p. 24). We might argue, similarly, that 'the movements of deterritorialization' and 'reterritorialization' within Welsh writing in English are symptomatic of, and inspired by, the depletion of the British Empire.

86 Glyn Jones, 'Autobiography', in *The Dragon has Two Tongues*, pp. 5–36 (p. 9).

87 Tony Brown, 'Introduction: The Making of a Writer', in *The Collected Stories of Glyn Jones*, ed. Tony Brown (Cardiff: University of Wales Press, 1999), pp. xiii–lxvi (p. xxiii). As Brown notes, 'by the time Glyn Jones became involved in the chapel, the week-night activities for the young people . . . were all conducted in English . . . although the Sunday services were still held in Welsh (pp. xxii–xxiii).

88 Glyn Jones, 'Autobiography', p. 37.

89 Glyn Jones, 'Autobiography', p. 37. As Dafydd Johnston notes, the *cywydd* form consisted of 'couplets of seven-syllable lines, with end-rhyme alternately stressed and unstressed'. Johnston explains how 'by the fifteenth century the *cywydd* had become established as the standard form for all types of poetry, so that the poets of the period are often referred to in Welsh as *Cywyddwyr*'; *The Literature of Wales: A Pocket Guide* (Cardiff: University of Wales Press, 1998), p. 34.

90 Tony Brown, 'Introduction', p. xxix.

91 Glyn Jones cited in Tony Brown, 'Introduction', p. xxix.

92 Glyn Jones, 'Conclusion', in *The Dragon has Two Tongues: Essays on Anglo-Welsh Writers and Writing*, ed. Tony Brown, 2nd edn (Cardiff: University of Wales Press, 2001), pp. 192–6 (p. 196).

93 Glyn Jones, 'Porth-y-Rhyd', in *The Collected Stories of Glyn Jones*, ed. Tony Brown (Cardiff: University of Wales Press, 1999), pp. 85–90 (p. 85). All further references are to this edition and are given in the text.

[94] Tony Brown, 'Notes', in *The Collected Stories of Glyn Jones*, pp. 354–402 (p. 365).
[95] Brown, 'Notes', p. 365.
[96] Brown, 'Notes', p. 365.
[97] As Johnston suggests, 'two essential features of the Welsh poetic tradition are its antiquity and the continuity of its central theme of praise'; *The Literature of Wales*, p. 1.
[98] Tony Brown points out that every August, throughout his life, 'Jones was in Carmarthenshire staying with his father's relatives, an annual visit to rural, Welsh-speaking Wales which . . . provided him with another world about which to write, far away from the scruffy urban world of Merthyr'; Brown, 'Introduction', p. xvii.
[99] Tony Brown, 'Glyn Jones and the "Uncanny"', *Almanac: A Yearbook of Welsh Writing in English – Critical Essays*, ed. Katie Gramich, n.s. 12 (2007–8), 89–114 (89).
[100] Nicholas Royle, *The Uncanny* (Manchester and New York: Manchester University Press, 2003), p. 6.
[101] Brown, 'Notes', p. 366.
[102] Entitled *Llyfr Gwyn Rhydderch* and *Llyfr Coch Hergest* in Welsh, these books contain the eleven tales that comprise the *Mabinogion*; Johnston, *The Literature of Wales*, p. 17.
[103] Johnston, *The Literature of Wales*, p. 17. As Johnston notes, the Welsh Triads are 'surviving fragments and allusions to lost [medieval] tales' in which 'characters and episodes are arranged in groups of three as a mnemonic device'; *The Literature of Wales*, p. 17.
[104] Glyn Jones, 'The Apple-Tree', in *The Collected Stories of Glyn Jones*, pp. 91–8 (p. 91). All further references are to this edition and are given in the text.
[105] Royle, *The Uncanny*, p. 2.
[106] Brown, 'Notes', p. 367.
[107] Wynn Thomas, *Corresponding Cultures*, p. 61.
[108] '*Cefn*' translates literally into English as 'back'; Brown, 'Notes', p. 365.
[109] Gerard Manley Hopkins, 'The Windhover', in *Gerard Manley Hopkins: Selected Poems*, ed. Catherine Phillips (Oxford and New York: Oxford University Press, 1998), p. 117, ll. 2–4.
[110] Catherine Phillips, 'Introduction', in *Gerard Manley Hopkins*, pp. xi–xvi (p. xv). Glyn Jones wrote an essay on 'Hopkins and Welsh Prosody' in *Life and Letters Today*, 21–2 (1939), 51–4.
[111] Glyn Jones, *The Valley, the City, the Village* (Cardigan: Parthian, Library of Wales Series, 2009), p. 5. All further references are to this edition and are given in the text.
[112] Stevie Davies, 'Foreword', in Glyn Jones, *The Valley, the City, the* Village, pp. ix–xv (p. xii).
[113] Meic Stephens, 'Notes on the Poems', in *The Collected Poems of Glyn Jones*, ed. Meic Stephens (Cardiff: University of Wales Press, 1996), pp. 133–66 (p. 140).
[114] Glyn Jones, 'Man', in *The Collected Poems of Glyn Jones*, p. 9. All further references to Jones's poems are to this edition and are given in the text.
[115] Breton, 'First Manifesto of Surrealism', p. 309.

116 Meic Stephens notes that 'he pointed out to GJ that there is a Sandde Bryd Angel (Sandde Angel-Face) in *The Mabinogion*, whom no one will engage in battle because he is so handsome, [and] he confirmed that it was there that he had found the name'; Stephens, 'Notes on the Poems', p. 140.
117 Stephens, 'Notes on the Poems', p. 140.
118 Glyn Jones, 'Sande', in *The Collected Poems of Glyn Jones*, ed. Meic Stephens (Cardiff: University of Wales Press, 1996), pp. 7–8.
119 *The Collected Poems of Glyn Jones*, p. 265.
120 *The Collected Poems of Glyn Jones*, p. 263.
121 Elfed Lewis, 'Poetry in the Thirties', p. 65.
122 Lewis, 'Is there an Anglo-Welsh Literature?', p. 13.
123 Bruce Griffiths, 'His Theatre', in *Presenting Saunders Lewis*, ed. Alun R. Jones and Gwyn Thomas (Cardiff: University of Wales Press, 1973), pp. 79–92 (p. 79).
124 Saunders Lewis, cited in Bruce Griffiths, '*The Eve of Saint John* and the Significance of the Stranger in the Plays of Saunders Lewis', in *Welsh Writing in English*, n.s. 3 (1997), 62–77 (66).
125 Saunders Lewis, cited in Bruce Griffiths, '*The Eve of Saint John*', 75. Lewis made this comment in an article entitled 'Anglo-Welsh theatre: the problem of language', in *Cambria Daily Leader* (10 September 1919).
126 Conran, *Frontiers in Anglo-Welsh Poetry*, p. 51.
127 Dafydd Johnston, 'Idris Davies's Life', in *The Complete Poems of Idris Davies*, ed. Dafydd Johnston (Cardiff: University of Wales Press 1994), pp. xi–xxxv (p. xiii).
128 Johnston, 'Idris Davies's Life', p. xiii.
129 Johnston, 'Idris Davies's Life', pp. xiii–xiv.
130 Idris Davies, 'I Was Born in Rhymney', in *The Complete Poems of Idris Davies*, p. 78. All further references to Davies's poems are to this edition and are given in the text.
131 Conran, *Frontiers in Anglo-Welsh Poetry*, p. 45.
132 Conran, *Frontiers in Anglo-Welsh Poetry*, p. 45.
133 Conran, *Frontiers in Anglo-Welsh Poetry*, p. 9. As Conran notes, the *buchedd* originated from 'the Methodist Awakening [in Wales] in the eighteenth century' (p. 2).
134 Conran, *Frontiers in Anglo-Welsh Poetry*, p. 1.
135 Johnston describes this technique as 'characteristic of the era of [governmental] Mass-Observation'; Dafydd Johnston, 'The Development of Idris Davies's Poetry', pp. xxxvi–lxxx (p. lvii).
136 Conran, *Frontiers in Anglo-Welsh Poetry*, pp. 43–4.
137 Idris Davies, *Gwalia Deserta*, p. 3. Conran notes that Welsh hymn-writers often used the phrase 'balm of Gilead' as 'a metaphor for healing – and particularly spiritual healing'; Conran, *Frontiers in Anglo-Welsh Poetry*, p. 44.
138 Conran, *Frontiers in Anglo-Welsh Poetry*, p. 9.
139 Conran, *Frontiers in Anglo-Welsh Poetry*, p. 10.
140 Daniel G. Williams, *Black Skin, Blue Books*, p. 114.
141 Davies's next poetic sequence, *The Angry Summer* (1943) – a text that is stylistically reminiscent of *Gwalia Deserta* – was accepted for publication by Eliot for his firm, Faber and Faber.
142 Conran, *Frontiers in Anglo-Welsh Poetry*, pp. 54–5.

[143] Glyn Jones, 'Notes on Surrealism', translated from the Welsh by Tony Brown, *The New Welsh Review*, 28 (1995) 20–2 (22).
[144] Dafydd Johnston points out that Davies admired the English Romantic poets, John Keats, William Wordsworth and Percy Bysshe Shelley; 'The Development of Idris Davies's poetry', p. xxxix.
[145] Johnston, 'The Development of Idris Davies's poetry', p. xlii.
[146] Wigginton, *Modernism from the Margins*, p. 30.
[147] Johnston, 'The Development of Idris Davies's poetry', p. xxxviii.
[148] This poem can also be viewed, as Johnston suggests, as a reflection of Davies's 'humanistic interpretation of Christianity'; 'The Development of Idris Davies's Poetry', p. xxxvii.
[149] Dafydd Johnston 'Notes to Section A', in *The Complete Poems of Idris Davies*, pp. 277–89 (p. 278). As Johnston notes, Davies's 'thoroughly religious upbringing provided a source for much of [his poetic] language and imagery, drawn both from the Bible and Welsh hymnology'; 'The Development of Idris Davies's Poetry', p. xxxvi.
[150] Tony Conran, 'Introduction', in Idris Davies, *The Angry Summer: A Poem of 1926* (Cardiff: University of Wales Press, 1993), pp. xiii–xxxii (p. xxvii).
[151] Conran, *Frontiers in Anglo-Welsh Poetry*, p. 52.
[152] John Fordham, *James Hanley: Modernism and the Working Class* (Cardiff: University of Wales Press, 2002), p. 90.
[153] European Expressionism is discussed in more detail in chapter five.
[154] Wynn Thomas, *Corresponding Cultures*, p. 53. For further discussions of Jones's relationship with Modernism, see M. Wynn Thomas, *Corresponding Cultures*, pp. 100–10 and Laura Wainwright, 'The huge upright Europe-reflecting mirror': The European Dimension in the Early Short Stories and Poems of Glyn Jones', in *Almanac: A Yearbook of Welsh Writing in English – Critical Essays*, ed. Katie Gramich, n.s. 12 (2007–8), 55–88.
[155] Doyle and Winkiel, 'Introduction', in *Geomodernisms*, p. 3.
[156] Doyle and Winkiel, 'Introduction', in *Geomodernisms*, p. 3.
[157] Deleuze and Guattari, *Kafka*, p. 25.
[158] Kronfeld, *On the Margins of Modernism*, p. 8. Kronfeld notes that 'clearly, minor writing existed before modernism . . . and will continue to exist after it', and therefore warns that 'to conflate the minor and the modernist without providing any historical criteria of contextualisation is to blur the temporality and cultural specificity of both' (p. 8).
[159] Conran, *Frontiers in Anglo-Welsh Poetry*, p. 71.
[160] Anne Price-Owen, 'Introduction', in *David Jones: Diversity in Unity* (Cardiff: University of Wales Press, 2000), pp. 1–10 (p. 3).
[161] Jeremy Hooker, 'David Jones and the Matter of Wales', in *David Jones: Diversity in Unity* (Cardiff: University of Wales Press, 2000), pp. 11–25 (p. 11).
[162] Conran, *Frontiers in Anglo-Welsh Poetry*, p. 71.
[163] Hooker, 'David Jones and the Matter of Wales', p. 11.
[164] Jeremy Hooker, *Imagining Wales: A View of Modern Welsh Writing in English* (Cardiff: University of Wales Press, 2001), p. 40.
[165] Patrick McGuinness, 'Preface', in *Lynette Roberts: Collected Poems*, ed. Patrick McGuinness (Manchester: Carcanet, 2005), pp. ix–xxxix (p. xii).
[166] Hooker, *Imagining Wales*, p. 11.

[167] David Jones, 'Preface' in David Jones, *In Parenthesis* (London: Faber and Faber, 1961), pp. ix–xv (p. x).
[168] Johnston, *The Literature of Wales*, p. 5.
[169] Johnston, *The Literature of Wales*, p. 5.
[170] David Jones, *In Parenthesis* (London: Faber and Faber, 1961), p. 133. All further references are to this edition and are given in the text.
[171] David Jones, 'Welsh Poetry', in *Epoch and Artist: Selected Writings by David Jones*, ed. Harman Grisewood (London: Faber and Faber, 1959), pp. 56–65 (pp. 57–8).
[172] David Jones, 'Welsh Poetry', p. 57.
[173] David Jones, 'Notes', p. 199.
[174] Paul Fussell, *The Great War and Modern Memory*, 2nd edn (New York: Oxford University Press, 1975), p. 154.
[175] David Jones, 'Notes', p. 199.
[176] Sioned Davies (trans.), *How Culhwch Won Olwen*, in *The Mabinogion* (Oxford: Oxford University Press, 2007), pp. 179–213 (p. 197).
[177] Sioned Davies (trans.), *How Culhwch Won Olwen*, p. 197.
[178] Johnston, *The Literature of Wales*, p. 22.
[179] This reference to *Culhwch ac Olwen* also seems to relate to Jones's ironic treatment of the theme of heroism. As Johnston notes, 'the action [of *Culhwch ac Olwen*] is often farcical, and gives the impression of being a burlesque of the traditional hero tales', *The Literature of Wales*, p. 22.
[180] David Jones, 'Preface', p. x.
[181] David Jones, 'Preface', p. xv.
[182] Taliesin, 'Book of Taliesin XXX', translated from the Welsh by R Williams, in William F. Skene, *The Four Ancient Books of Wales: Containing the Cymric Poems attributed to the Bards of the Sixth Century* (Edinburgh: Edmonston and Douglas, 1868), I. 265. All further references are to this edition and are given in the text.
[183] David Jones, 'Notes', p. 200.
[184] David Jones, 'Notes', p. 200.
[185] 'Uffern' is the usual Welsh word for Hell, cognate with 'inferno'.
[186] David Jones, 'Notes', p. 200. Lady Charlotte Guest was the first translator of the *Mabinogion* into English (1849).
[187] Caradoc Evans, 'Be this Her Memorial', in *My People* (Bridgend: Seren, 1987), pp. 108–12 (p. 108). All further references to Evans's stories are to this edition and are given in the text.
[188] Conran, *The Cost of Strangeness*, p. 161.
[189] Conran, *The Cost of Strangeness*, p. 161.
[190] Conran, *The Cost of Strangeness*, p. 161.
[191] David Jones, 'Notes, p. 199.
[192] David Jones, 'Notes, p. 199.
[193] Samuel Taylor Coleridge, 'The Rime of the Ancient Mariner', in *Samuel Taylor Coleridge: Poems*, ed. John Beer (London: Dent, 1963), I. 51–78. All further references are to this edition and are given in the text.
[194] David Jones, 'Notes', p. 201.
[195] D. S. Evans (trans.), 'Red Book of Hergest IV', in William F. Skene, *The Four Ancient Books of Wales*, I. 589.

[196] Aneirin, *Y Gododdin: Britain's Oldest Heroic Poem*, translated from the Welsh by A. O. H. Jarman (Llandysul: Gomer, 1988), p. 64, ll. 947–69.

[197] David Jones, 'Notes', p. 220.

[198] David Jones, 'Notes', p. 220.

[199] William Shakespeare, *Henry V*, ed. Gary Taylor (Oxford and New York: Oxford University Press, 1984), II. iii. ll. 1–10. Jones invokes Henry V throughout *In Parenthesis*, drawing parallels between the British army in the First World War and the uniting, in Shakespeare's play, of soldiers from various parts of the British Isles in battle against the French. Among the soldiers in *Henry V* is a Welshman, Captain Fluellen, who is aligned with the figure of Dai Greatcoat in Jones's poem.

[200] Fussell, *The Great War and Modern Memory*, p. 145.

[201] David Jones, 'Notes', p. 211.

[202] Wigginton, *Modernism from the Margins*, p. 111.

[203] Joe Cleary, 'Introduction: Ireland and Modernity', in *The Cambridge Companion to Modern Irish Culture*, ed. Joe Cleary and Claire Connolly (Cambridge: Cambridge University Press, 2005), pp. 1–21 (p. 2).

[204] Hooker, *Diversity in Unity*, p. 12.

[205] Thomas Dilworth, *Reading David Jones* (Cardiff: University of Wales Press, 2008), p. 20.

[206] Duncan Campbell, 'David Jones: "No End to these Wars, No End, No End/At All"', in *Wales at War: Critical Essays on Literature and Art*, ed. Tony Curtis (Bridgend: Seren, 2007), pp. 25–38 (p. 31).

[207] David Jones, 'Notes', p. 211.

[208] D. S. Evans (trans.), 'The Black Book of Carmarthen XXXVIII', in William F. Skene, *The Four Ancient Books of Wales*, I. 302.

[209] As Jones points out in his notes, *Sospan Fach* is 'associated with Rugby Football matches'. Jones adds, 'I am indebted to the secretary of Llanelly Rugby Football club, who kindly provided me with a copy of this song'; 'Notes', p. 201. John Davies describes how 'the rugby clubs could draw upon the strong tradition of communal activity which had taken root in the industrial districts of Wales'; *A History of Wales*, p. 440.

[210] In accordance with the Futurist philosophy, however, Tullio Crali's painting is a celebration rather than an indictment of war.

[211] August Stramm, 'Guard-Duty', translated from the German by Patrick Bridgewater, in *The Penguin Book of First World War Poetry*, ed. Jon Silkin, 2nd edn (Harmondsworth: Penguin, 1979), p. 240.

[212] Richard Sheppard, 'The Poetry of August Stramm: A Suitable Case for Deconstruction', *Journal of European Studies*, n.s. 15/261 (1985). Available at *http://jes.sagepub.com/cgi/reprint/15/4/261* (accessed 18 January 2008).

[213] Georg Trakl, 'Night', translated from the German by David McDuff, Jon Silkin and R. S. Furness, in *The Penguin Book of First World War Poetry*, p. 231.

[214] Malcolm Bradbury and James Mcfarlane, 'Brief Biographies', in *Modernism: A Guide to European Literature 1890–1930*, pp. 613–40 (p. 637). Trakl committed suicide in 1914 while serving on the Eastern Front; Bradbury and Mcfarlane, 'Brief Biographies', p. 637.

[215] Kronfeld, *On the Margins of Modernism*, p. 4.

216 Gwyn Jones, 'Editorial', *The Welsh Review*, n.s. 1 (February 1939), 3–7 (3–4).
217 Peter Nicholls, 'Preface to the Second Edition', in *Modernisms: A Literary Guide*, 2nd edn (Basingstoke and New York: Palgrave Macmillan, 2009), p. viii.

Chapter 2: 'Always observant and slightly obscure': Lynette Roberts as Welsh Modernist

1 Patrick McGuinness, 'Introduction', in *Lynette Roberts: Diaries, Letters and Recollections*, ed. Patrick McGuinness (Manchester: Carcanet, 2008), pp. vii–xvii (p. viii).
2 Patrick McGuinness, 'Introduction', in *Lynette Roberts: Diaries, Letters and Recollections*, p. ix.
3 Patrick McGuinness, 'Introduction', in *Lynette Roberts: Diaries, Letters and Recollections*, p. x.
4 Lynette Roberts, 'Poem from Llanybri', in *Lynette Roberts: Collected Poems*, ed. Patrick McGuinness (Manchester: Carcanet, 2005), p. 3. All further references to Roberts's poems are to this edition and are given in the text.
5 Tony Conran, 'Lynette Roberts: The Lyric Pieces', *Poetry Wales*, n.s. 19/2, 125–33 (132).
6 Johnston, *The Literature of Wales*, p. 42.
7 Johnston, *The Literature of Wales*, p. 35.
8 Conran, 'Lynette Roberts: The Lyric Pieces', p. 131.
9 Hooker, *Imagining Wales*, p. 40.
10 Lynette Roberts, 'The Circle of C', in *Lynette Roberts: Collected Poems*, p. 7.
11 Lynette Roberts, 'Notes on Legend and Form', in *Lynette Roberts: Collected Poems*, pp. 38–40 (p. 38).
12 The *englyn* is 'the oldest recorded Welsh metrical form'; Meic Stephens (ed.), *The New Companion to the Literature of Wales* (Cardiff: University of Wales Press, 1998).
13 See *Lynette Roberts: Collected Poems*, pp. 127–38.
14 Lynette Roberts, 'An Introduction to Welsh Dialect', in *Lynette Roberts: Collected Poems*, pp. 107–24 (p. 124). As Patrick McGuinness notes, 'this article precedes . . . seven stories in *An Introduction to Village Dialect*, which were conceived originally as illustrations of the continuities between the living speech of Llanybri and the ancient forms of Welsh'; 'Notes', in *Lynette Roberts: Diaries, Letters and Recollections*, pp. 221–9 (p. 223).
15 Lynette Roberts, 'An Introduction to Welsh Dialect', p. 124.
16 Lynette Roberts, 'Lamentation', p. 8.
17 Lynette Roberts, 'A Carmarthenshire Diary', in *Lynette Roberts: Diaries, Letters and Recollections*, pp. 3–93 (p. 32).
18 Lynette Roberts, 'A Carmarthenshire Diary', p. 33.
19 Lynette Roberts, *Gods With Stainless Ears: A Heroic Poem*, pp. 60–1.
20 *Gods With Stainless Ears* is framed by a series of prose 'arguments', which Roberts included on the advice of the text's editor, T. S. Eliot; Patrick McGuinness, 'Notes', in *Lynette Roberts: Collected Poems*, pp. 135–50 (p. 143).

[21] Lynette Roberts, 'Notes on Legend and Form', p. 38.
[22] John Pikoulis, 'Lynette Roberts and Alun Lewis', in *Poetry Wales*, n.s. 19/2, 9–29 (p. 9).
[23] Patrick McGuinness, 'Introduction', in *Lynette Roberts: Collected Poems*, pp. xi–xxxix (p. xviii).
[24] Lynette Roberts, 'Raw Salt on Eye', pp. 6–7.
[25] Jean Rhys, 'I Spy A Stranger', in *Jean Rhys: Collected Stories* (New York and London: Norton, 1987), pp. 232–55 (p. 251).
[26] Lilian Pizzichini, *The Blue Hour: A Portrait of Jean Rhys* (London: Bloomsbury, 2009), p. 7.
[27] Pizzichini, *The Blue Hour*, pp. 46–280.
[28] Jean Rhys, *Voyage in the Dark* (London: Penguin, 1969), p. 7.
[29] Lynette Roberts, 'Royal Mail', p. 27.
[30] Kronfeld, *On the Margins of Modernism*, p. 2.
[31] McGuinness, 'Introduction', in *Lynette Roberts: Diaries, Letters and Recollections*, p. xii.
[32] Lynette Roberts, 'A Carmarthenshire Diary', p. 9.
[33] Conran, 'Lynette Roberts: The Lyrical Pieces', p. 131.
[34] T. S. Eliot, cited in Patrick McGuinness, 'Introduction', in *Lynette Roberts: Diaries, Letters and Recollections*, p. ix.
[35] Robert Graves cited in Patrick McGuinness, 'Introduction', in *Lynette Roberts: Collected Poems*, p. xxxiii.
[36] Wynn Thomas, *Internal Difference*, p. 26.
[37] Deleuze and Guattari, *Kafka*, p. 26.
[38] Lynette Roberts, 'An Introduction to Welsh Dialect', p. 107.
[39] Lynette Roberts simply writes that 'Miss Lynette Roberts published her second book of poetry last year'; 'The Welsh Dragon', pp. 139–42 (p. 140).
[40] Lynette Roberts, 'The Welsh Dragon', p. 142.
[41] McGuinness, 'Introduction', in *Lynette Roberts: Collected Poems*, p. xii.
[42] Saunders Lewis, 'Is there an Anglo-Welsh Literature?', p. 11.
[43] Lynette Roberts, 'A Carmarthenshire Diary', p. 46.
[44] Lynette Roberts, 'Crossed and Uncrossed', p. 20.
[45] Lynette Roberts, 'Notes on Legend and Form', p. 38.
[46] H.D., 'The Walls Do Not Fall', in H.D., *Trilogy* (New York: New Directions Publishing, 1973), pp. 3–4. All further references to H.D.'s poems are to this edition and are given in the text.
[47] Lynette Roberts, 'Seagulls', p. 16.
[48] Keidrych Rhys, 'Poem for a Green Envelope', in Keidrych Rhys, *The Van Pool and Other Poems* (London: Routledge, 1942), p. 25.
[49] Gill Plain, *Women's Fiction of the Second World War: Gender, Power and Resistance* (Edinburgh: Edinburgh University Press, 1996), p. 11.
[50] Lynette Roberts, 'Plasnewydd', p. 5.
[51] Lynette Roberts, 'A Carmarthenshire Diary', p. 16.
[52] Lynette Roberts, 'An Introduction to Village Dialect', p. 118.
[53] Glyn Jones, '18 Poems Again', 22–6 (24).
[54] Lynette Roberts, 'Visit to T. S. Eliot', in *Lynette Roberts: Diaries, Letters and Recollections*, pp. 149–53 (p. 150).
[55] Katie Gramich, 'Welsh Women Writers and War', in *Wales at War: Critical*

Essays on Literature and Art, ed. Tony Curtis (Bridgend: Seren, 2007), pp. 122–41 (p. 128).

56 Plain, *Women's Fiction of the Second World War*, p. 20.

57 Gramich, 'Welsh Women Writers and War', p. 132.

58 Plain, *Women's Fiction of the Second World War*, p. 20.

59 Lynette Roberts, 'Curlew', p. 15.

60 Lynette Roberts, 'Letters to Robert Graves', in *Lynette Roberts: Diaries, Letters and Recollections*, pp. 167–88 (p. 181).

61 Tony Brown, 'Introduction: The Making of a Writer', p. lix.

62 Branwen's marriage to Matholwch, king of Ireland, ultimately leads to war between Ireland and Wales.

63 *Oxford English Dictionary Online* (accessed 4 February 2010).

64 Catherine Soanes and Angus Stevenson (eds), *Concise Oxford English Dictionary*, 11th edn (Oxford: Oxford University Press, 2004).

65 Gramich, 'Welsh Women Writers and War', p. 132.

66 Pierre Grimal, *The Penguin Dictionary of Classical Mythology*, ed. Stephen Kershaw, trans. A. R. Maxwell-Hyslop (London: Penguin, 1990), p. 94.

67 Lynette Roberts, 'Notes to *Gods With Stainless Ears: A Heroic Poem*', in *Lynette Roberts: Collected Poems*, pp. 70–8 (p. 71).

68 Patrick McGuinness, 'Notes', in *Lynette Roberts: Collected Poems*, p. 143.

69 Patrick McGuinness, 'Notes', in *Lynette Roberts: Collected Poems*, p. 143.

70 Roland Barthes, *The Pleasure of the Text*, translated from the French by Richard Miller (New York: Hill and Wang, 1975), p. 42.

71 Barthes, *The Pleasure of the Text*, p. 42.

72 Lynette Roberts, 'Notes to *Gods With Stainless Ears*', p. 71.

73 Conran, *The Cost of Strangeness*, pp. 19–1.

74 Lynette Roberts, 'Notes to *Gods With Stainless Ears*', p. 71.

75 Lynette Roberts, 'Notes to *Gods With Stainless Ears*', p. 71.

76 Taliesin, 'The Battle of the Trees', translated from the Welsh by D. W. Nash, in Robert Graves, in *The White Goddess: A Historical Grammar of Poetic Myth* (London: Faber and Faber, 1948), pp. 31–2, ll. 57–87.

77 Taliesin, 'The Battle of the Trees', p. 46.

78 Robert Graves, *The White Goddess*, p. 38.

79 Katie Gramich also comments on the 'fictionalised, surrealist and often hallucinatory style' of *Gods With Stainless Ears*; 'Welsh Women Writers and War', p. 132.

80 Patrick McGuinness, 'Notes', in *Lynette Roberts: Collected Poems*, p. 143.

81 Sharon Ouditt, *Fighting Forces, Writing Women* (London: Routledge, 1994), p. 14.

82 Brecht's phrase is used loosely here. Its actual meaning is discussed in chapter one.

83 Wheale, p. 102.

84 Barthes, *The Pleasure of the Text*, p. 20.

85 Patrick McGuinness, *Maurice Maeterlinck and the Making of Modern Theatre* (Oxford and New York: Oxford University Press, 2000), p. 7.

86 McGuinness, 'Notes', in *Lynette Roberts: Collected Poems*, p. 144.

87 McGuinness, 'Notes', in *Lynette Roberts: Collected Poems*, p. 146.

88 Wheale, p. 99.

[89] *Oxford English Dictionary Online* (accessed 10 February 2010).
[90] Conran, 'Lynette Roberts: War Poet', p. 202.
[91] Kronfeld, *On the Margins of Modernism*, p. 57.
[92] Kronfeld, *On the Margins of Modernism*, p. 2.

Chapter 3: Vernon Watkins's 'Modern Country of the Arts'

[1] Rowan Williams, 'Swansea's Other Poet: Vernon Watkins and the Threshold between Worlds', *Welsh Writing in English: A Yearbook of Critical Essays*, n.s. 8 (2003), 107–20 (p. 107).
[2] Richard Ramsbotham, 'Introduction', in *Vernon Watkins: Selected Poems*, ed. Richard Ramsbotham (Manchester: Carcanet Press, 2006), pp. xi–xxviii (p. xii).
[3] Roland Mathias, *Vernon Watkins: Writers of Wales* (Cardiff: University of Wales Press, 1974), pp. 4–5.
[4] Glyn Jones, 'Whose Flight is Toil', in *Vernon Watkins 1906–1967*, ed. Leslie Norris (London: Faber and Faber, 1970), pp. 23–6 (p. 25).
[5] As Mathias notes, Watkins's mother 'enjoyed an educational experience unusual in that day for a girl from a West Wales town like Carmarthen'. Not only was she sent to a school in London, but she was also afforded the opportunity to develop her interest in languages by attending, for a time, 'a school at Bolkenhein, in one of the German-speaking regions later known as Sudetenland'. Mathias suggests that 'it was probably this that disposed her to wish for her son a wider education than a purely Welsh background might allow'; Mathias, p. 6.
[6] Mathias, *Vernon Watkins,* p. 9.
[7] Mathias, *Vernon Watkins*, p. 9.
[8] Mathias, *Vernon Watkins*, p. 9.
[9] Ramsbotham, 'Introduction', in *Vernon Watkins*, p. xii.
[10] Mathias, *Vernon Watkins*, p. 9.
[11] Mathias, *Vernon Watkins*, p. 21.
[12] Mathias, *Vernon Watkins*, p. 21.
[13] Ramsbotham, 'Introduction', in *Vernon Watkins*, p. xii.
[14] Mathias, *Vernon Watkins*, p. 117.
[15] Mathias, *Vernon Watkins*, p. 10.
[16] Glyn Jones, 'Whose Flight is Toil', p. 25. As Dafydd Johnston notes (and previously mentioned), *cynghanedd* 'refers to the complex system of sound correspondences which adorns Welsh strict-metre poetry'; *The Literature of Wales*, p. 34.
[17] Vernon Watkins, 'Taliesin and the Spring of Vision', in *The Collected Poems of Vernon Watkins* (Ipswich: Golgonooza, Press, 1986), p. 224. All further references to Watkins's poems are to this edition and are given in the text.
[18] Dafydd Johnston, *The Literature of Wales*, p. 16.
[19] Wynn Thomas, *Internal Difference*, p. 36.
[20] Wynn Thomas, *Corresponding Cultures*, p. 69.
[21] Lynette Roberts, 'An Introduction to Welsh Dialect', p. 107.
[22] Watkins cited in Mathias, *Vernon Watkins*, p. 1.

23. For a discussion of the various affinities between the lives and works of Friedrich Hölderlin and Vernon Watkins, see Ian Hilton, 'Vernon Watkins and Hölderlin', in *Poetry Wales*, n.s. 12/4 (Spring 1977), 101–17.
24. Wynn Thomas, *Corresponding Cultures*, p. 71.
25. Vernon Watkins, 'The Translation of Poetry', in *Vernon Watkins: Selected Verse*, ed. Ruth Pryor (London: Enitharmon Press, 1977), pp. 15–22 (p. 15).
26. Ian Hilton, 'Vernon Watkins as Translator', in *Vernon Watkins 1906–1967*, ed. Leslie Norris, pp. 74–89 (p. 85).
27. Vernon Watkins, 'Discoveries', p. 38.
28. Meic Stephens (ed.), *The New Companion to the Literature of Wales*, p. 220. Stephens notes that in these poems, 'the vigour of the hero in life [is often] contrasted with the desolation of his grave' (p. 220).
29. Jonathan Swift cited in David Nokes, *Jonathan Swift: A Hypocrite Reversed – A Critical Biography* (Oxford and New York: Oxford University Press, 1987), p. 412.
30. Grimal, *The Penguin Dictionary of Classical Mythology*, p. 439.
31. Grimal, *The Penguin Dictionary of Classical Mythology*, p. 440.
32. W. B. Yeats, 'Swift's Epitaph', in *The Collected Poems of W. B. Yeats*, 2nd edn, ed. Richard J. Finneran (New York: Simon and Schuster, 1996), pp. 245–6. All further references to Yeats's poems, unless stated otherwise, are to this edition and are given in the text.
33. W. B. Yeats, 'Under Ben Bulben', p. 328, ll. 84–94.
34. Peter Armour, 'Notes: *Paradiso*', in Dante Alighieri, *The Divine Comedy*, translated from the Italian by Allen Mandelbaum (London: Everyman's Library, 1995), pp. 707–91 (p. 707).
35. Patricia Fara, *Science: A Four Thousand Year History* (Oxford and New York: Oxford University Press, 2009), p. 21.
36. Fara, *Science*, p. 22.
37. Fara, *Science*, p. 24.
38. Fara, *Science*, p. 24.
39. Fara, *Science*, p. 22.
40. Fara, *Science*, p. 108.
41. John A. Scott, *Understanding Dante* (Notre Dame, Indiana: University of Notre Dame Press, 2004), p. 233.
42. Armour, 'Notes: *Paradiso*', p. 707.
43. Armour, 'Notes: *Paradiso*', p. 778.
44. Joseph Gallagher, *A Modern Reader's Guide to Dante's The Divine Comedy* (Liguori, MO: Liguori/Triumph, 1996), p. 64.
45. Gallagher, *A Modern Reader's Guide to Dante's The Divine Comedy*, p. 64.
46. Peter Armour, 'Notes: *Purgatorio*', in Dante Alighieri, *The Divine Comedy*, pp. 625–706 (p. 706).
47. Dante Aligheri, *The Divine Comedy*, translated by Allen Mandelbaum (New York: Alfred A. Knopf, 1995), *Paradiso*, xxviii. 16-20.
48. S. Foster Damon, *A Blake Dictionary: The Ideas and Symbols of William Blake*, 2nd edn (Hanover, NH: University of New England, 1988), p. 191.
49. Foster Damon, *A Blake Dictionary*, p. 192.
50. Robert Ryan, 'Blake and Religion', in *The Cambridge Companion to William Blake*, ed. Morris Eaves (Cambridge: Cambridge University Press, 2003), pp. 150–68 (p. 62).

[51] William Blake, 'The Divine Image', in *Blake: The Complete Poems*, ed. W. H. Stevenson, 3rd edn (Harlow: Pearson, 2007), p. 75, ll. 13–20. All further references to Blake's poems are to this edition and are given in the text.

[52] William Blake, 'Auguries of Innocence', p. 612, ll. 1–4.

[53] Foster Damon, *A Blake Dictionary*, p. 96.

[54] Foster Damon, *A Blake Dictionary*, p. 96.

[55] Foster Damon, *A Blake Dictionary*, p. 96.

[56] Bradley W. Carroll and Dale A. Ostlie, *An Introduction to Modern Astrophysics* (Reading, MA: Addison-Wesley Publishing, 1996), p. 25.

[57] John Carey, *John Donne: Life, Mind and Art* (London: Faber and Faber, 1981), p. 251.

[58] Fara, *Science*, p. 26.

[59] Carey, *John Donne*, p. 252. Carey notes that 'Tycho's pupil, [Johannes] Kepler [1571–1630] identified two other new stars, one in . . . 1600, and one . . . in 1604. Kepler published his observations in the *De Stella Nova* of 1606', which Donne mentions in *Biathanatos*. Carey points out that 'then came Galileo with his telescope and the map of the heavens was revolutionized. In his *Siderius Nunicus* of 1610, Galileo announced that he had discovered multitudes of stars never suspected before, and also the four satellites of Jupiter', pp. 251–2.

[60] Carey, *John Donne*, pp. 251–2. It should be noted, however, that Donne did not express this view in all of his writings; p. 18.

[61] According to Carey, Donne was 'one of the few Englishmen of his day to know Dante in the original'; *John Donne*, p. 18.

[62] John Donne, 'The Canonization', in *John Donne's Poetry: A Norton Critical Edition*, ed. Donald R. Dickson (New York and London: Norton, 2007), p. 78, l. 21. All further references to Donne's poems are to this edition and are given in the text.

[63] Margaret Ferguson, Mary Jo Salter and Jon Stallworthy (eds), *The Norton Anthology of Poetry*, 5th edn (London and New York: Norton, 2005), p. 297.

[64] Foster Damon, *A Blake Dictionary*, p. 191.

[65] Donne cited in Carey, *John Donne*, p. 204.

[66] Carey, *John Donne*, p. 204. Carey notes that *Biathanatos* was 'probably composed in 1608, [and was] the first English defence of suicide to be published'; p. 204.

[67] Dickson, *John Donne's Poetry*, p. 78.

[68] Dickson, *John Donne's Poetry*, p. 110.

[69] Donne, 'The Expiration', p. 114, ll. 7-12.

[70] John Keats, 'On First Looking into Chapman's Homer', in *John Keats: The Complete Poems*, ed. John Barnard, 2nd edn (Harmondsworth: Penguin, 1977), p. 72, ll. 1–14.

[71] Carey, *John Donne*, p. 15.

[72] Dickson, 'Preface', in *John Donne's Poetry*, pp. xi–xiv (p. xi).

[73] Andrew Mousley, 'Introduction', in *New Casebooks: John Donne – Contemporary Critical Essays*, ed. Andrew Mousley (Basingstoke: Palgrave, 1999), pp. 1–24 (p. 3). As Carey suggests, canonisation or 'the intercession of saints was Catholic doctrine, disowned by Anglicans'; *John Donne*, p. 43.

[74] Carey, *John Donne*, p. 57.

[75] As Carey suggests, Donne, 'like every other Protestant of his day, was deeply influenced by Calvinism'; *John Donne*, p. 240.
[76] Donne, 'Holy Sonnet 19', p. 145, ll. 10–11.
[77] Donne, 'Holy Sonnet 1', p. 136, ll. 12–14.
[78] D. J. Enright (ed.), *The Oxford Book of Death* (Oxford and New York: Oxford University Press, 1983), p. 330.
[79] Enright, *The Oxford Book of Death*, p. 330.
[80] Enright, *The Oxford Book of Death*, p. 330.
[81] As Ian Davidson notes, 'throughout his life, Voltaire's iconoclasm had frequently got him into trouble with Church and State'; *Voltaire in Exile: The Last Years, 1753–78* (London: Atlantic Books, 2004), p. xvi.
[82] Voltaire, 'Reflections on Religion', in *The Portable Enlightenment Reader*, ed. Isaac Kramnick (London: Penguin, 1996), pp. 115–33 (p. 131).
[83] Davidson, *Voltaire in Exile*, p. xvi.
[84] Donne, 'The Will', p. 106, ll. 46–51.
[85] Christopher Fox, 'Introduction', in *The Cambridge Companion to Jonathan Swift*, ed. Christopher Fox (Cambridge: Cambridge University Press, 2003), pp. 1–13 (p. 1). Swift was buried 'in the great aisle of the cathedral'; Nokes, *Jonathan Swift*, p. 412.
[86] See A. Owen Aldridge, *Voltaire and the Century of Light* (Princeton, NJ: Princeton University Press, 1975), pp. 64–5.
[87] Aldridge, *Voltaire and the Century of Light*, p. 64.
[88] Joseph McMinn, 'Swift's Life', in *The Cambridge Companion to Jonathan Swift*, ed. Christopher Fox, pp. 14–30 (p. 20).
[89] Judith C. Mueller, '*A Tale of Tub* and early prose', in *The Cambridge Companion to Jonathan Swift*, ed. Christopher Fox, pp. 202–15 (p. 207).
[90] As Davidson notes, 'through the medium of a knowingly unrealistic and picaresque international travel adventure', which Swift also uses in *Gulliver's Travels*, *Candide* 'makes sceptical fun of the pretensions of all institutions of Church and State, starting with the theologians, metaphysicians, Jesuits and inquisitors'; *Voltaire in Exile*, p. 54.
[91] Fox, 'Introduction', p. 3.
[92] Swift cited in Nokes, *Jonathan Swift*, p. 412.
[93] John Milton, *Paradise Lost*, ed. John Leonard (London: Penguin, 2000), iii. 21–36. All further references are to this edition and are given in the text.
[94] John Leonard, 'Introduction', in John Milton, *Paradise Lost*, ed. John Leonard (London: Penguin, 2000), pp. vii–xliii (p. xviii).
[95] Leonard, 'Introduction', p. xxi. As Leonard points out, 'the old astronomy held that the darkness of night was an illusion. The darkness is not really out there between the stars. The night sky just looks dark because we see it through our earth's shadow. This view of the universe was standard in ancient and medieval times and it survived into the Renaissance. The celestial heavens above and around the earth's shadow are a brilliant blue, with sun, moon, planets and stars all visible at once'; Leonard, 'Introduction', p. xxi.
[96] Leonard, 'Introduction', p. xxii.
[97] Leonard, 'Introduction', p. xxi.
[98] John Leonard, 'Notes', in John Milton, *Paradise Lost*, pp. 289–453 (p. 325).
[99] Blake, 'The Tiger', p. 163, ll. 1–6.

[100] Blake, *The Marriage of Heaven and Hell*, in *Poetry and Prose of William Blake*, ed. Geoffrey Keynes (London: The Nonesuch Press, 1948), pp. 181–93 (p. 182).
[101] Foster Damon, p. 274.
[102] Foster Damon, *A Blake Dictionary*, p. 275.
[103] Keith Alldritt, *W. B. Yeats: The Man and the Milieu* (London: John Murray, 1997), p. 86.
[104] Alldritt, *W. B. Yeats*, p. 87.
[105] Foster Damon, *A Blake Dictionary*, pp. 280-281.
[106] Margaret Drabble (ed.), *The Oxford Companion to English Literature*, 6th edn (Oxford and New York: Oxford University Press, 2000), p. 108.
[107] W. B. Yeats, 'The Song of Wandering Aengus', p. 59, ll. 5–8.
[108] Bradbury, 'The Cities of Modernism', p. 100.
[109] Peter Ackroyd, *T. S. Eliot* (London: Hamish Hamilton, 1984), p. 88.
[110] Ackroyd, *T. S. Eliot*, p. 101.
[111] T. S. Eliot, 'Tradition and the Individual Talent', in *T.S. Eliot: Selected Writings*, pp. 13–33 (p. 14).
[112] T. S. Eliot, 'Tradition and the Individual Talent', p. 14.
[113] T. S. Eliot, 'Tradition and the Individual Talent', p. 14.
[114] Vernon Watkins, 'Prose: excerpts from Vernon Watkins's lecture notes used at University College, Swansea, in 1966', *Poetry Wales*, n.s. 12/4 (Spring 1977), 52– 6 (p. 52).
[115] Vernon Watkins, 'Ode: to T. S. Eliot', p. 294.
[116] *The Oxford English Dictionary Online* (accessed 15 March 2010).
[117] T. S. Eliot, 'The Hollow Men', p. 81.
[118] Bradbury, 'The Cities of Modernism', p. 101.
[119] Deleuze and Guattari, *Kafka*, p. 24.
[120] Wynn Thomas, *Internal Difference*, p. 37.
[121] Wynn Thomas, *In the Shadow of the Pulpit*, p. 235.
[122] John Xiros Cooper, *The Cambridge Companion to T. S. Eliot* (Cambridge and New York: Cambridge University Press, 2006), p. 2.
[123] F.O. Matthiessen, 'The Quartets', in *T. S. Eliot Four Quartets: A Casebook*, ed. Bernard Bergonzi (London: Macmillan, 1969), pp. 88–104 (p. 89– 90).
[124] Eliot, 'Burnt Norton', p. 179.
[125] Matthiessen, 'The Quartets', p. 94.
[126] Eliot, 'The Dry Salvages', p. 199.
[127] Eliot, 'The Dry Salvages', p. 193.
[128] Eliot, 'Little Gidding', p. 208.
[129] Vernon Watkins, 'The Collier', pp. 3– 4.
[130] *The Oxford English Dictionary Online* (accessed 10 March 2010).
[131] Rowan Williams, 'Swansea's Other Poet', p. 115.
[132] Richard Ramsbotham, 'Notes', in *Vernon Watkins: New Selected Poems*, ed. Richard Ramsbotham (Manchester: Carcanet, 2006), pp. 103– 12 (p. 103).
[133] Watkins cited in Ramsbotham, 'Notes', p. 103.
[134] William Wordsworth, *The Prelude*, in *The Oxford Authors: William Wordsworth*, ed. Stephen Gill (Oxford and New York: Oxford University Press, 1984), i. 375. All further references to Wordsworth's poems are to this edition and are given in the text.

[135] Ackroyd, *T. S. Eliot*, p. 138.
[136] Vernon Watkins, 'Yeats in Dublin', p. 59.
[137] Rowan Williams, 'Swansea's Other Poet', p. 14.
[138] Vernon Watkins, 'Ophelia', pp. 114–15.
[139] Christopher Wood, *The Pre-Raphaelites* (London: Seven Dials, 2000), p. 33.
[140] Hilton, 'Vernon Watkins as Translator', p. 80.
[141] William Shakespeare, *Hamlet: A Norton Critical Edition*, ed. Cyrus Hoy, 2nd edn (New York and London: Norton, 1991), III. i. 119.
[142] Arthur Rimbaud, 'Ophelia', pp. 29– 31.
[143] Wynn Thomas, *Corresponding Cultures*, p. 70.
[144] James A. Davies, 'Dylan Thomas and his Welsh Contemporaries', in *A Guide to Welsh Literature*, pp. 120–64 (p. 149).
[145] James A. Davies, 'Dylan Thomas and his Welsh Contemporaries', p. 152.

Chapter 4: Cadaqués and Carmarthenshire: The Modernist 'Heterotopias' of Salvador Dalí and Dylan Thomas

[1] Wigginton, *Modernism from the Margins*, p. 43.
[2] Wigginton, *Modernism from the Margins*, p. 41.
[3] Dylan Thomas, Letter to Edith Sitwell, 17 January 1936, in *Dylan Thomas: The Collected Letters*, ed. Paul Ferris (London: Paladin, 1987), p. 210.
[4] Glyn Jones, 'Notes on Surrealism', p. 22.
[5] Wigginton, *Modernism from the Margins*, p. 49.
[6] John Goodby, *The Poetry of Dylan Thomas: Under the Spelling Wall* (Liverpool: Liverpool University Press, 2013), p. 278.
[7] Jonathan Jones, 'The Riddle of the Rocks', *The Guardian*, 5 March 2007. Available at *http://www.guardian.co.uk/world/2007/mar/05/spain.art* (accessed 31 March 2008).
[8] Ian Gibson, *The Shameful Life of Salvador Dalí* (London: Faber and Faber, 1997), p. 4.
[9] Gibson, *The Shameful Life of Salvador Dalí*, p. 35.
[10] Gibson, *The Shameful Life of Salvador Dalí*, p. 35.
[11] Salvador Dalí quoted in Robert Descharnes and Gilles Néret, *Salvador Dalí: The Paintings 1904–1946* (Cologne: Benedikt Taschen, 1997), p. 41.
[12] Cleary, 'Introduction: Ireland and Modernity', p. 5.
[13] See Goodby, *The Poetry of Dylan Thomas: Under the Spelling Wall*, p. 278.
[14] Michel Foucault, 'Different Spaces', translated from the French by Robert Hurley and others, in *Essential Works of Foucault 1954–1984*, ed. James D. Fausion (New York: The New Press, 1998), II, 175–185.
[15] Andrew Thacker, *Moving through Modernity: Space and Geography in Modernism* (Manchester: Manchester University Press, 2003), pp. 24–5.
[16] Katie Gramich, *Twentieth-Century Women's Writing in Wales: Land, Gender, Belonging* (Cardiff: University of Wales Press, 2007), p. 201.
[17] André Breton, 'First Manifesto of Surrealism', p. 309.
[18] Dalí's use of the name Gradiva was inspired by Wilhelm Jensen's short story, 'Gradiva' and Sigmund Freud's analysis of that text; Gibson, *The Shameful Life of Salvador Dalí*, p. 220.

[19] Gibson, *The Shameful Life of Salvador Dalí*, p. 167.
[20] Foucault 'Different Spaces', p. 180.
[21] Dylan Thomas, Letter to John Goodland, 22 December 1938, in *The Collected Letters*, p. 345.
[22] Paul Ferris, *Dylan Thomas: The Biography* (Talybont: Y Lolfa, 2006), p. 29.
[23] Dylan Thomas, 'The Peaches', pp. 122–37 (p. 132).
[24] Dalí quoted in Descharnes and Néret, *Salvador Dalí: The Paintings*, p. 25.
[25] Ferris touches on the 'movement between the real and the unreal' in 'The Peaches' in his biography of Dylan Thomas. Gibson notes that 'curiously, [given his 'love of the macabre',] in "The Peaches" Thomas made scarcely any capital from the fact that, as he knew, the Carmarthen hangman was supposed to have lived in the house [at Fernhill], as recently as the end of the nineteenth century . . . In "The Peaches" Thomas identifies the hangman's home as a deserted house down the road; probably he wanted to confuse local readers and stop them recognising Fernhill too easily'; *Dylan Thomas: The Biography*, p. 31.
[26] Ferris, *Dylan Thomas: The Biography*, p. 31.
[27] Gibson, *The Shameful Life of Salvador Dalí*, p. 167.
[28] As Jeni Williams notes, 'Questions . . . arise over the role and status of texts which deploy a child protagonist for an *adult* audience. By blurring the categories of innocence and experience, child and adult, such a text destabilises a belief in a trustworthy adult world'; '"Oh, for our vanished youth": Avoiding Adulthood in the Later Stories of Dylan Thomas', in *New Casebooks: Dylan Thomas*, ed. John Goodby and Chris Wigginton (Basingstoke: Palgrave, 2001), pp. 172–91 (p. 174).
[29] John Goodby and Christopher Wigginton, '"Shut, too, in a tower of words": Dylan Thomas' modernism', in *Locations of Literary Modernism: Region and Nation in British and American Modernist Poetry*, ed. Alex Davis and Lee M. Jenkins (Cambridge: Cambridge University Press, 2000), pp. 89–112 (p. 104). Ferris details the frequent censorship of Thomas's stories in his biography. He describes, for example, how when, in 1939, 'a new book of prose and poems, *The Map of Love*, was being discussed with Dent, [Thomas's publisher,] Richard Church refused to print some of [the stories], in particular the one that Thomas regarded as the best, 'A Prospect of the Sea', because it contained 'unwarrantable moments of sensuality'; Ferris, *Dylan Thomas: The Biography*, p. 178.
[30] Conran, *Frontiers in Anglo-Welsh Poetry*, p. 2.
[31] Ferris, *Dylan Thomas: The Biography*, p. xvii. Ferris notes that, in particular, Thomas's 'autobiographical stories make symbols of sinful pleasure out of actresses and dancers, once good for a delicious shudder in nonconformist Wales' (p. 66).
[32] Federico García Lorca, *The House of Bernarda Alba: A Drama about Women in the Villages of Spain*, translated from the Spanish by James Graham-Luján and Richard L. O'Connell, in *Federico García Lorca: Collected Plays* (London: Secker and Warburg, 1976), pp. 398–453 (p. 404).
[33] Linda Williams, *Figures of Desire: A Theory and Analysis of Surrealist Film* (Berkley and Los Angeles: University of California Press, 1981), p. 90.
[34] Gibson, *The Shameful Life of Salvador Dalí*, p. 51.

[35] Gibson, *The Shameful Life of Salvador Dalí*, pp. 245–49.
[36] Dylan Thomas, 'I see the boys of summer', in *Dylan Thomas: Collected Poems 1934–1953*, ed. Walford Davies and Ralph Maud (London: Phoenix, 2000), p. 7.
[37] Dalí cited in Gibson, *The Shameful Life of Salvador Dalí*, p. 71.
[38] Goodby and Wigginton, '"Shut, too, in a tower of words": Dylan Thomas' modernism', p. 104.
[39] Walford Davies, 'The Poetry of Dylan Thomas: Welsh Contexts, Narrative and the Language of Modernism', p. 122.
[40] Katie Gramich, 'Daughters of Darkness', in *Dylan Thomas: Contemporary Critical Essays*, ed. John Goodby and Christopher Wigginton (Basingstoke: Palgrave, 2001), pp. 65–84 (p. 70).
[41] Dylan Thomas, 'The Enemies', pp. 16–20 (p. 17).
[42] Wynn Thomas, *Internal Difference*, p. 31. According to Wynn Thomas, 'the whole farm [i.e. Fernhill] as portrayed in the *Portrait* is a splendid adventure playground for the ebullient young imagination . . . Later . . . this corner of rural Carmarthenshire became, in "Fern Hill", the simply enchanted country of childhood, just as in the thirties it obligingly served as a surrealist landscape moulded to fit the contours of the subconscious' (p. 31).
[43] Williams, '"Oh, for our vanished youth": Avoiding Adulthood in the Later Stories of Dylan Thomas', p. 175.
[44] Williams, '"Oh, for our vanished youth"', p. 175.
[45] Dylan Thomas, 'The Holy Six', pp. 95–103 (p. 95).
[46] Dylan Thomas, 'A Prospect of the Sea', pp. 87–94 (p. 90).
[47] Annis Pratt, *Dylan Thomas: Early Prose: A Study in Creative Mythology* (Pittsburgh: University of Pittsburgh Press, 1970), p. 36. Pratt cites the lines, 'Here seed, up the tide, broke on the boiling coasts; the sand grains multiplied'; see Dylan Thomas, 'The Map of Love', pp. 109–14 (p. 109).
[48] Jerome Neu, 'Introduction', in *The Cambridge Companion to Freud* (Cambridge: Cambridge University Press, 1991), pp. 1–7 (p. 3).
[49] Gibson, *The Shameful Life of Salvador Dalí*, p. 380.
[50] As Bennett Simon and Rachel B. Blass note, the Oedipus complex 'was coined and defined as a constellation of desire for the mother as a sexual object and hate of the father as a rival'; 'The development and vicissitudes of Freud's ideas on the Oedipus complex', in *The Cambridge Companion to Freud*, ed. Jerome Neu (Cambridge: Cambridge University Press, 1991), pp. 161–74 (p. 163).
[51] Dylan Thomas cited in Ferris, *Dylan Thomas: The Collected Letters*, p. 311.
[52] Jennifer Church'Morality, and the internalized other', in *The Cambridge Companion to Freud*, ed. Jerome Neu (Cambridge: Cambridge University Press, 1991), pp. 209–23 (p. 209).
[53] Church, 'Morality, and the internalized other', p. 217.
[54] Pratt, *Dylan Thomas: Early Prose*, p. 67.
[55] Church, 'Morality, and the internalized other', p. 216. As Church notes, 'Freud considered the presence of a superego – an inner critic and ideal – and the presence of a moral sense to be one and the same' (p. 219).
[56] John Davies, *A History of Wales*, p. 391.
[57] This view of Wales emerged from the 'campaign to redeem Wales, and the

Welsh woman particularly, from the condemnation expressed in . . . [the Blue Books Report]'; Gramich, *Twentieth-Century Women's Writing in Wales*, p. 53.

[58] Alison Benjamin, 'Mixed Metaphor', *The Guardian*, 14 March 2001. Available at *http://www.guardian.co.uk/society/2001/mar/14/guardiansocietysupplement5* (accessed 6 September 2008).

[59] Mark Spilka, 'Turning the Freudian Screw: How Not to Do It', in Henry James, *The Turn of the Screw*, ed. Robert Kimbrough (New York: Norton, 1966), pp. 245–53 (p. 251).

[60] Spilka, 'Turning the Freudian Screw', p. 247

[61] Henry James, *The Turn of the Screw*, ed. Robert Kimbrough (New York: Norton, 1966), p. 22.

[62] Descharnes and Néret, *Salvador Dalí: 1904–1989* (Cologne: Taschen, 2006), p. 51.

[63] Dylan Thomas, Letter to Pamela Hansford Johnson, 15 April 1934, in *Dylan Thomas: The Collected Letters*, p. 111.

[64] Katie Gramich, Unpublished paper: '"Sick to death of Hot Salt": The Mother's Body in the Poetry of Dylan Thomas' (presented at the annual Association for Welsh Writing in English conference, Gregynog Hall, Powys, 1996).

[65] Dalí cited in Gibson, *The Shameful Life of Salvador Dalí*, p. 313.

[66] Ferris, *Dylan Thomas: The Biography*, p. 26.

[67] Ferris, *Dylan Thomas: The Biography*, p. 26.

[68] Sigmund Freud, 'Lecture XXXII: Anxiety and Instinctual Life', in Peter Gay (ed.), *The Freud Reader* (London: Vintage, 1995), pp. 773–83 (p. 778). Freud suggests that thumb-sucking is a manifestation of 'pregenital sexual organisation' and signifies the point at which 'the sexual activity, detached from the nutritive activity [that is, sucking at the mother's breast], has substituted for the extraneous object one situated in the subject's own body'; Sigmund Freud, 'Three Essays on the Theory of Infantile Sexuality', in Peter Gay (ed.), *The Freud Reader* (London: Vintage, 1995), pp. 239–93 (p. 273).

[69] Freud, 'Anxiety and Instinctual Life', pp. 777–8.

[70] Descharnes and Néret, *Salvador Dalí: 1904–1989*, p. 50.

[71] Salvador Dalí, *The Secret Life* (New York: Dover, 1993), p. 248.

[72] Gibson, *The Shameful Life of Salvador Dalí*, p. 217.

[73] Sigmund Freud, 'Beyond the Pleasure Principle', in Peter Gay (ed.), *The Freud Reader* (London: Vintage, 1995), pp. 594–627 (p. 620).

[74] Freud, 'Beyond the Pleasure Principle', p. 620.

[75] Freud, 'Beyond the Pleasure Principle', p. 612.

[76] Dylan Thomas, 'The force that through the green fuse', p. 13.

[77] Ivan Phillips, '"Death is all metaphor": Dylan Thomas's Radical Morbidity', in *Dylan Thomas: Contemporary Critical Essays*, pp. 124–39 (p. 126).

[78] As Linda Williams suggests, 'this transformation begins a pattern of association linking passion with the paroxysms of violence and death'; *Figures of Desire*, p. 87.

[79] Dylan Thomas, 'A process in the weather of the heart', p. 10.

[80] John Deigh, 'Freud's later theory of civilisation: changes and implications', in *The Cambridge Companion to Freud*, pp. 287–308 (p. 307).

[81] Deigh, 'Freud's later theory of civilisation', p. 307.

82 Dylan Thomas, Letter to Trevor Hughes, summer 1934, in *Dylan Thomas: The Collected Letters*, p. 162.

83 Doyle and Winkiel, 'Introduction', in *Geomodernisms*, p. 3.

84 Goodby and Wigginton, 'Welsh Modernist Poetry: Dylan Thomas, David Jones and Lynette Roberts', in *Regional Modernisms*, p. 163.

Chapter 5: 'Hellish Funny': The Grotesque Modernism of Gwyn Thomas and Rhys Davies

1 Tyrus Miller, *Late Modernism: Politics, Fiction, and the Arts Between the World Wars* (Berkeley, Los Angeles and London: University of California Press, 1999), p. 14.

2 Terence Brown, 'Ireland, Modernism and the 1930s', in *Modernism and Ireland: The Poetry of the 1930s* (Cork: Cork University Press, 1995), pp. 24–42 (p. 24).

3 Brown, 'Ireland, Modernism and the 1930s', p. 24.

4 Brown, 'Ireland, Modernism and the 1930s', p. 24.

5 Meic Stephens (ed.), 'What was before the Big Bang?: Extracts from the 1980s jottings of Glyn Jones', *The New Welsh Review*, n.s. 39 (Winter, 1997–8), 40–2 (p. 41).

6 Pascale Casanova, *The World Republic of Letters*, translated from the French by M. B. Debevoise (Cambridge, MA, and London: Harvard University Press, 2004), p. 43.

7 Conran, *Frontiers in Anglo-Welsh Poetry*, p. 113.

8 Conran, *Frontiers in Anglo-Welsh Poetry*, p. 113.

9 Conran, *Frontiers in Anglo-Welsh Poetry*, p. 113.

10 Wynn Thomas argues, for example, that 'Gwyn Thomas, Rhys Davies, even to some extent Idris Davies and Glyn Jones, attended chapel services in a language (Welsh) of which they had at best only an incomplete grasp . . . And given the nature of what they vaguely apprehended – the perfervid imagery of damnation, the ecstatic rhetoric of salvation – no wonder the whole event appeared to them as the equivalent of the sublimely apocalyptic landscapes of a huge John Martin painting crossed with the grotesque world of a Hieronymus Bosch'; see Wynn Thomas, *In the Shadow of the Pulpit*, p. 219.

11 Thomas, *Oscar*, p. 5.

12 Lynette Hunter, '*Animal Farm*: From Satire to Allegory', in *George Orwell: Contemporary Critical Essays*, ed. Graham Holderness, Bryan Loughrey and Nahem Yousaf (Basingstoke: Macmillan, 1998), pp. 31–46 (p. 34).

13 Fordham, *James Hanley*, p. 90.

14 György M. Vajda, 'Outline of the Philosophic Backgrounds of Expressionism', in *Expressionism as an International Literary Phenomenon*, ed. Ulrich Weisstein, translated from the German by Linda Brust (Paris: Librairie Marcel Didier, 1973), pp. 45–58 (p. 48).

15 Vajda, 'Outline of the Philosophic Backgrounds of Expressionism', p. 58. The Expressionist movement came to prominence in Germany around 1910. The first group of Expressionist painters were the Dresden-based Die Brücke group, comprising Ernst Ludwig Kirchner, Emil Nolde, Karl

Schmidt-Rottluff, Max Pechstein, Erich Heckel and Otto Mueller. The Munich-based Blaue Reiter group, consisting of Franz Marc, the Russian painter, Wassili Kandinsky, and Auguste Macke, followed in 1912–13. During the interwar years, Expressionism infiltrated other artistic media in Germany, including the theatre of Ernst Toller and Georg Kaiser, the poetry of Johannes R. Becher and the prose of Kasimir Edschmid. Paul Wegener's *The Golem* (1920), Robert Wiene's *The Cabinet of Dr Caligari* (1920) and Fritz Lang's *Metropolis* (1927) are important German Expressionist films. Expressionism significantly influenced the arts in other European countries, especially in France, Italy, Belgium, Spain and Czechoslovakia.

16 Wynn Thomas, *Internal Difference*, p. 43.

17 Norbert Wolf identifies 'the factors of exaggeration, distortion and grotesqueness' as central to Expressionism; *Expressionism*, ed. Uta Grosenick (Cologne and London: Taschen, 2004), p. 38.

18 Raymond Williams, 'Language and the Avant-Garde', in *Raymond Williams, Politics of Modernism: Against the New Conformists*, ed. Tony Pinkney, 2nd edn (London and New York: Verso, 2007), pp. 65–80 (p. 74).

19 Thomas's expression of political outrage seems to refer to the effects of the Depression in industrial south Wales, particularly the Rhondda Valley where he was born and brought up during the 1930s. John Davies notes that 'the fate of thousands of Welsh people in the 1930s was to stay at home in idleness. In 1938, 62 per cent of the Rhondda had been out of work for three years or more, and life on the dole was the reality for vast numbers of the people of Wales . . . Rising late, loitering on street corners, scratching for coal on the tips . . . these were the experiences of perhaps the majority of unemployed men'; *A History of Wales*, pp. 579–80.

20 Raymond Williams, 'Language and the Avant-Garde', p. 75.

21 Knight, *A Hundred Years of Fiction*, p. 99.

22 George Grosz cited in Wolf, *Expressionism*, p. 42.

23 George Grosz cited in Wolf, *Expressionism*, p. 42.

24 Glyn Jones, 'Gwyn Thomas', p. 101.

25 Conran, *Frontiers in Anglo-Welsh Poetry*, p. 3.

26 Thomas studied Spanish at Oxford University, and spent six months at Madrid's *Universidad Complutense* in 1934. When he graduated in 1936, he returned to Wales to become a teacher of Spanish and French; Parnell, *Laughter from the Dark*, p. 23. Thomas admitted his particular interest in the literature, and especially the theatre, of the Spanish Romantic period; *Laughter from the Dark*, p. 188. His knowledge of Spanish writing, however, was clearly wide-ranging. In 1965, for example, he published an essay on Spanish literature in the magazine *Holiday* entitled 'The Passionate Authors'. The article 'reviewed the whole range of narrative writing from the medieval epic of The Song of El Cid to [José] Ortega y Gasset [– a key member of the Spanish avant-garde generation of 1919 –] and [the nineteenth-century realist novelist] Benito Pérez Galdós'; *Laughter from the Dark*, p. 187. Thomas also wrote a novel, *The Love Man* (1958), which was set in Spain and based on the Spanish legend of Don Juan.

27 John Lyon, *The Theatre of Valle-Inclán* (Cambridge: Cambridge University Press, 1983), p. 107. As Maria Delgado notes, 'although the [First World] War

had initially brought prosperity to Spain – she was able to supply the allies with much needed raw materials – the boom had been short lived and had led to inflation, political instability and industrial problems. In effect these events politicised [Valle-Inclán], creating an awareness of the need to express his disenchantment with the political regime and its brutal handling of proletarian disputes witnessed in Madrid and Barcelona in 1919. Domestic unrest was also aggravated by the impact of the Russian revolution, felt in Spain more deeply than in any other European country: the impact of Socialism evident not only in the labour disputes which rocked Spain's two major cities but also in the increasing hostility to the monarchy which was eventually to lead to the exile of the King and the establishment of the Second Republic in 1931'; 'Introduction', in *Ramón del Valle-Inclán, Valle-Inclán Plays: One*, translated from the Spanish by Maria Delgado (London: Methuen Drama, 1993), pp. xiii–xlii (p. xxi).

28 Ramón del Valle-Inclán, *Bohemian Lights*, in *Valle-Inclán Plays: One*, pp. 91–184 (p. 160). All further references are to this edition and are given in the text.

29 Derek Harris, 'Squared horizons: the hybridization of the avant-garde in Spain', in Derek Harris (ed.), *The Spanish Avant-Garde* (Manchester and New York: Manchester University Press, 1995), pp. 1–14 (p. 6).

30 The Collins Spanish Dictionary Plus Grammar (Glasgow: HarperCollins, 1998).

31 Friedrich Nietzsche, *Thus Spake Zarathustra: A Book For All And None*, translated from the German by Thomas Wayne (New York: Algora, 2003), p. 9.

32 Delgado, 'Introduction', p. xxiii.

33 Many of Goya's paintings contain elements of social and political satire.

34 As Gwynne Edwards suggests, 'the world of *Luces de Bohemia* look[s] back . . . to [the Spanish Golden Age poet, Francisco de] Quevedo and Goya'; *Dramatists in Perspective: Spanish Theatre in the Twentieth Century* (Cardiff: University of Wales Press, 1985), p. 60.

35 Delgado,'Introduction', p. xxiii.

36 Mikhail Bakhtin, *Rabelais and his World*, translated from the Russian by Hélène Iswolsky (Bloomington: Indiana University Press, 1984), p. 49.

37 Susan Stewart, *On Looking: Narratives of the Miniature, the Gigantic, the Souvenir, the Collection* (Durham, NC, and London: Duke University Press, 1993), p. 105.

38 David Smith, 'The Early Gwyn Thomas', p. 74.

39 Gwyn Thomas, *Simeon*, in *The Dark Philosophers* (Cardigan: Parthian, Library of Wales Series, 2006), pp. 243–95 (p. 261). All further references are to this edition and are given in the text.

40 Some critics even translate *esperpento* figuratively, as 'puppet' or, in the case of Delgado, 'scarecrow'; Delgado,'Introduction', p. xxxiii.

41 As Gwynne Edwards notes, 'the puppet-theatre . . . has been popular in Spain for centuries. [Miguel de] Cervantes [for example] had introduced a puppet show – El retablo de Maese Pedro – (Master Peter's Puppet Show) – into the second part of Don Quixote [1615]'; *Dramatists in Perspective*, p. 85. Edwards also points out that 'in the Madrid of [Valle-Inclán's] time there were frequent

puppet-shows' and that 'the tradition of farce [is] also an old one in Spanish literary history', p. 85.

[42] The British Punch and Judy puppet-show also features grotesque puppets, farcical violence and slapstick comedy.

[43] Frederico García Lorca, *The Billy-Club Puppets: Tragicomedy of Don Cristóbal and Miss Rosita*, in *Frederico García Lorca: Collected Plays*, translated from the Spanish by James Graham-Luján and Richard L. O'Connell (London: Secker and Warburg, 1976), pp. 77–119 (p. 115). All further references to Lorca's plays are to this edition and are given in the text.

[44] As Gwynne Edwards notes, 'Lorca's opposition to the naturalistic theatre is reflected . . . in his allegiance to the traditions and techniques of puppet-theatre and farce; *Dramatists in Perspective*, p. 84.

[45] Parnell, *Laughter from the Dark*, p. 35.

[46] G.G. Brown describes 'the extraordinary veneration in which . . . Chaplin and Keaton [in particular] were held by many Spanish writers' during this period. 'The tragic undertones of their melancholy alienation from modern society, in the midst of grotesque slapstick', Brown suggests, 'appealed to Spanish taste . . . and the . . . puppet-like movements and gestures of these films seemed to many thoughtful Spaniards to reflect the absurdity of modern existence'; G.G. Brown, *A Literary History of Spain: The Twentieth Century* (London: Ernest Benn, 1972), p. 9.

[47] G.G. Brown, *A Literary History of Spain*, p. 9.

[48] Edwards, *Dramatists in Perspective*, p. 69.

[49] Edwards, *Dramatists in Perspective,* p. 69.

[50] Lorca, *The Shoemaker's Prodigious Wife: A Violent Farce in Two Acts and a Prologue*, pp. 125–172 (p. 135).

[51] As Edwards suggests, in *The Shoemaker's Prodigious Wife* the 'puppets have become more human' (p. 93). Edwards also identifies Valle-Inclán as an important influence on Lorca; see Edwards, *Dramatists in Perspective*, p. 85.

[52] Edwards, *Dramatists in Perspective*, p. 98.

[53] Caradoc Evans, 'Lamentations', pp. 140–4 (p. 144).

[54] Ramón del Valle-Inclán, cited in Edwards, *Dramatists in Perspective*, p. 70. The extract is translated from the Spanish by Edwards.

[55] Lyon, *The Theatre of Valle-Inclán*, p. 109.

[56] Lyon notes that 'the vision of man and society formulated in scene 12 of *Luces* is a complete reversal of the heroic view'; *The Theatre of Valle-Inclán*, p. 109.

[57] Lyon, *The Theatre of Valle-Inclán*, p. 109.

[58] Edwards, *Dramatists in Perspective*, p. 71.

[59] Gwyn Thomas, 'The Central Wound', in *A Welsh Eye* (London: Hutchinson, 1964), pp. 9–24 (p. 18). Thomas uses this analogy to convey his personal experience of the climate of industrial strife and socio-economic adversity in the Rhondda Valley during the 1920s and 1930s.

[60] Gwyn Thomas cited in Jones, 'Gwyn Thomas', p. 103.

[61] Victor Golightly, 'Gwyn Thomas's American "'Oscar'"', *New Welsh Review*, n.s. 22 (Autumn, 1993) 26–31 (30). Golightly argues that Lewis embodies 'two coincidental and antagonistic narrators'. One of these narrators, he suggests, appropriates 'the laconic style of the American detective hero that had been developed by [Dashiell] Hammett and [Raymond] Chandler', and the other

is a 'buffoon [who also] has an American accent . . . and . . . is derived from the cinema and popular fiction', particularly the novels of Damon Runyon'; pp. 27–30.

62 Golightly,'Gwyn Thomas's American "Oscar"', p. 30.

63 Jean Baudrillard, *Simulacra and Simulation*, translated from the French by Sheila Faria Glaser (Michigan: University of Michigan Press, 1994), p. 1.

64 Thomas's technique can also be compared to that of Lorca in *The Shoemaker's Prodigious Wife*, where, as Edwards suggests, 'the idea of manipulation has [also] acquired resonances beyond the traditions of the puppet-theatre, touching instead on the nature of human life itself and on the theme of man manipulated by his nature and his circumstances'; Edwards, *Dramatists in Perspective*, p. 93.

65 Stephen Knight, '"Not a Place for Me": Rhys Davies's Fiction and the Coal Industry', in *Rhys Davies: Decoding the Hare*, ed. Meic Stephens (Cardiff: University of Wales Press, 2001), pp. 54–70 (p. 55).

66 Rhys Davies, 'Arfon', in *Rhys Davies: Collected Stories*, ed. Meic Stephens (Llandysul: Gomer, 1996), I. 17–43 (p. 17). All further references to Davies's stories are to this edition and are given in the text.

67 Rhys Davies, *Print of a Hare's Foot: An Autobiographical Beginning* (Bridgend: Seren, 1998), p. 95.

68 Rhys Davies, *Print of a Hare's Foot*, p. 112.

69 Meic Stephens, 'Introduction', in *Rhys Davies: Decoding the Hare*, pp. 1–28 (p. 6).

70 Meic Stephens points out that Davies wrote the short story, 'Cherry-Blossom on the Rhine' (1936) 'after a visit to Germany . . . in 1927'. He also notes that Davies visited Nice in 1928 and Paris in 1929; Stephens, 'Introduction', in *Decoding the Hare*, p. 6.

71 J. Lawrence Mitchell notes, for example, that Davies read and admired Gustave Flaubert's novel, *Madame Bovary* (1857) – see J. Lawrence Mitchell, '"I Wish I Had a Trumpet": Rhys Davies and the Creative Impulse', in *Rhys Davies: Decoding the Hare*, pp. 147–61 (p. 151) – while Barbara Prys Williams discusses Davies's enjoyment of Oscar Wilde's play *Salome*, illustrated by Aubrey Beardsley (1894); see Barbara Prys Williams, 'Rhys Davies as Autobiographer: Hare or Houdini?', in *Rhys Davies: Decoding the Hare*, pp. 104–37 (p. 110). Davies particularly admired the novels and short stories of his friend D. H. Lawrence, however. The relationship between Davies's work and that of Lawrence is explored in detail by Jeff Wallace in 'Lawrentianisms: Rhys Davies and D. H. Lawrence', in *Rhys Davies: Decoding the Hare*, pp. 175–90.

72 Conran, *Frontiers in Anglo-Welsh Poetry*, pp. 2–3.

73 As Meic Stephens notes, Rhys Davies's own family, 'on both his father's and his mother's side', 'had their remote origins in north-west [rural] Carmarthenshire'; Meic Stephens, 'Introduction', in *Rhys Davies: Collected Stories*, ed. Meic Stephens (Llandysul: Gomer, 1996), I. 7–16 (p. 9).

74 Rhys Davies, 'Resurrection', pp. 166–71 (p. 166).

75 José Ortega y Gasset, 'The Dehumanisation of Art', in *'The Dehumanisation of Art' and Other Essays on Art, Culture, and Literature*, translated from the Spanish by Helene Weyl (Princeton: Princeton University Press, 1968), pp. 3–54 (p. 38).

[76] Günter Grass, *The Tin Drum*, translated from the German by Ralph Manheim (London: Vintage, 1998), p. 46.

[77] As Conran notes, 'the buchedd was not as homogenous as it tried to make out. There were class divisions, particularly in the industrial areas'; *Frontiers in Anglo-Welsh Poetry*, p. 3.

[78] M. Wynn Thomas, '"Never Seek to Tell thy Love": Rhys Davies's Fiction', in *Rhys Davies: Decoding the Hare*, pp. 260–82 (p. 263).

[79] Wynn Thomas, *Corresponding Cultures*, p. 80. Wynn Thomas suggests that this Nonconformist 'awareness of the sinister potency of the imagination' is evident throughout Dylan Thomas's *Portrait of the Artist as a Young Dog*; *Corresponding Cultures*, p. 80.

[80] Wynn Thomas, *Corresponding Cultures*, p. 95.

[81] Wynn Thomas, '"Never Seek to Tell thy Love": Rhys Davies's Fiction', p. 261.

[82] Joseph Allen Boone, *Libidinal Currents: Sexuality and the Shaping of Modernism* (Chicago and London: University of Chicago Press, 1998), p. 210. As Boone notes, 'the term queer emerged in the interwar period among homosexuals to signal an innate orientation toward persons of the same sex'; Boone, p. 208.

[83] Wynn Thomas, '"Never Seek to Tell thy Love": Rhys Davies's Fiction', p. 268.

[84] Simon Baker and Joanna Furber, '"Unspeakable Rites": Writing the Unspeakable in Rhys Davies', in *Rhys Davies: Decoding the Hare*, pp. 244–59 (p. 247).

[85] This second example, however, could also be interpreted – like the boy's vision of the monstrous girl in Dylan Thomas's 'A Prospect of the Sea' discussed in the previous chapter – in terms of the Freudian 'fear of castration as a motive for repression'.

[86] Aubrey Beardsley was associated with Oscar Wilde's circle of aesthetes in the 1890s. Ian Fletcher describes how 'Wilde's circle . . . was composed of homoerotics, most of whom were practising homosexuals.' Fletcher points out that 'Beardsley's sexual tastes were either muted or equivocal', but 'he showed no signs of actually "coming out"'; *Aubrey Beardsley*, ed. Herbert Sussman (Boston, MA: Twayne Publishers, 1987), p. 11.

[87] As Ian Chilvers notes, 'the scandal of Wilde's arrest for homosexual offences in 1895 led to his [Beardsley's] dismissal from [his position as art editor of the periodical] *The Yellow Book*'; Ian Chilvers, *The Concise Oxford Dictionary of Art and Artists*, 3rd edn (Oxford and New York: Oxford University Press, 2003).

[88] Davies, *Print of a Hare's Foot*, p. 95.

[89] Judith Butler, 'Imitation and Gender Insubordination', in *The Routledge Critical and Cultural Theory Reader*, ed. Neil Badmington and Julia Thomas (London and New York: Routledge, 2008), pp. 365–80 (p. 368).

[90] Butler, 'Imitation and Gender Insubordination', p. 372.

[91] Butler, 'Imitation and Gender Insubordination', p. 371.

[92] Butler, 'Imitation and Gender Insubordination', p. 371.

[93] Butler, 'Imitation and Gender Insubordination', p. 372.

[94] Katherine Mansfield, 'The Woman at the Store', in *Katherine Mansfield: Selected Stories*, ed. Angela Smith (Oxford and New York: Oxford University Press, 2002), pp. 10–19 (p. 17). All further references to Mansfield's stories are to this edition and are given in the text.

[95] Linden Peach, 'Eccentricity and Lawlessness in Rhys Davies's Fiction', in *Rhys Davies: Decoding the Hare*, pp. 162–74 (p. 168).
[96] Andrew Bennett, *Katherine Mansfield* (Tavistock: Northcote House, 2004), p. 54.
[97] Katherine Mansfield, 'Frau Brechenmacher Attends a Wedding', pp. 3–9 (p. 9).
[98] Oscar Wilde, *Salome*, illustrated by Aubrey Beardsley and translated from the French by Lord Alfred Douglas (New York: Dover, 1967), p. 67.
[99] Bennett, *Katherine Mansfield*, p. 45.
[100] Bennett, *Katherine Mansfield*, p. 45.
[101] Adrienne Rich, 'Compulsory Heterosexuality and Lesbian Existence', in *Adrienne Rich's Poetry and Prose*, ed. Barbara Charlesworth Gelpi and Albert Gelpi (New York and London: Norton, 1993), pp. 203–24 (p. 203).
[102] Williams, *Black Skin, Blue Books*, p. 87.
[103] Keith Williams and Steven Matthews, 'Introduction', in *Rewriting the Thirties: Modernism and After*, ed. Keith Williams and Steven Matthews (New York: Longman, 1997), pp. 1–4 (p. 1).
[104] Kristin Bluemel, *George Orwell and the Radical Extremists: Intermodernism in Literary London* (New York and Basingstoke: Palgrave Macmillan, 2004), p. 5.

Conclusion

[1] Kronfeld, *On the Margins of Modernism*, p. 57.
[2] Daniel G. Williams has begun research into these areas and demonstrates their complexity and scope in *Black Skin, Blue Books*, pp. 76–141 and 'Welsh Modernism', in *The Oxford Handbook of Modernisms*, pp. 797–816.

Bibliography

Primary Texts

Alighieri, Dante, *The Divine Comedy*, translated by Allen Mandelbaum (New York: Alfred A. Knopf, 1995)

Aneirin, *Y Gododdin: Britain's Oldest Heroic Poem*, translated from the Welsh by A. O. H. Jarman (Llandysul: Gomer, 1988)

Blake, William, 'Auguries of Innocence', in *Blake: The Complete Poems*, ed. W. H. Stevenson, 3rd edn (Harlow: Pearson, 2007), pp. 612–15

Blake, William, 'The Divine Image', in *Blake: The Complete Poems*, ed. W. H. Stevenson, 3rd edn (Harlow: Pearson, 2007), pp. 74–5

Blake, William, *The Marriage of Heaven and Hell*, in *Poetry and Prose of William Blake*, ed. Geoffrey Keynes (London: Nonesuch Press, 1948), pp. 181–93

Blake, William, 'The Tiger', in *Blake: The Complete Poems*, ed. W. H. Stevenson, 3rd edn (Harlow: Pearson, 2007), pp. 163–4

Coleridge, Samuel Taylor, 'The Rime of the Ancient Mariner', in *Samuel Taylor Coleridge: Poems*, ed. John Beer (London: Dent, 1963), pp. 173–89

Davies, Idris, *Gwalia Deserta*, *The Complete Poems of Idris Davies*, ed. Dafydd Johnston (Cardiff: University of Wales Press, 1994), pp. 3–20

Davies, Idris, 'I Was Born in Rhymney', in *The Complete Poems of Idris Davies*, ed. Dafydd Johnston (Cardiff: University of Wales Press, 1994), pp. 76–90

Davies, Rhys, 'Arfon', in *Rhys Davies: Collected Stories*, ed. Meic Stephens (Llandysul: Gomer, 1996), I. 17–43

Davies, Rhys, *Print of a Hare's Foot: An Autobiographical Beginning* (Bridgend: Seren, 1998)

Davies, Rhys, 'Resurrection', in *Rhys Davies: Collected Stories*, ed. Meic Stephens (Llandysul: Gomer, 1996), I. 166–71

Davies, Sioned (trans.), *How Culhwch Won Olwen*, in *The Mabinogion* (Oxford: Oxford University Press, 2007), pp. 179–213

Donne, John, 'Holy Sonnet 1', in *John Donne's Poetry: A Norton Critical Edition*, ed. Donald R. Dickson (New York and London: Norton, 2007), p. 136

Donne, John, 'Holy Sonnet 6', in *John Donne's Poetry: A Norton Critical Edition*, ed. Donald R. Dickson (New York and London: Norton, 2007), pp. 138–9

Donne, John, 'Holy Sonnet 19', in *John Donne's Poetry: A Norton Critical Edition*, ed. Donald R. Dickson (New York and London: Norton, 2007), pp. 144–5

Donne, John, 'The Canonization', in *John Donne's Poetry: A Norton Critical Edition*, ed. Donald R. Dickson (New York and London: Norton, 2007), pp. 77–8

Donne, John, 'The Expiration', in *John Donne's Poetry: A Norton Critical Edition*, ed. Donald R. Dickson (New York and London: Norton, 2007), p. 114

Donne, John, 'The Will', in *John Donne's Poetry: A Norton Critical Edition*, ed. Donald R. Dickson (New York and London: Norton, 2007), pp. 105–7

Eliot, T. S., 'Burnt Norton', in *T. S. Eliot: Collected Poems 1909–1962* (London: Faber and Faber, 1974), pp. 177–83

Eliot, T. S., 'East Coker', in *T. S. Eliot: Collected Poems 1909–1962* (London: Faber and Faber, 1974), pp. 184–91

Eliot, T. S., 'Little Gidding', in *T. S. Eliot: Collected Poems 1909–1962* (London: Faber and Faber, 1974), pp. 201–9

Eliot, T. S., 'The Dry Salvages', in *T. S. Eliot: Collected Poems 1909–1962* (London: Faber and Faber, 1974), pp. 192–200

Eliot, T. S., 'The Hollow Men', in *T. S. Eliot: Collected Poems 1909–1962* (London: Faber and Faber, 1974), pp. 77–82

Eliot, T. S., 'The Love Song of J. Alfred Prufrock', in *T. S. Eliot: Collected Poems 1909–1962* (London: Faber and Faber, 1974), pp. 3–7

Eliot, T. S. *The Waste Land*, in *T.S. Eliot: Collected Poems 1909-1962* (London: Faber and Faber, 1974), pp. 51–76

Evans, Caradoc, 'Be This Her Memorial', in *My People* (Bridgend: Seren, 1987), pp. 108–12

Evans, Caradoc, 'Lamentations', in *My People* (Bridgend: Seren, 1987), pp. 140–4

Evans, D. S. (trans.), 'The Black Book of Carmarthen XXXVIII', in William F. Skene, *The Four Ancient Books of Wales: Containing the Cymric Poems attributed to the Bards of the Sixth Century* (Edinburgh: Edmonston and Douglas, 1868), I. 302

Evans, D. S. (trans.), 'Red Book of Hergest IV', in William F. Skene, *The Four Ancient Books of Wales: Containing the Cymric Poems attributed to the Bards of the Sixth Century* (Edinburgh: Edmonston and Douglas, 1868), I. 586–90

García Lorca, Federico, *The Billy-Club Puppets: Tragicomedy of Don Cristóbal and Miss Rosita*, in *Frederico García Lorca: Collected Plays*, translated from the Spanish by James Graham-Luján and Richard L. O'Connell (London: Secker and Warburg, 1976), pp. 77–119

García Lorca, Federico, *The House of Bernarda Alba: A Drama about Women in the Villages of Spain*, in *Federico García Lorca: Collected Plays*, translated from the Spanish by James Graham-Luján and Richard L. O'Connell (London: Secker and Warburg, 1976), pp. 398–453

García Lorca, Federico, *The Shoemaker's Prodigious Wife: A Violent Farce in Two Acts and a Prologue*, in *Federico García Lorca: Collected Plays*, translated from the Spanish by James Graham-Luján and Richard L. O'Connell (London: Secker and Warburg, 1976), pp. 125–72

Grass, Günter, *The Tin Drum*, translated from the German by Ralph Manheim (London: Vintage, 1998)

H.D., 'The Walls Do Not Fall', in H.D., *Trilogy* (New York: New Directions Publishing, 1973), pp. 1–59

Hopkins, Gerard Manley, 'The Windhover', in *Gerard Manley Hopkins: Selected Poems*, ed. Catherine Phillips (Oxford and New York: Oxford University Press, 1998), p. 117

James, Henry, *The Turn of the Screw*, ed. Robert Kimbrough (New York: Norton, 1966)

Jones, David, *In Parenthesis* (London: Faber and Faber, 1963)

Jones, David, 'Preface', in David Jones, *In Parenthesis* (London: Faber and Faber, 1963), pp. ix–xv

Jones, Glyn, 'Man', in *The Collected Poems of Glyn Jones*, ed. Meic Stephens (Cardiff: University of Wales Press, 1996), p. 9

Jones, Glyn, 'Porth-y-Rhyd', in *The Collected Stories of Glyn Jones*, ed. Tony Brown (Cardiff: University of Wales Press, 1999), pp. 85–90

Jones, Glyn, 'Sande', in *The Collected Poems of Glyn Jones*, ed. Meic Stephens (Cardiff: University of Wales Press, 1996), pp. 7–8

Jones, Glyn, 'The Apple-Tree', in *The Collected Stories of Glyn Jones*, ed. Tony Brown (Cardiff: University of Wales Press, 1999), pp. 91–8

Jones, Glyn, *The Valley, the City, the Village* (Cardigan: Parthian, Library of Wales, 2009)

Joyce, James, *Ulysses* (London: Minerva, 1992)

Kafka, Franz, 'In the Penal Colony', in *The Complete Short Stories of Franz Kafka*, ed. Nahum N. Glatzer, translated from the German by Willa and Edwin Muir (London: Vintage, 1999), pp. 140–67

Kafka, Franz, 'The Metamorphosis', in *The Complete Short Stories of Franz Kafka*, ed. Nahum N. Glatzer, translated from the German by Willa and Edwin Muir (London: Vintage, 1999), pp. 89–139

Keats, John, 'On First Looking into Chapman's Homer', in *John Keats: The Complete Poems*, ed. John Barnard, 2nd edn (Harmondsworth: Penguin, 1977), p. 72

Mansfield, Katherine, 'Frau Brechenmacher Attends a Wedding', in *Katherine Mansfield: Selected Stories*, ed. Angela Smith (Oxford and New York: Oxford University Press, 2002), pp. 3–9

Mansfield, Katherine, 'The Woman at the Store', in *Katherine Mansfield: Selected Stories*, ed. Angela Smith (Oxford and New York: Oxford University Press, 2002), pp. 10–19

Milton, John, *Paradise Lost*, ed. John Leonard (London: Penguin, 2000)

Rhys, Jean, 'I Spy A Stranger', in *Jean Rhys: Collected Stories* (New York and London: Norton, 1987), pp. 232–55

Rhys, Jean, *Voyage in the Dark* (London: Penguin, 1969)

Rhys, Keidrych, 'Poem for a Green Envelope', in Keidrych Rhys, *The Van Pool and Other Poems* (London: Routledge, 1942), pp. 25–8

Rimbaud, Arthur, *A Season in Hell*, in *Arthur Rimbaud: Collected Poems*, translated from the French by Martin Sorrell (Oxford and New York: Oxford University Press, 2001), pp. 210–55

Rimbaud, Arthur, 'Ophelia', in *Arthur Rimbaud: Collected Poems*, translated from the French by Martin Sorrell (Oxford and New York: Oxford University Press, 2001), pp. 29–31

Roberts, Lynette, 'Crossed and Uncrossed', in *Lynette Roberts: Collected Poems*, ed. Patrick McGuinness (Manchester: Carcanet, 2005), pp. 20–1

Roberts, Lynette, 'Curlew', in *Lynette Roberts: Collected Poems*, ed. Patrick McGuinness (Manchester: Carcanet, 2005), p. 15

Roberts, Lynette, *Gods With Stainless Ears: A Heroic Poem*, in *Lynette Roberts: Collected Poems*, ed. Patrick McGuinness (Manchester: Carcanet, 2005), pp. 41–69

Roberts, Lynette, 'Lamentation', in *Lynette Roberts: Collected Poems*, ed. Patrick McGuinness (Manchester: Carcanet, 2005), pp. 8–9

Roberts, Lynette, 'Notes on Legend and Form', in *Lynette Roberts: Collected Poems*, ed. Patrick McGuinness (Manchester: Carcanet, 2005), pp. 38–40

Roberts, Lynette, 'Notes to *Gods With Stainless Ears: A Heroic Poem*', in *Lynette Roberts: Collected Poems*, ed. Patrick McGuinness (Manchester: Carcanet, 2005), pp. 70–8

Roberts, Lynette, 'Plasnewydd', in *Lynette Roberts: Collected Poems*, ed. Patrick McGuinness (Manchester: Carcanet, 2005), pp. 4–5

Roberts, Lynette, 'Poem from Llanybri', in *Lynette Roberts: Collected Poems*, ed. Patrick McGuinness (Manchester: Carcanet, 2005), p. 3

Roberts, Lynette, 'Raw Salt on Eye', in *Lynette Roberts: Collected Poems*, ed. Patrick McGuinness (Manchester: Carcanet, 2005), pp. 6–7

Roberts, Lynette, 'Royal Mail', in *Lynette Roberts: Collected Poems*, ed. Patrick McGuinness (Manchester: Carcanet, 2005), p. 27

Roberts, Lynette, 'Seagulls', in *Lynette Roberts: Collected Poems*, ed. Patrick McGuinness (Manchester: Carcanet, 2005), p. 16

Roberts, Lynette, 'The Circle of C', in *Lynette Roberts: Collected Poems*, ed. Patrick McGuinness (Manchester: Carcanet, 2005), p. 7

Shakespeare, William, *Hamlet: A Norton Critical Edition*, ed. Cyrus Hoy, 2nd edn (New York and London: Norton, 1991)

Shakespeare, William, *Henry V*, ed. Gary Taylor (Oxford and New York: Oxford University Press, 1984)

Stramm, August, 'Guard-Duty', translated from the German by Patrick Bridgewater, in *The Penguin Book of First World War Poetry*, ed. Jon Silkin, 2nd edn (Harmondsworth: Penguin, 1979), p. 240

Taliesin, 'Book of Taliesin XXX', translated from the Welsh by R. Williams, in William F. Skene, *The Four Ancient Books of Wales: Containing the Cymric Poems attributed to the Bards of the Sixth Century* (Edinburgh: Edmonston and Douglas, 1868), I. 264–6

Taliesin, 'The Battle of the Trees', translated from the Welsh by D. W. Nash, in Robert Graves, *The White Goddess: A Historical Grammar of Poetic Myth* (London: Faber and Faber, 1948), pp. 30–6

Taliesin, 'The Battle of the Trees', translated from the Welsh by Robert Graves, in Robert Graves, *The White Goddess: A Historical Grammar of Poetic Myth* (London: Faber and Faber, 1948), pp. 44–7

Thomas, Dylan, 'A process in the weather of the heart', in *Dylan Thomas: Collected Poems 1934–1953*, ed. Walford Davies and Ralph Maud (London: Phoenix, 2000), pp. 10–11

Thomas, Dylan, 'A Prospect of the Sea', in *Dylan Thomas: The Collected Stories* (London: J. M. Dent, 1983), pp. 87–94

Thomas, Dylan, 'Ceremony After a Fire Raid', in *Dylan Thomas: Collected Poems 1934–1953*, ed. Walford Davies and Ralph Maud (London: Phoenix, 2000), pp. 107–9

Thomas, Dylan, 'I see the boys of summer', in *Dylan Thomas: Collected Poems 1934–1953*, ed. Walford Davies and Ralph Maud (London: Phoenix, 2000), pp. 7–8

Thomas, Dylan, 'The Enemies', in *Dylan Thomas: The Collected Stories* (London: J. M. Dent, 1983), pp. 16–20

Thomas, Dylan, 'The force that through the green fuse', in *Dylan Thomas: Collected Poems 1934–1953*, ed. Walford Davies and Ralph Maud (London: Phoenix, 2000), p. 13

Thomas, Dylan, 'The Holy Six', in *Dylan Thomas: The Collected Stories* (London: J. M. Dent, 1983), pp. 95–103

Thomas, Dylan, 'The Lemon', in *Dylan Thomas: The Collected Stories* (London: J. M. Dent, 1984), pp. 54–8

Thomas, Dylan, 'The Map of Love', in *Dylan Thomas: The Collected Stories* (London: J. M. Dent, 1983), pp. 109–14

Thomas, Dylan, 'The Peaches', in *Dylan Thomas: The Collected Stories* (London: J. M. Dent, 1983), pp. 122–37

Thomas, Gwyn, 'And a Spoonful of Grief to Taste', in *Where did I put Pity? Folk Tales from the Modern Welsh* (London: Progress Publishing, 1946), pp. 171–82

Thomas, Gwyn, 'Dust in the Lonely Wind', in *Where did I put Pity?: Folk Tales from the Modern Welsh* (London: Progress Publishing, 1946), pp. 148–70

Thomas, Gwyn, 'Myself My Desert', in *Where did I put Pity?: Folk Tales from the Modern Welsh* (London: Progress Publishing, 1946), pp. 183–93

Thomas, Gwyn, *Oscar*, in *The Dark Philosophers* (Cardigan: Parthian, Library of Wales Series, 2006), pp. 3–101

Thomas, Gwyn, *Simeon*, in *The Dark Philosophers* (Cardigan: Parthian, Library of Wales Series, 2006), pp. 243–95

Thomas, Gwyn, *Sorrow for thy Sons* (London: Lawrence and Wishart, 1986)

Trakl, Georg, 'Night', translated from the German by David McDuff, Jon Silkin and R. S. Furness, in *The Penguin Book of First World War Poetry*, ed. Jon Silkin, 2nd edn (Harmondsworth: Penguin, 1979), p. 231

Valle-Inclán, Ramón del, *Bohemian Lights*, in *Valle-Inclán Plays: One*, translated from the Spanish by Maria Delgado (London: Methuen Drama, 1993), pp. 91–184

Watkins, Vernon, 'Discoveries', in *The Collected Poems of Vernon Watkins* (Ipswich: Golgonooza, Press, 1986), pp. 38–9

Watkins, Vernon, 'Ode: to T. S. Eliot', in *The Collected Poems of Vernon Watkins* (Ipswich: Golgonooza, Press, 1986), pp. 293–5
Watkins, Vernon, 'Ophelia', in *The Collected Poems of Vernon Watkins* (Ipswich: Golgonooza, Press, 1986), pp. 114–15
Watkins, Vernon, 'Taliesin and the Spring of Vision', in *The Collected Poems of Vernon Watkins* (Ipswich: Golgonooza, Press, 1986), pp. 224–5
Watkins, Vernon, 'The Collier', in *The Collected Poems of Vernon Watkins* (Ipswich: Golgonooza, Press, 1986), pp. 3–4
Watkins, Vernon, 'Yeats in Dublin', in *The Collected Poems of Vernon Watkins* (Ipswich: Golgonooza, Press, 1986), pp. 59–68
Wilde, Oscar, *Salome*, illustrated by Aubrey Beardsley and translated from the French by Lord Alfred Douglas (New York: Dover, 1967)
Wordsworth, William, *The Prelude*, in *The Oxford Authors: William Wordsworth*, ed. Stephen Gill (Oxford and New York: Oxford University Press, 1984), pp. 375–590
Yeats, W. B., 'Brown Penny', in *The Collected Poems of W. B Yeats*, 2nd edn, ed. Richard J. Finneran (New York: Simon and Schuster, 1996), p. 98
Yeats, W. B., 'Swift's Epitaph', in *The Collected Poems of W. B Yeats*, 2nd edn, ed. Richard J. Finneran (New York: Simon and Schuster, 1996), pp. 245–6
Yeats, W.B., 'The Song of Wandering Aengus', in *The Collected Poems of W. B Yeats*, 2nd edn, ed. Richard J. Finneran (New York: Simon and Schuster, 1996), pp. 59–60
Yeats, W.B., 'Under Ben Bulben', in *The Collected Poems of W.B Yeats*, 2nd edn, ed. Richard J. Finneran (New York: Simon and Schuster, 1996), pp. 325–8
Yeats, W. B., 'When You are Old', in *The Collected Poems of W.B Yeats*, 2nd edn, ed. Richard J. Finneran (New York: Simon and Schuster, 1996), p. 41

Films

L'Age d'or, dir. Luis Buñuel (1930)
Un Chien Andalou, dir. Luis Buñuel and Salvador Dalí (1929)

Paintings and Images

Beardsley, Aubrey, *The Toilette of Salome* (1893), The British Museum, London
Carrà, Carlo, *Interventionist Manifestation* (1914), Collezione Gianni Mattioli, Venice, Peggy Guggenheim Collection – The Solomon R. Guggenheim Foundation, New York

Crali, Tullio, *Air Battle I* (1936–8), Private collection
Dalí, Salvador, *Average Atmospherocephalic Bureaucrat in the Act of Milking a Cranial Harp* (1933), The Salvador Dalí Museum, St Petersberg, FL
Dalí, Salvador, *Illuminated Pleasures* (1929), The Museum of Modern Art, New York
Dalí, Salvador, *The Enigma of Desire – My Mother, My Mother, My Mother* (1929), Staatsgalerie moderner Kunst, Munich
Dalí, Salvador, *The Great Masturbator* (1929), Museo Nacional Reina Sofía, Madrid
Dalí, Salvador, *The Hand – Remorse* (1930), The Salvador Dalí Museum, St Petersberg, FL
Dalí, Salvador, *The Persistence of Memory (Soft Watches)* (1931), The Museum of Modern Art, New York
Dalí, Salvador, *The Red Tower (Anthropomorphic Tower)* (1930), Mrs Edwin A. Bergman Collection, Chicago
Dalí, Salvador, *The Spectre of Sex Appeal* (1934), Fundación Gala-Salvador Dalí, Figueras
Dalí, Salvador, *Untitled (William Tell and Gradiva)* (1933), Private collection
Dalí, Salvador, *Vertigo – Tower of Pleasure* (1930), Private collection
Dalí, Salvador, *View of Cadaqués from Mount Pani* (1921), The Salvador Dalí Museum, St Petersberg, FL
Dalí, Salvador, *View of Cadaqués from Playa Poal* (1920), Fundación Gala-Salvador Dalí, Figueras
Dix, Otto, *Prager Strasse* (1920), Galerie der Stadt Stuttgart, Stuttgart
Dix, Otto, *Self-Portrait as a Soldier* (1914–15), Galerie der Stadt Stuttgart, Stuttgart
Dix, Otto, *The Skat Players* (1920), Galerie der Stadt Stuttgart, Stuttgart
Felixmüller, Conrad, *Industrie – Regenlandschaft* (1922), Hessisches Landesmuseum, Darmstadt
Felixmüller, Conrad, *Ruhrrevier I* (1920), Private collection
Grosz, George, *Dedicated to Oscar Panizza* (1917–18), Staatsgalerie Stuttgart, Stuttgart
Heckel, Erich, *Portrait of a Man (Self-Portrait)* (1919), Brücke-Museum, Berlin
Millais, Sir John Everett, *Ophelia* (1852), Tate Gallery, London

Secondary Sources

Ackroyd, Peter, *T. S. Eliot* (London: Hamish Hamilton, 1984)
Aldridge, A. Owen, *Voltaire and the Century of Light* (Princeton, NJ: Princeton University Press, 1975)

Alldritt, Keith, *W. B. Yeats: The Man and the Milieu* (London: John Murray, 1997)

Alexander, Neal, and James Moran (eds), *Regional Modernisms* (Edinburgh: Edinburgh University Press, 2013)

Armour, Peter, 'Notes: *Paradiso*', in Dante Alighieri, *The Divine Comedy*, translated from the Italian by Allen Mandelbaum (London: Everyman's Library, 1995), pp. 707–91

Armour, Peter, 'Notes: *Purgatorio*', in Dante Alighieri, *The Divine Comedy*, translated from the Italian by Allen Mandelbaum (London: Everyman's Library, 1995), pp. 625–706

Baker, Simon, and Joanna Furber, '"Unspeakable Rites": Writing the Unspeakable in Rhys Davies', in *Rhys Davies: Decoding the Hare*, ed. Meic Stephens (Cardiff: University of Wales Press, 2001), pp. 244–59

Bakhtin, Mikhail, *Rabelais and his World*, translated from the Russian by Hélène Iswolsky (Bloomington: Indiana University Press, 1984)

Barthes, Roland, 'from *Writing Degree Zero*', in *A Barthes Reader*, ed. Susan Sontag (London: Vintage, 1993), pp. 31–61

Barthes, Roland, *The Pleasure of the Text*, translated from the French by Richard Miller (New York: Hill and Wang, 1975)

Baudrillard, Jean, *Simulacra and Simulation*, translated from the French by Sheila Faria Glaser (Michigan: University of Michigan Press, 1994)

Benjamin, Walter, 'Surrealism: The Last Snapshot of the European Intelligentsia', in *Walter Benjamin: Selected Writings 1927–1934*, ed. Michael W. Jennings, Howard Eiland and Gary Smith (Cambridge, MA, and London: Harvard University Press, 1999), II. 207–21

Bennett, Andrew, *Katherine Mansfield* (Tavistock: Northcote House, 2004)

Bluemel, Kristin, *George Orwell and the Radical Extremists: Intermodernism in Literary London* (New York and Basingstoke: Palgrave Macmillan, 2004)

Boone, Joseph Allen, *Libidinal Currents: Sexuality and the Shaping of Modernism* (Chicago and London: The University of Chicago Press, 1998)

Bradbury, Malcolm, 'The Cities of Modernism', in *Modernism: A Guide to European Literature 1890–1930*, ed. Malcolm Bradbury and James McFarlane (London: Penguin, 1976), pp. 96–104

Bradbury, Malcolm, and James Mcfarlane, 'Brief Biographies', in *Modernism: A Guide to European Literature 1890–1930*, ed. Malcolm Bradbury and James McFarlane (London: Penguin, 1976), pp. 613–40

Brecht, Bertolt, 'A Short Organum for the Theatre', in *Brecht on Theatre: The Development of an Aesthetic*, translated from the German by John Willet (London: Methuen, 1964), pp. 179–205

Brecht, Bertolt, 'Short Description of a New Technique of Acting which Produces an Alienation Effect', in *Brecht on Theatre: The Development of an Aesthetic*, translated from the German by John Willet (London: Methuen, 1964), pp. 136–47

Breton, André, 'First Manifesto of Surrealism', translated from the French by Richard Seaver and Helen R. Lane, in *Modernism: An Anthology of Sources and Documents*, ed. Vassiliki Kolocotroni, Jane Goldman and Olga Taxidou (Edinburgh: Edinburgh University Press, 1998), pp. 307–11

Brown, G. G., *A Literary History of Spain: The Twentieth Century* (London: Ernest Benn, 1972)

Brown, Terence, 'Ireland, Modernism and the 1930s', in *Modernism and Ireland: The Poetry of the 1930s* (Cork: Cork University Press, 1995), pp. 24–42

Brown, Tony, 'Glyn Jones and the "Uncanny"', in *Almanac: A Yearbook of Welsh Writing in English – Critical Essays*, ed. Katie Gramich, n.s. 12 (2007–8), 89–114

Brown, Tony, 'Introduction: The Making of a Writer', in *The Collected Stories of Glyn Jones*, ed. Tony Brown (Cardiff: University of Wales Press, 1999), pp. xiii–lxvi

Brown, Tony, 'Notes', in *The Collected Stories of Glyn Jones*, ed. Tony Brown (Cardiff: University of Wales Press, 1999), pp. 354–402

Butler, Judith, 'Imitation and Gender Insubordination', in *The Routledge Critical and Cultural Theory Reader*, ed. Neil Badmington and Julia Thomas (London and New York: Routledge, 2008), pp. 365–80

Campbell, Duncan, 'David Jones: "No End to these Wars, No End, No End/ At All"', in *Wales at War: Critical Essays on Literature and Art*, ed. Tony Curtis (Bridgend: Seren, 2007), pp. 25–38

Carey, John, *John Donne: Life, Mind and Art* (London: Faber and Faber, 1981)

Carroll, Bradley W., and Dale A. Ostlie, *An Introduction to Modern Astrophysics* (Reading, MA: Addison-Wesley Publishing, 1996)

Casanova, Pascale, *The World Republic of Letters*, translated from the French by M. B. Debevoise (Cambridge, MA, and London: Harvard University Press, 2004)

Chilvers, Ian, *The Concise Oxford Dictionary of Art and Artists*, 3rd edn (Oxford and New York: Oxford University Press, 2003)

Church, Jennifer, 'Morality and the internalized other', in *The Cambridge Companion to Freud*, ed. Jerome Neu (Cambridge: Cambridge University Press, 1991), pp. 209–23

Cleary, Joe, 'Introduction: Ireland and Modernity', in *The Cambridge Companion to Modern Irish Culture*, ed. Joe Cleary and Claire Connolly (Cambridge: Cambridge University Press, 2005), pp. 1–21

Conran, Anthony, *The Cost of Strangeness: Essays on the English Poets of Wales* (Llandysul: Gomer Press, 1982)

Conran, Tony, *Frontiers in Anglo-Welsh Poetry* (Cardiff: University of Wales Press, 1997)

Conran, Tony, 'Introduction' in Idris Davies, *The Angry Summer: A Poem of 1926* (Cardiff: University of Wales Press, 1993), pp. xiii–xxxii

Conran, Tony, 'Lynette Roberts: The Lyric Pieces', *Poetry Wales*, n.s. 19/2, 125–33

Cooper, John Xiros, *The Cambridge Companion to T. S. Eliot* (Cambridge and New York: Cambridge University Press, 2006)

Cork, Richard, *Vorticism and Abstract Art in the First Machine Age* (London: Gordon Fraser, 1976)

Crawford, Robert, *Identifying Poets: Self and Territory in Twentieth-Century Poetry* (Edinburgh: Edinburgh University Press, 1993)

Dalí, Salvador, *The Secret Life* (New York: Dover, 1993)

Damon, S. Foster, *A Blake Dictionary: The Ideas and Symbols of William Blake*, 2nd edn (Hanover, NH: University of New England, 1988)

Davidson, Ian, *Voltaire in Exile: The Last Years, 1753–78* (London: Atlantic Books, 2004)

Davies, James A., 'Dylan Thomas and his Welsh Contemporaries', in *A Guide to Welsh Literature: Welsh Writing in English*, ed. M. Wynn Thomas (Cardiff: University of Wales Press, 2003), VII. 120–64

Davies, John, *A History of Wales* (London: Penguin, 1994)

Davies, Stevie, 'Foreword', in Glyn Jones, *The Valley, the City, the Village* (Cardigan: Parthian, Library of Wales Series, 2009), pp. ix–xv

Davies, Walford, 'The Poetry of Dylan Thomas: Welsh Contexts, Narrative and the Language of Modernism', in *Dylan Thomas: Contemporary Critical Essays*, ed. John Goodby and Chris Wigginton (Basingstoke: Palgrave, 2001), pp. 106–23

Davies, Walford, and Ralph Maud (eds), 'Notes', in *Dylan Thomas: Collected Poems 1934–1953* (London: Phoenix, 2000), pp. 175–258

Deigh, John, 'Freud's later theory of civilisation: changes and implications', in *The Cambridge Companion to Freud*, ed. Jerome Ness (Cambridge: Cambridge University Press, 1991), pp. 287–308

Deleuze, Gilles, and Félix Guattari, *Kafka: Toward a Minor Literature*, translated from the French by Dana Polan (Minneapolis: University of Minnesota Press, 1986)

Delgado, Maria, 'Introduction', in Ramón del Valle-Inclán, *Valle-Inclán Plays: One*, translated from the Spanish by Maria Delgado (London: Methuen Drama, 1993), pp. xiii–xlii

Descharnes, Robert, and Gilles Néret, *Salvador Dalí: 1904–1989* (Cologne: Taschen, 2006)

Descharnes, Robert, and Gilles Néret, *Salvador Dalí: The Paintings 1904–1946* (Cologne: Benedikt Taschen, 1997)

Dickson, Donald R. (ed.), 'Preface', in *John Donne's Poetry: A Norton Critical Edition* (New York and London: Norton, 2007), pp. xi–xiv

Dilworth, Thomas, *Reading David Jones* (Cardiff: University of Wales Press, 2008)

Doyle, Laura, and Laura Winkiel, 'Introduction', in Laura Doyle and Laura Winkiel (eds), *Geomodernisms: Race, Modernism, Modernity* (Bloomington and Indianapolis: Indiana University Press, 2005), pp. 1–14

Drabble Margaret (ed.), *The Oxford Companion to English Literature*, 6th edn (Oxford and New York: Oxford University Press, 2000)

Edwards, Gwynne, *Dramatists in Perspective: Spanish Theatre in the Twentieth Century* (Cardiff: University of Wales Press, 1985)

Elger, Dietmar, *Expressionism: A Revolution in German Art* (Cologne: Taschen, 2007)

Eliot, T. S., 'The Metaphysical Poets', in *T.S. Eliot: Selected Essays*, 2nd edn (London: Faber and Faber, 1934), pp. 281–91

Eliot, T. S., 'Tradition and the Individual Talent', in *T. S. Eliot: Selected Writings* (London: Faber and Faber, 1932), pp. 13–33

Enright, D. J. (ed.), *The Oxford Book of Death* (Oxford and New York: Oxford University Press, 1983)

Fara, Patricia, *Science: A Four Thousand Year History* (Oxford and New York: Oxford University Press, 2009)

Ferguson, Margaret, Mary Jo Salter and Jon Stallworthy (eds), *The Norton Anthology of Poetry*, 5th edn (London and New York: Norton, 2005)

Ferris, Paul, *Dylan Thomas: The Biography* (Talybont: Y Lolfa, 2006)

Ferris, Paul (ed.), *Dylan Thomas: The Collected Letters* (London: Paladin, 1987)

Fletcher, Ian, *Aubrey Beardsley*, ed. Herbert Sussman (Boston, MA: Twayne Publishers, 1987)

Fordham, John, *James Hanley: Modernism and the Working Class* (Cardiff: University of Wales Press, 2002)

Foucault, Michel, 'Different Spaces', translated from the French by Robert Hurley and others, in *Essential Works of Foucault 1954–1984*, ed. James D. Fausion (New York: The New Press, 1998), II. 175–85

Fox, Christopher, 'Introduction', in *The Cambridge Companion to Jonathan Swift*, ed. Christopher Fox (Cambridge: Cambridge University Press, 2003), pp. 1–13

Freud, Sigmund, 'Beyond the Pleasure Principle', in *The Freud Reader*, ed. Peter Gay (London: Vintage, 1995), pp. 594–627

Freud, Sigmund, 'Lecture XXXII: Anxiety and Instinctual Life', in *The Freud Reader*, ed. Peter Gay (London: Vintage, 1995), pp. 773–83

Freud, Sigmund, 'Three Essays on the Theory of Infantile Sexuality', in *The Freud Reader*, ed. Peter Gay (London: Vintage, 1995), pp. 239–93

Fussell, Paul, *The Great War and Modern Memory*, 2nd edn (New York: Oxford University Press, 1975)

Gallagher, Joseph, *A Modern Reader's Guide to Dante's The Divine Comedy* (Liguori, MI: Liguori/Triumph, 1996)

Gasiorek, Andzej, *Wyndham Lewis and Modernism* (Tavistock: Northcote House, 2004)

Gibson, Ian, *The Shameful Life of Salvador Dalí* (London: Faber and Faber, 1997)

Golightly, Victor, 'Gwyn Thomas's American 'Oscar'', *New Welsh Review*, n.s. 22 (Autumn 1993), 26–31

Goodby, John, *The Poetry of Dylan Thomas Under the Spelling Wall* (Liverpool: Liverpool University Press, 2013)

Goodby, John, and Christopher Wigginton, '"Shut, too, in a tower of words': Dylan Thomas' modernism', in *Locations of Literary Modernism: Region and Nation in British and American Modernist Poetry*, ed. Alex Davis and Lee M. Jenkins (Cambridge: Cambridge University Press, 2000), pp. 89–112

Goodby, John, and Chris Wigginton, 'Welsh Modernist Poetry: Dylan Thomas, David Jones and Lynette Roberts', in *Regional Modernisms*, ed. Neal Alexander and James Moran (Edinburgh: Edinburgh University Press, 2013), pp. 160–83

Gramich, Katie, 'Daughters of Darkness', in *Dylan Thomas: Contemporary Critical Essays*, ed. John Goodby and Christopher Wigginton (Basingstoke: Palgrave, 2001), pp. 65–84

Gramich, Katie, Unpublished paper: '"Sick to death of Hot Salt": The Mother's Body in the Poetry of Dylan Thomas' (presented at the annual Association for Welsh Writing in English conference, Gregynog Hall, Powys, 1996)

Gramich, Katie, *Twentieth-Century Women's Writing in Wales: Land, Gender, Belonging* (Cardiff: University of Wales Press, 2007)

Gramich, Katie, 'Welsh Women Writers and War', in *Wales at War: Critical Essays on Literature and Art*, ed. Tony Curtis (Bridgend: Seren, 2007), pp. 122–41

Graves, Robert, *The White Goddess: A Historical Grammar of Poetic Myth* (London: Faber and Faber, 1948)

Gregson, Ian, *The New Poetry in Wales* (Cardiff: University of Wales Press, 2007)

Griffiths, Bruce, 'His Theatre', in *Presenting Saunders Lewis*, ed. Alun R. Jones and Gwyn Thomas (Cardiff: University of Wales Press, 1973), pp. 79–92

Griffiths, Bruce, '*The Eve of Saint John* and the Significance of the Stranger in the Plays of Saunders Lewis', in *Welsh Writing in English*, n.s. 3 (1997), 62–77

Grimal, Pierre, *The Penguin Dictionary of Classical Mythology*, ed. Stephen Kershaw, translated from the French by A. R. Maxwell-Hyslop (London: Penguin, 1990)

Grimme, Karin H., *Impressionism*, ed. Norbert Wolf (Cologne: Taschen, 2007)

Harris, Derek, 'Squared horizons: the hybridization of the avant-garde in Spain', in Derek Harris (ed.), *The Spanish Avant-Garde* (Manchester and New York: Manchester University Press, 1995), pp. 1–14

Hilton, Ian, 'Vernon Watkins and Hölderlin', in *Poetry Wales*, n.s. 12/4 (Spring 1977), 101–17

Hilton, Ian, 'Vernon Watkins as Translator', in *Vernon Watkins 1906–1967*, ed. Leslie Norris (London: Faber and Faber, 1970), pp. 74–89

Hooker, Jeremy, 'David Jones and the Matter of Wales', in *David Jones: Diversity in Unity* (Cardiff: University of Wales Press, 2000), pp. 11–25

Hooker, Jeremy, *Imagining Wales: A View of Modern Welsh Writing in English* (Cardiff: University of Wales Press, 2001)

Hunter, Lynette, '*Animal Farm*: From Satire to Allegory', in *George Orwell: Contemporary Critical Essays*, ed. Graham Holderness, Bryan Loughrey and Nahem Yousaf (Basingstoke: Macmillan, 1998), pp. 31–46

Johnston, Dafydd, 'Idris Davies's Life', in *The Complete Poems of Idris Davies*, ed. Dafydd Johnston (Cardiff: University of Wales Press 1994), pp. xi–xxxv

Johnston, Dafydd, 'Notes to Section A', *The Complete Poems of Idris Davies*, ed. Dafydd Johnston (Cardiff: University of Wales Press, 1994), pp. 277–89

Johnston, Dafydd, 'The Development of Idris Davies's Poetry', *The Complete Poems of Idris Davies*, ed. Dafydd Johnston (Cardiff: University of Wales Press, 1994), pp. xxxvi–lxxx

Johnston, Dafydd, *The Literature of Wales: A Pocket Guide* (Cardiff: University of Wales Press, 1998)

Jones, David, 'Preface' in David Jones, *In Parenthesis* (London: Faber and Faber, 1963), pp. ix–xv

Jones, David, 'Welsh Poetry', in *Epoch and Artist: Selected Writings by David Jones*, ed. Harman Grisewood (London: Faber and Faber, 1959), pp. 56–65

Jones, Glyn, '18 Poems Again', *Poetry Wales*, n.s. 9 (1973–4), 22–6

Jones, Glyn, 'Autobiography', in Glyn Jones, *The Dragon has Two Tongues: Essays on Anglo-Welsh Writers and Writing*, ed. Tony Brown, 2nd edn (Cardiff: University of Wales Press, 2001), pp. 5–36

Jones, Glyn, 'Conclusion', in Glyn Jones, *The Dragon has Two Tongues: Essays on Anglo-Welsh Writers and Writing*, ed. Tony Brown, 2nd edn (Cardiff: University of Wales Press, 2001), pp. 192–6

Jones, Glyn, 'Gwyn Thomas', in Glyn Jones, *The Dragon has Two Tongues: Essays on Anglo-Welsh Writers and Writing*, ed. Tony Brown, 2nd edn (Cardiff: University of Wales Press, 2001), pp. 100–16

Jones, Glyn, 'Notes on Surrealism', translated from the Welsh by Tony Brown, *The New Welsh Review* 28 (1995) 20–2

Jones, Glyn, 'Whose Flight is Toil', in *Vernon Watkins 1906-1967*, ed. Leslie Norris (London: Faber and Faber, 1970), pp. 23–6

Jones, Gwyn, 'Editorial', *The Welsh Review*, n.s. 1 (February 1939), 3–4

Karcher, Eva, *Otto Dix 1891–1969*, 2nd edn (Cologne: Taschen, 2002)

Klonsky, Milton, *Blake's Dante: The Complete Illustrations to the Divine Comedy* (London: Sidgwick and Jackson, 1981)

Knight, Stephen, *A Hundred Years of Fiction: Writing Wales in English* (Cardiff: University of Wales Press, 2004)

Knight, Stephen, '"Not a Place for Me": Rhys Davies's Fiction and the Coal Industry', in *Rhys Davies: Decoding the Hare*, ed. Meic Stephens (Cardiff: University of Wales Press, 2001), pp. 54–70

Krempel, Ulrich (ed.), *Conrad Felixmüller: Die Dresdner Jahre 1910–1934* (Cologne: Druck- and Verlagshaus Wiend, 1997)

Kronfeld, Chana, *On the Margins of Modernism: Decentering Literary Dynamics* (Berkeley and London: University of California Press, 1996)

Leonard, John, 'Introduction', in John Milton, *Paradise Lost*, ed. John Leonard (London: Penguin, 2000), pp. vii–xliii

Leonard, John, 'Notes', in John Milton, *Paradise Lost*, ed. John Leonard (London: Penguin, 2000), pp. 289–453

Lewis, Peter Elfed, 'Poetry in the Thirties: A View of the "First Flowering"', *The Anglo-Welsh Review*, n.s. 71 (1982), 50–74

Lewis, Saunders, *Is there an Anglo-Welsh Literature? Being the Annual Lecture Delivered to the Branch on December 10th, 1938* (Cardiff: Urdd Graddedigion Prifysgol Cymru, 1939)

Lyon, John, *The Theatre of Valle-Inclán* (Cambridge: Cambridge University Press, 1983)

Marinetti, Filippo Tommaso, 'Technical Manifesto of Futurist Literature', in *Marinetti: Selected Writings*, translated from the Italian by R. W. Flint and Arthur A. Coppotelli (New York: Farrar, Straus and Giroux, 1972), pp. 8493

Marinetti, Filippo Tommaso, 'The Founding and Manifesto of Futurism', translated from the French by R. W. Flint, in *Modernism: An Anthology of Sources and Documents*, ed. Vassiliki Kolocotroni, Jane Goldman and Olga Taxidou (Edinburgh: Edinburgh University Press, 1998), pp. 249–53

Martin, Sylvia, *Futurism* (Cologne: Taschen, 2006)

Mathias, Roland, *Vernon Watkins* (Cardiff: University of Wales Press, Writers of Wales Series, 1974)

Matthiessen, F.O., 'The Quartets', in *T. S. Eliot Four Quartets: A Casebook*, ed. Bernard Bergonzi (London: Macmillan, 1969), pp. 88–104

McCombie, Elizabeth, 'Introduction', in *Stéphane Mallarmé: Collected Poems and Other Verse*, translated from the French by E. H. and A. M. Blackmore (Oxford and New York: Oxford University Press, 2006), pp. ix–xxvii

McGuinness, Patrick, 'Introduction', in *Lynette Roberts: Collected Poems*, ed. Patrick McGuinness (Manchester: Carcanet, 2005), pp. xi–xxxix

McGuinness, Patrick, 'Introduction', in *Lynette Roberts: Diaries, Letters and Recollections*, ed. Patrick McGuinness (Manchester: Carcanet, 2008), pp. vii–xvii

McGuinness, Patrick, *Maurice Maeterlinck and the Making of Modern Theatre* (Oxford and New York: Oxford University Press, 2000)

McGuinness, Patrick, 'Notes', in *Lynette Roberts: Collected Poems*, ed. Patrick McGuinness (Manchester: Carcanet, 2005), pp. 135–50

McGuinness, Patrick, 'Notes', in *Lynette Roberts: Diaries, Letters and Recollections*, ed. Patrick McGuinness (Manchester: Carcanet, 2008), pp. 221–9

McGuinness, Patrick, 'Preface', in *Lynette Roberts: Collected Poems*, ed. Patrick McGuinness (Manchester: Carcanet, 2005), pp. ix–xxxix

McMinn, Joseph, 'Swift's Life', in *The Cambridge Companion to Jonathan Swift*, ed. Christopher Fox (Cambridge: Cambridge University Press, 2003), pp. 14–30

Miller, Tyrus, *Late Modernism: Politics, Fiction, and the Arts Between the World Wars* (Berkley, Los Angeles and London: University of California Press, 1999)

Mitchell, J. Lawrence, '"I Wish I Had a Trumpet": Rhys Davies and the Creative Impulse', in *Rhys Davies: Decoding the Hare*, ed. Meic Stephens (Cardiff: University of Wales Press, 2001), pp. 147–61

Mousley, Andrew, 'Introduction', in *John Donne: Contemporary Critical Essays*, ed. Andrew Mousley (Basingstoke: Palgrave, 1999), pp. 1–24

Mueller, Judith C., '*A Tale of a Tub* and early prose', in *The Cambridge Companion to Jonathan Swift*, ed. Christopher Fox (Cambridge: Cambridge University Press, 2003), pp. 202–15

Neu, Jerome, 'Introduction', in *The Cambridge Companion to Freud* (Cambridge: Cambridge University Press, 1991), pp. 1–7

Nicholls, Peter, *Modernisms: A Literary Guide*, 2nd edn (Basingstoke and New York: Palgrave Macmillan, 2009)

Nietzsche, Friedrich, *Thus Spake Zarathustra: A Book For All And None*, translated from the German by Thomas Wayne (New York: Algora, 2003)

Nokes, David, *Jonathan Swift: A Hypocrite Reversed – A Critical Biography* (Oxford and New York: Oxford University Press, 1987)

Norris, Leslie (ed.), *Vernon Watkins 1906–1967* (London: Faber and Faber, 1970)

Ortega y Gasset, José, 'The Dehumanisation of Art', in *'The Dehumanisation of Art' and Other Essays on Art, Culture, and Literature*, translated from the Spanish by Helene Weyl (Princeton: Princeton University Press, 1968), pp. 3–54

Ouditt, Sharon, *Fighting Forces, Writing Women* (London: Routledge, 1994)

Parnell, Michael, *Laughter from the Dark: A Life of Gwyn Thomas* (London: John Murray, 1988)

Peach, Linden, 'Eccentricity and Lawlessness in Rhys Davies's Fiction', in *Rhys Davies: Decoding the Hare*, ed. Meic Stephens (Cardiff: University of Wales Press, 2001), pp. 162–74

Phillips, Catherine, 'Introduction', in *Gerard Manley Hopkins: Selected Poems*, ed. Catherine Phillips (Oxford and New York: Oxford University Press, 1998), pp. xi–xvi

Phillips, Ivan, '"Death is all metaphor": Dylan Thomas's Radical Morbidity', in *Dylan Thomas: Contemporary Critical Essays*, ed. John Goodby and Christopher Wigginton (Basingstoke: Palgrave, 2001), pp. 124–39

Pikoulis, John, 'Lynette Roberts and Alun Lewis', in *Poetry Wales*, n.s. 19/2 (1983), 9–29

Pizzichini, Lilian, *The Blue Hour: A Portrait of Jean Rhys* (London: Bloomsbury, 2009)

Plain, Gill, *Women's Fiction of the Second World War: Gender, Power and Resistance* (Edinburgh: Edinburgh University Press, 1996)

Pratt, Annis, *Dylan Thomas' Early Prose: A Study in Creative Mythology* (Pittsburgh: University of Pittsburgh Press, 1970)

Price-Owen, Anne, 'Introduction', in *David Jones: Diversity in Unity* (Cardiff: University of Wales Press, 2000), pp. 1–10

Prys Williams, Barbara, 'Rhys Davies as Autobiographer: Hare or Houdini?', in *Rhys Davies: Decoding the Hare*, ed. Meic Stephens (Cardiff: University of Wales Press, 2001), pp. 104–37

Ramsbotham, Richard, 'Introduction', in *Vernon Watkins: New Selected Poems*, ed. Richard Ramsbotham (Manchester: Carcanet Press, 2006), pp. xi–xxviii

Ramsbotham, Richard, 'Notes', in *Vernon Watkins: New Selected Poems*, ed. Richard Ramsbotham (Manchester: Carcanet, 2006), pp. 103–12

Rich, Adrienne, 'Compulsory Heterosexuality and Lesbian Existence', in *Adrienne Rich's Poetry and Prose*, ed. Barbara Charlesworth Gelpi and Albert Gelpi (New York and London: Norton, 1993), pp. 203–24

Roberts, Lynette, 'A Carmarthenshire Diary', in *Lynette Roberts: Diaries, Letters and Recollections*, ed. Patrick McGuinness (Manchester: Carcanet, 2008), pp. 393

Roberts, Lynette, 'An Introduction to Welsh Dialect', in *Lynette Roberts: Collected Poems*, ed. Patrick McGuinness (Manchester: Carcanet, 2005), pp. 107–24

Roberts, Lynette, 'Letters to Robert Graves', in *Lynette Roberts: Diaries, Letters and Recollections*, ed. Patrick McGuinness (Manchester: Carcanet, 2008), pp. 167–88

Roberts, Lynette, 'The Welsh Dragon', in *Lynette Roberts: Diaries, Letters and Recollections*, ed. Patrick McGuinness (Manchester: Carcanet, 2008), pp. 139–42

Roberts, Lynette, 'Visit to T. S. Eliot', in *Lynette Roberts: Diaries, Letters and Recollections*, ed. Patrick McGuinness (Manchester: Carcanet, 2008), pp. 149–53

Royle, Nicholas, *The Uncanny* (Manchester: Manchester University Press, 2002)

Ryan, Robert, 'Blake and Religion', in *The Cambridge Companion to William Blake*, ed. Morris Eaves (Cambridge: Cambridge University Press, 2003), pp. 150–68

Saussure, Ferdinand de, *Course in General Linguistics*, ed. Charles Bally and Albert Sechehaye, translated from the French by Wade Baskin (New York: McGraw-Hill, 1966)

Scott, Clive, 'Symbolism, Decadence and Impressionism', in *Modernism: A Guide to European Literature 1890V1930*, ed. Malcolm Bradbury and James McFarlane (London: Penguin, 1976), pp. 206–27

Scott, John A., *Understanding Dante* (Notre Dame, Indiana: University of Notre Dame Press, 2004)

Sheppard, Richard, 'The Crisis of Language', in *Modernism: A Guide to European Literature 1890–1930*, ed. Malcolm Bradbury and James McFarlane (London: Penguin, 1976), pp. 323–36

Simon, Bennett, and Rachel B. Blass, 'The development and vicissitudes of Freud's ideas on the Oedipus complex', in *The Cambridge Companion to Freud*, ed. Jerome Neu (Cambridge: Cambridge University Press, 1991), pp. 161–74

Sinclair, Lorna (ed.), *The Collins Spanish Dictionary Plus Grammar* (Glasgow: HarperCollins, 1998)

Smith, David, 'The Early Gwyn Thomas', *Transactions of the Honourable Society of Cymmrodorion* (1985), 71–8

Soanes, Catherine, and Angus Stevenson (eds), *Concise Oxford English Dictionary*, 11th edn (Oxford: Oxford University Press, 2004)

Spilka, Mark, 'Turning the Freudian Screw: How Not to Do It', in Henry James, *The Turn of the Screw*, ed. Robert Kimbrough (New York: Norton, 1966), pp. 245–53

Stephens, Meic, 'Introduction', in *Rhys Davies: Collected Stories*, ed. Meic Stephens (Llandysul: Gomer, 1996), I. 7–16

Stephens, Meic, 'Introduction', in *Rhys Davies: Decoding the Hare*, ed. Meic Stephens (Cardiff: University of Wales Press, 2001), pp. 1–28

Stephens, Meic, 'Notes on the Poems', in *The Collected Poems of Glyn Jones*, ed. Meic Stephens (Cardiff: University of Wales Press, 1996), pp. 133–66

Stephens, Meic (ed.), *The New Companion to the Literature of Wales* (Cardiff: University of Wales Press, 1998)

Stephens, Meic (ed.), 'What was before the Big Bang?: Extracts from the 1980s jottings of Glyn Jones', in *The New Welsh Review*, n.s. 39 (Winter, 1997–8), 40–2

Stewart, Susan, *On Looking: Narratives of the Miniature, the Gigantic, the Souvenir, the Collection* (Durham, NC, and London: Duke University Press, 1993)

Thacker, Andrew, *Moving through Modernity: Space and Geography in Modernism* (Manchester: Manchester University Press, 2003)

Thomas, Gwyn, 'The Central Wound', in *A Welsh Eye* (London: Hutchinson, 1964), pp. 9–24

Thomas, M. Wynn, *Corresponding Cultures: The Two Literatures of Wales* (Cardiff: University of Wales Press, 1999)

Thomas, M. Wynn, *Internal Difference: Literature in Twentieth-Century Wales* (Cardiff: University of Wales Press, 1992)

Thomas, M. Wynn, *In the Shadow of the Pulpit: Literature and Nonconformist Wales* (Cardiff: University of Wales Press, 2010)

Thomas, M. Wynn, "Never Seek to Tell thy Love': Rhys Davies's Fiction', in *Rhys Davies: Decoding the Hare*, ed. Meic Stephens (Cardiff: University of Wales Press, 2001), pp. 260–82

Vajda, György M., 'Outline of the Philosophic Backgrounds of Expressionism', in *Expressionism as an International Literary Phenomenon*, ed. Ulrich Weisstein, translated from the German by Linda Brust (Paris: Librairie Marcel Didier, 1973), pp. 45–58

Voltaire, 'Reflections on Religion', in *The Portable Enlightenment Reader*, ed. Isaac Kramnick (London: Penguin, 1996), pp. 115–33

Wainwright, Laura, '"The huge upright Europe-reflecting mirror"': The European Dimension in the Early Short Stories and Poems of Glyn Jones', in *Almanac: A Yearbook of Welsh Writing in English – Critical Essays*, ed. Katie Gramich, n.s. 12 (2007–8), 55–88

Walker, R.A. (ed.), *The Best of Beardsley* (London: The Bodley Head, 1948)

Wallace, Jeff, 'Lawrentianisms: Rhys Davies and D. H. Lawrence', in *Rhys Davies: Decoding the Hare*, ed. Meic Stephens (Cardiff: University of Wales Press, 2001), pp. 175–90

Watkins, Vernon, 'Prose: excerpts from Vernon Watkins's lecture notes used at University College, Swansea, in 1966', *Poetry Wales*, n.s. 12/4 (Spring 1977), 52–6

Watkins, Vernon, 'The Translation of Poetry', in *Vernon Watkins: Selected Verse*, ed. Ruth Pryor (London: Enitharmon Press, 1977), pp. 15–22

Wheale, Nigel, 'Beyond the Trauma Stratus: Lynette Roberts's *Gods With Stainless Ears* and the Post-War Cultural Landscape', in *Welsh Writing in English: A Yearbook of Critical Essays*, n.s. 3 (1997), 98–117

Wigginton, Chris, "Birth and copulation and death': Gothic Modernism and Surrealism in the Poetry of Dylan Thomas', in *Dylan Thomas: Contemporary Critical Essays*, ed. John Goodby and Chris Wigginton (Basingstoke: Palgrave, 2001), pp. 85–105

Wigginton, Christopher, *Modernism from the Margins: The 1930s Poetry of Louis MacNeice and Dylan Thomas* (Cardiff: University of Wales Press, 2007)

Williams, Daniel G., *Black Skin, Blue Books: African Americans and Wales, 1845–1945* (Cardiff: University of Wales Press, 2012)

Williams, Daniel G., 'Welsh Modernism', in *The Oxford Handbook of Modernisms*, ed. Peter Brooker, Andrzej Gasiorek, Deborah Longworth and Andrew Thacker (Oxford and New York: Oxford University Press, 2010), pp. 797–816

Williams, Jeni, '"Oh, for our vanished youth": Avoiding Adulthood in the Later Stories of Dylan Thomas', in *Dylan Thomas: Contemporary Critical Essays*, ed. John Goodby and Chris Wigginton (Basingstoke: Palgrave, 2001), pp. 172–19

Williams, Keith, and Steven Matthews, 'Introduction', in *Rewriting the Thirties: Modernism and After*, ed. Keith Williams and Steven Matthews (New York: Longman, 1997), pp. 1–4

Williams, Linda, *Figures of Desire: A Theory and Analysis of Surrealist Film* (Berkley and Los Angeles: University of California Press, 1981)

Williams, Raymond, 'Language and the Avant-Garde', in *Raymond Williams, Politics of Modernism: Against the New Conformists*, ed. Tony Pinkney, 2nd edn (London and New York: Verso, 2007), pp. 65–80

Williams, Raymond, 'When Was Modernism?', in *Politics of Modernism: Against the New Conformists*, ed. Tony Pinkney (London and New York: Verso, 2007), pp. 31–5

Williams, Rowan, 'Swansea's Other Poet: Vernon Watkins and the Threshold between Worlds', *Welsh Writing in English: A Yearbook of Critical Essays*, n.s. 8 (2003), 107–20

Wolf, Norbert, *Expressionism*, ed. Uta Grosenick (Cologne and London: Taschen, 2004)

Internet Sources and Websites

Benjamin, Alison, 'Mixed Metaphor', *The Guardian*, 14 March 2001. Available at http://www.guardian.co.uk/society/2001/mar/14/guardiansocietysupplement5

Jones, Jonathan, 'The Riddle of the Rocks', *The Guardian*, 5 March 2007. Available at http://www.guardian.co.uk/world/2007/mar/05/spain.art

Sheppard, Richard, 'The Poetry of August Stramm: A Suitable Case for Deconstruction', *Journal of European Studies*, n.s. 15/261 (1985). Available at http://jes.sagepub.com/cgi/reprint/15/4/261

Simpson, John (ed.), *Oxford English Dictionary Online*. Available at http://dictionary.oed.com/

Index

S